SELLING BOOKS

IN THE BAY AREA

A Marketing Directory for Small Press and Self-publisher

Karen Misuraca, Editor

Jessica Misuraca, Ass't. Editor

Lagoon Publications
9 Channel Landing
Tiburon, CA 94920

To Michael, the wind in my sails.

Acknowledgements: Many thanks to Dan Poynter for heading me in the right direction, to Jayne Murdock for much encouragement, and to my invaluable assistant, Jessica Misuraca, for all the care and all the hours.

Cover design: Robert Howard Design, (805) 569-0801
Design, layout and desktop publishing: The Creative Type, (415) 383-2095
Printing and binding: Spilman Printing, (800) 448-3511
Production notes: 60 lb. white offset paper, 12 pt. UV coated cover
Typeset on a Macintosh SE using PageMaker, Word and Works
Typefaces: Bookman and Helvetica
Camera-ready copy printed on a LaserWriter II NTX

Inquiries: Lagoon Publications
             9 Channel Landing
             Tiburon, CA 94920

ISBN 0-923823-10-7
Library of Congress Catalog Card No. 88-084036

Contents

Contents
(continued)

INTRODUCTION
How To Use This Book

For you, the small press or entrepreneurial publisher, this marketing directory and guide is the key to selling your books in the Greater San Francisco Bay Area.

As a small publisher putting my own marketing plan together, I found it necessary to compile this information myself, from a wide variety of sources.

This book will save you months of research and fact-checking.

Selling Books In The Bay Area is an all-in-one compendium of regional publications, editors, reviewers, resources, libraries, media, book buyers and sellers and marketing ideas. You also get advice from the publishing pros and a calendar of important events and activities.

It's the only comprehensive marketing directory designed specifically for producers, sellers and distributors of books in the Greater San Francisco Bay Area.

To get you started on your book selling campaign, here's what I suggest:

1. Study the recommendations offered herein by the publishing pros.

2. Join the appropriate networking and support organizations in Section

3. Order what you need from Books for Publishers, Section 12.

4. Note on your calendar the meetings, trade shows, classes and events for publishers in Section 11.

5. Design a news release program for your targeted mailing lists of periodicals and media programs; follow up with phone calls (consider using the services of a syndicate and/or wire service, Section 9).

6. Look through the co-op marketing opportunities (Section 10) and directory of mailing lists (Section 7) for ideas on trade show exhibits and direct mail promotions to bookstores, libraries and other markets.

7. Make appointments with bookstore buyers (Section 4); bring along boxes of books, point of purchase aids (counter display boxes, posters, flyers, etc.), copies of reviews and invoices. (Distributors and wholesalers will be more interested in stocking and promoting your product if you're already placed in several stores.)

8. In Section 6, locate and contact those distributors and/or wholesalers appropriate to your type of book.

9. When your book is stocked by distributors/wholesalers, plan an author's tour of the Bay Area; an experienced publicist can be of invaluable assistance here (Section 8). Or, you can handle it yourself, send a package of information to selected radio and TV producers and assignment editors, including news release, copies of reviews, copy of your book and cover letter; follow up with phone calls.

Last, but not least, keep your copy of *Selling Books in the Bay Area* chained to your desk, within easy reach and safe from the clutches of your competition.

1

Bay Area Periodicals:
Newspapers, Magazines, Newsletters and Journals

Free Publicity for Your Book with News Releases

By Karen Misuraca, Lagoon Publications, editor, Selling Books in the Bay Area and editor, SPEX, the newsletter of the Marin Self-Publishers Association.

For the price of a few 25-cent stamps and several phone calls, you could generate enough book sales to cover your printing bills and pay your way to the next ABA.

All you have to do is send issue-oriented or benefit-oriented news releases, written in clear, down-to-earth newspaper style, to a targeted list of publications and other media, whether or not they have traditional book review columns or book review editors.

Just one paragraph in one newspaper can be worth thousands of dollars of advertising to you. If you plan to make a profit in publishing, you should take advantage of this free publicity before, during and after the printing of your book.

Send news releases to announce an upcoming publication date, a "back-to-the-presses" date, accomplishments of the author (speaking engagements, courses completed, appointment to office or boards of directors, TV, radio appearances, autograph parties, book promo tours).

Do you publish cookbooks? Make your release a gift idea and send before Mother's or Father's Day. Travel books? Herald the onset of summer vacation, Christmas vacation, Easter vacation. Poetry? Find out the birthdates of famous poets and link up your book. New Age? Write up your own definition of the term and how the movement got started, link to your book.

Many periodicals and non-print media listed in this directory will mention your book if you let them know about it. At least ten to twenty-five percent of their editorial space results from unsolicited news releases.

First, catch the editor's eye with a title and a lead tying your book to current events, new trends, people-oriented stories, fads, interesting statistics - anything happening in your field which showcases your new book.

Keep your eye open for local and national events, holidays, new products and social issues you can use to create a news angle.

Focus on reader or listener benefits and news value, rather than describing the book itself. Editors are not interested in selling your book for you, but in publishing the kind of information and news their readers expect.

When newspaper editors were asked by the Wall Street Journal to name their gripes about news releases, they said, ". . . content lacking relevance and significance," ". . . important information is buried," ". . . no local connection."

With your trusty computer, it's easy to direct your message to the readers of each specific periodical. It's important to do this, so editors don't get the idea you've sent an identical, blanket release to everyone in sight. It's a strong possiblity your release will be published verbatim, so tailor-make it for each newspaper, magazine, newsletter, and trade journal, if you possibly can.

Assignment editors for metropolitan dailies receive literally hundreds of news leads and releases each day, by mail, FAX, phone and wire service.

How to attract attention to your offering of newsworthy material? Start with a smashing title and a subtitle.

How about this one from author John Kremer: "A Cast of Thousands!," about his trivia book *Tinseltowns, U.S.A.*, featuring towns from famous movies and TV shows.

Start with a one or two sentence lead - a question perhaps, a statistic, an interesting fact, a link to current events.

For a book on singles' lifestyle: "Stouffers now makes 86 different frozen entrees designed for one person."

Focus on one main idea, issue or event and keep it simple. Imagine you are writing this for one other person. Read it out loud to yourself. Would you actually use those phrases? Instead of "Nouvelle cuisine is sweeping the nation," say, "We're all eating lighter foods these days."

The release should be no more than one and a half to two pages, double-spaced, and written in typical, inverted triangle newspaper style, including the five W's: who, what, when, where, why.

Your piece will likely be cut to fit space available, and it will be cut from the bottom up with little or no editing.

For your "most likely to be interested" editors, enclose a 5 X 7 black and white photo from the book or of the author (candid, not posed). A good photo can sell the editor on using your material.

Use quotes and anecdotes whenever possible, from the book, the author, or another expert. Notice how many popular periodicals pepper their articles with quotes. People like to read about people. If you don't have appropriate quotes, interview someone. You won't be refused - everyone likes to see their words in print.

Quotes help you promote the book without it seeming like advertising. Don't say, "This is the best book every written on cross-country skiing." Promote the subject, not the book; i.e., "Ski store owner, Sam Jones, said, 'Cross-country skiing is the fastest growing winter sport in the U.S.' "

Make a free offer if you can think of one. A free information kit, a free how-to article, a free resource list, a free map. Editors are more apt to include your address or phone if there's a benefit to their readers.

Biographical information about the author? Be very brief, and consider attaching a separate sheet of background notes, "About the Author."

Equally as important as the straight forward, concisely written release and the photos are the follow-up phone calls to a carefully chosen list of editors. Without follow-up phone calls, your response will be disappointing, to say the least.

Get each editor's correct name, give them a call a week or so after mailing and ask if they received it. Would they like additional information? a different angle? more photos to choose from?

Get your editor talking, give him/her a reason to remember you. Don't waste their time. Be ready to zero in on the most interesting facet of the book you're producing, why it's new, why it's important, why the readers will want to know about it.

If your editor is out when you call a time or two, leave a complete message of why you called and encourage a collect call back.

Don't give up if your response to a particular news release is disappointing. Regular mailings will eventually get you some free space.

It's the cheapest and best advertising you'll ever get.

Bay Area Periodicals:
Newspapers, Magazines, Newsletters and Journals

ACTS: A Journal of New Writing
514 Guerrero St.
San Francisco, CA 94110
(415) 431-8297
David Levi Strauss, Ed, Benjamin Hollander, Books Ed. 2x/year. Poetry, criticism, essays, reviews, translations, graphics/artwork, photographs. 1,600 circ, 6 rev/issue, favors Bay Area authors, interna readership.

Adweek West
410 Pacific
San Francisco, CA 94133-4607
(415) 986-4374
John Berry, Ed. Advertising trade journal.

AGADA
2020 Essex St.
Berkeley, CA 94703
(415) 848-0965
Reuven Goldfarb, Ed. 2x/year. Poetry, fict., essay, graphics, artwork. 750 circ.

Alameda Times Star
1516 Oak St.
Alameda, CA 94501
(415) 523-1205
Thomas Tuttle, Ed. 9,400 circ.

American Indian Quarterly
Univ. of Cal., NAS/3415 Dwinelle Hall
Berkeley, CA 94720-9989
(415) 642-6607
Robert Black, Ed. Quarterly, Anthropology, history, literature related to Amer. Indians. 1,000 circ, 30-35 rev/issue, mentions books/authors, na readership.

Anderson Valley Advertiser
Box 246
Boonville, CA 95415-0246
Bruce Anderson, Ed, Dr J David Colfax, Books Ed. Weekly newspaper, community & na news. 5,000 circ, 5 rev/issue.

Animal Tracks
171 Bel Marin Keys
Novato, CA 94949
(415) 883-4621
Judy Carroll, Ed. Quarterly. Domestic animals & horses, care, wildlife issues. 10,000 circ, no reviews, mentions books/authors, na readership.

Antiques West
3315 Sacramento St., #618
San Francisco, CA 94118
(415) 621-2906
Toby Rose, Ed. Monthly. Antiques, early fine art and related subjects. 21,000 circ, 1 rev/issue, mentions books/authors, na readership.

Argus Courier
830 Petaluma Blvd. North
Petaluma, CA 94952
(707) 762-4541
Chris Samson, Ed. Daily newspaper, community & na news. 10,000 circ, no reviews, mentions Petaluma authors, So. Sonoma County readership.

Art Com
Box 3123, Rincon Annex
San Francisco, CA 94119
(415) 431-7524
Carl Loeffler, Ed. Non-traditional art forms, news. 11,000 circ.

Arts & Books, SJ Mercury News
750 Ridder Park Dr.
San Jose , CA 95190
(408) 920-5000
Lee Grant, Ed. Sunday section.

Artweek
1628 Telegraph
Oakland, CA 94612
(415) 763-0422
Cecile McCann, Ed. Weekly tabloid, art. 16,000 circ.

Asian Week
809 Sacramento
San Francisco, CA 94108
(415) 397-0221
Patrick Andersen, Ed. Weekly newspaper, Asian Amer. in English. 31,000 circ, some reviews, mentions books/authors, na readership.

ASMP
10 Cleveland St.
San Francisco, CA 94103
(415) 863-8395
Barrie Rokeach, Ed. 10x/year. No. Cal. Society of Magazine Photographers Newsletter. 3,000 circ, some reviews, mentions books/authors,.

Athena Incognito
2555 29th Ave.
San Francisco, CA 94122
Chris Custer, Books Ed. Experimental writing, poetry, art. 2 rev/issue, mentions books/authors, f na readership.

Bam Magazine
5951 Canning St.
Oakland, CA 94609
(415) 652-3810
Keith Moerer, Ed. Biweekly music, entertainment magazine 140,000 circ, no reviews, mentions books/authors, Bay Area, So. Cal. readership.

Bananas Newsletter
6501 Telegraph Ave.
Oakland, CA 94609
(415) 658-7101
Child-care, parent support. 9,000 circ, Grtr Bay Area readership.

Bay Area Baby
455 Los Gatos Blvd, #103
Los Gatos, CA 95030
(408) 358-1414
Lynn Berardo, Ed. Semiannual magazine for expectant & new parents. 35,000 circ, 3 rev/issue, mentions books/authors, Grtr Bay Area readership.

Bay Area Computer Currents
5720 Hollis
Emeryville, CA 94608
(415) 547-6800
David Needle, Ed. Semiweekly, 67,000 circ.

Bay Area Parent
455 Los Gatos Blvd., #103
Los Gatos, CA 95030
(408) 358-1414
Lynn Berardo, Ed. Monthly magazine for parents & kids. 60,000 circ, 3 rev/issue, mentions books/authors, favors Bay Area authors, Santa Clara County readership.

Bay Area Reporter
1528 15th St.
San Francisco, CA 94103
(415) 861-5019
Ray O'Laughlin, Ed. Weekly newspaper, free, gay-related. 36,000 circ.

Bay Area Writer
236 West Portal Ave., #232
San Francisco, CA 94127
(415) 285-6946
Kathleen White, Ed. Quarterly. National Writers' Union Newsletter, Local 3. 350 circ, no reviews, but mentions books by members, favors Bay Area authors,.

BBMS, M & T Publishing
501 Galveston Dr.
Redwood City, CA 94063
(415) 366-3600
Wendy Hart, Books Ed. Monthly review of books and software of interest to businesses.

Berkeley Press, Press Publications
Box 10151
Oakland , CA 94610
(415) 547-4000
Perry David, Ed, Ray Epstein, Jan Miller, Books Eds. 2x/Month. Tabloid newspaper, community news; also Oakland Press, Piedmont Press, Montclair Press. 27,000 circ, 1 review/issue, favors Bay Area authors, review copies welcomed, Grtr Bay Area readership.

Berkeley Tri City Post
630 20th St.
Oakland, CA 94612
(415) 763-1120
Gail Berkley, Ed. 2x/week. Local newspaper, also Oakland Post, Richmond Post. 200,000 combined circ.

Berkeley Voice
6208 LaSalle St
Oakland, CA 94611
(415) 339-8777
Andy Whipple, Ed. Weekly.

Better Homes & Gardens
2226 Beach St.
San Francisco, CA 94123
(415) 346-0193
Kathryn Stechert, Books Ed. Monthly. Family & regional travel books; 4-color glossy. Some reviews, na readership.

Blue Unicorn
22 Avon Rd.
Kensington, CA 94707
(415) 526-8439
Ruth G Iodice, Ed. 3x/year. Poetry, translation, artwork. 500 circ, no reviews, mentions books/authors, interna, na readership.

BMUG Newsletter
1442A Walnut St.,#62
Berkeley, CA 94709
(415) 549-BMUG
Randy Simon, Ed. Semiannual newsletter for microcomputer users. 8,000 circ, 2 rev/ issue, mentions books/authors, favors authors with BMUG membership, interna readership.

Bodega Bay Navigator
Box 865
Bodega Bay, CA 94923
(707) 875-3574
Newspaper, community news.

Bodega Bay Signal
555 Highway 1
Bodega Bay, CA 94923
(707) 875-2255
Kathie Morgan, Ed. Weekly newspaper, community news. No reviews, Grtr Bay Area readership.

Bookbuilders West Newsletter
Box 883666
San Francisco, CA 94188-3666
(415) 995-4208
Pat Brewer, Ed. Bi-monthly newsletter of organization of book producers & related professionals.

Bookreader
942 Market St., #611
San Francisco CA 94102
(414) 982-7619
Jay Bail, Ed. Bimonthly tabloid, 20 pg, several dozen reviews, distributed to 800 bookstores.

Bookwatch
166 Miramar Ave.
San Francisco, CA 94112
(415) 221-0414
Diane C. Donovan, Ed. Monthly newsletter of Midwest Book Review, reviews of large & small press. 90,000 circ, 75 rev/issue, na readership.

Brentwood News
654 Third St.
Brentwood, CA 94513
(415) 643-2125
Theresa Keegan, Ed. Weekly, 3,600 circ.

Business Software
501 Galveston Dr.
Redwood City, CA 94063
(415) 366-3600
James Fawcette, Ed. Monthly, 46,000 circ.

Business West
450 Sansome St., Suite 210
San Francisco, CA 94111
(415) 956-6262
Sipora Gruskin, Ed, Deborah Collins, Books Ed. . Monthly magazine re Pacific Rim, Calif, Western states business news; banking, shipping, travel, advertising, ports & harbors, labor, medicine, high tech. 66,000 circ, some reviews, mentions books/authors, na, interna readership. "Total coverage of Pac. Rim & how it relates to Calif. business person."

Business Wire Newsletter
44 Montgomery St.
San Francisco, CA 94104
(415) 986-4422
Lorry I Lokey, Ed. Monthly newsletter from a news syndicate: public relations, journalism, communications news. 7,300 circ, no reviews, infrequent mention of books re journalism & PR, na, interna readership.

California Bicyclist
1149 Folsom St.
San Francisco, CA 94103
(415) 864-8670
Ms Shawn McAndrew, Ed, Roy Wallack, Books Ed. Monthly cycling magazine 104,000 circ, infrequent reviews, mentions books/authors, Cal. readership.

California Explorer
Box 6449
Tahoe City, CA 95130
(916) 581-3820
Stuart Weiss, Ed. Hiking, outdoors, ghost towns, back roads. Bimonthly, 10,000 circ, no reviews, mentions books/authors, West. U.S. readership.

California Farmer
731 Market
San Francisco, CA 94103
(415) 495-3340
Len Richardson, Ed. Semiweekly, 57,000 circ.

Cal. Fed. of Business & Professional Women's Clubs newsletter
833 Market St., Suite 809
San Francisco, CA 94103
Quarterly magazine for business women.

California History
2090 Jackson
San Francisco, CA 94109
(415) 567-1848
Dr Richard Orsi, Ed., James Rawls, Books Ed.. Quarterly, reviews books and articles onCalif. hist. 11,000 circ, 8 rev/issue, mentions books/authors, west. U. S. readership.

California Journal
1714 Capitol Ave.
Sacramento, CA 94814
(916) 444-2840
Richard Zeiger, Ed. Regional magazine, state capitol, politics. 21,000 circ.

California Lawyer
1390 Market St., Suite 1016
San Francisco, CA 94102
(415) 558-9888
Ray Reynolds, Ed, Peter Allen, Books Ed. Monthly. Professional & personal lives of lawyers. 14,000 circ, 2 rev/issue, mentions books/authors, na readership.

California Magazine
325 Pacific Ave.
San Francisco, CA 94111
(415) 986-5196
Tracy Johnston, Ed, Greil Marcus, Books Ed. Monthly magazine, lifestyles, general interest, upscale. 5-10 books reviewed or mentioned each issue, also serial excerpts. 90 days lead time.

California Management Review c/o UC
350 Barrows Hall, Univ. of Cal.
Berkeley, CA 94720
(415) 642-7159
David Vogel, Ed. Quarterly. Research, thought in business. 6,000 circ, no reviews, does not mention books/authors, interna readership.

California Monthly
University of California
Berkeley, CA 94720
(415) 642-5781
Russell Schoch, Ed. Alumni magazine. 99,000 circ.

California Physician
Box 7690
San Francisco, CA 94120-7690
(415) 882-5118
Kelly F Guncheon, Ed. Monthly socioeconomic magazine for physicians. 32,000 circ, no reviews, mentions books/authors, West. U. S. readership.

California Tomorrow
Fort Mason Center
San Francisco, CA 94123
(415) 441-7631
Carol Dowell, Ed, Ruth Kelly, Books Ed.
Quarterly multi racial magazine.

California Visitors' Review
Box 92
El Verano, CA 95433
(707) 928-0780
Julia Tapia, Ed. Weekly Northern Calif
tabloid for tourists. 46,000 circ.

California Voice
2956 Sacramento
Berkeley, CA 94703
(415) 644-2446
Ruth B Love, Ed, Charles E Aikens, Books
Ed. Weekly newspaper, black audience.
30,000 circ, 3 rev/issue, mentions books/
authors, Grtr Bay Area readership.

California Waterfront Age
1330 Broadway #1100
Oakland, CA 94612
(415) 464-0736
Rasa Gustaitis, Ed. Quarterly magazine,
book review section, waterfront restoration
& construction, coastal issues, environ-
ment. 7,000 circ, 4 rev/issue, U.S.,
Canada readership.

California Writers Club Bulletin
2214 Derby St.
Berkeley, CA 94705
Dorothy Benson, Ed. Monthly newsletter
for all No. Cal. branches of CWC. 800 circ,
no reviews, members' books mentioned,
na readership.

Cambio
4215 Montgomery St., #A
Oakland, CA 94611-4709
(415) 420-8030
Alberto Ampuero, Ed, Carlos Barón, Books
Ed. Monthly newspaper, bilingual. 26,000
circ, 2 rev/issue, Grtr Bay Area reader-
ship.

Cardio
c/o Miller Freeman Publications Inc
500 Howard St.
San Francisco, CA 94105-3002
(415) 397-1881
Don Gibbons, Ed. Semimonthly medical
magazine No reviews, does not mention
books/authors, na readership.

Carlmont Enquirer Bulletin
961 Laurel St.
San Carlos, CA 94070
(415) 593-1997
Lara Kaborycha, Ed. Weekly newspaper,
South Bay area. 22,000 circ.

Cathay Times
27 Hang Ah St.
San Francisco, CA 94108
(415) 391-0499
Fung Lee, Ed. Weekly, 35,000 circ.

CenterVoice
110 Sutter St., Suite #200
San Francisco, CA 94104
(415) 398-1854
Richard Keeler, Ed. Monthly. Lifestyle,
downtown SF. 40,000 circ, no reviews,
mentions books/authors, Grtr Bay Area
readership.

Centre Daily News
602 Kearny St.
San Francisco, CA 94108
(415) 648-3693
Daily, New York based Chinese newspa-
per, local & interna news. 21,000 circ.

Children's Advocate
1700 Broadway, Suite 300
Oakland, CA 94612
(415) 444-7136
Daphne Muse, Ed, Elizabeth Boyd, Books
Ed. Bimonthly, children's issues. 20,000
circ, 1 rev/issue, mentions books/authors,
na readership.

Children's Album / Children's Crafts
Box 6086
Concord , CA 94524
(415) 671-9852
Kathy Madsen, Ed. Bimonthly, children's
crafts & creative writing, poetry. 3 rev/
issue, mentions books/authors.

China Times
3410 Geary, Room 240
San Francisco, CA 94118
(415) 751-9066
Mr Chen, Ed. Weekly, 30,000 circ.

Chinese Times
686 Sacramento St.
San Francisco, CA 94111
(415) 982-6206
Lawrence Tan, Ed. Weekly, 10,000 circ.

Chopmark
460 Magnolia
Larkspur, CA 94939
(415) 924-3801
*Maryjane Dunstan, Ed. Monthly. Book-
store newsletter; reviews. 800 circ, 20 rev/
issue, Grtr Bay Area readership.*

City Bike
1126 Kearny St.
San Francisco, CA 94133
(415) 982-7242
*Brian Halton, Ed. Monthly tabloid re
motorcycles.17,500 circ.*

City Living
853 Howard St.
San Francisco, CA 94103
(415) 982-8030
*Thomas York, Ed. Bimonthly, 4-color
magazine, home & garden, interior design,
real estate, remodeling, homeowners &
renters issues at City Hall.*

City Sports Magazine
Box 3693
San Francisco, CA 94119
(415) 546-6150
*Jane McConnell, Ed, David Smethurst,
Books Ed. Monthly, California sports
tabloid, fitness. 200,000 circ, no reviews,
mentions books/authors, Cal. readership.*

Cloverdale Revielle
207 North Cloverdale Blvd.
Cloverdale, CA 95425
(707) 894-3339
Newspaper.

Coastal Post
Box 31
Bolinas, CA 94924
(415) 868-1600
*Don Deane, Ed. Weekly tabloid local
newspaper. 12,000 circ, some reviews,
Marin County readership.*

Coastal Traveller
Box 210
Point Reyes Station, CA 94956
(415) 663-8404
*David V Mitchell, Ed. Quarterly tabloid
publication by Point Reyes Light; natural &
regional history, environment, recreation,
West Marin & Sonoma counties.*

Coastside Chronicle
1331 San Mateo Ave.
South San Francisco, CA 94080
(415) 266-9600
*Will Thomas, Ed. Biweekly newspaper,
West San Mateo county. 7,500 circ.*

Coming Up
592 Castro St.
San Francisco, CA 94114
(415) 626-8121
*Kim Corsaro, Ed. Monthly newspaper, gay
& lesbian, na & interna news, events.
100,000 circ, 7 rev/issue, Grtr Bay Area
readership.*

Common Ground
305 San Anselmo Ave., #217
San Anselmo, CA 94960
(415) 459-4900
*Baha' uddin Alpine, Ed. Quarterly, New
Age newspaper. 80,000 circ, na readership.*

Communication World
870 Market St. #940
San Francisco, CA 94102
(415) 433-3400
*Gloria Gordon, Ed. Monthly. Business
communications.*

Communications Arts
410 Sherman Ave., Box 10300
Palo Alto , CA 94303-0807
(415) 326-6040
*Richard Coyne, Ed, Patrick Coyne, Books
Ed. 8x/year. Visual communications trade
magazine 8,000 circ, 6 rev/issue, interna
readership.*

Computer Currents
Box 2339
Berkeley, CA 94702
(415) 547-6800
*Stan Politi, Ed. Biweekly, Business
microcomputers.*

Consumer Action News
116 New Montgomery St
San Francisco, CA 94105
(415) 777-9635
Phone & banking, primarily.

Contra Costa Sun
3678A Mt. Diablo Blvd.
Lafayette, CA 94549
(415) 284-4444
Jane Putnam, Ed. Weekly, 20,000 circ.

Contra Costa Times
Box 5088
Walnut Creek, CA 94596
(415) 935-2525
*Ernie Hines, Ed, Carol Fowler, Books Ed.
Daily, 100,000 circ.*

COSMEP Newsletter
Box 703
San Francisco, CA 94101
(415) 922-9490
*Richard Morris, Ed, Henry Berry, Books
Ed. Monthly newsletter of International
Association of Independent Publishers;
information & events; send your an-
nouncements of publishing activities, offer
your mailing lists, etc. Book reviews re
publishing, writing, promotion. 2,000 circ,
1 rev/issue, interna readership.*

Country Almanac
Box 98
Menlo Park, CA 94026
(415) 328-1600
*Elaine Levine, Ed. Weekly. Local,
Woodside/Menlo Park. 23,000 circ.*

Creation
Box 19216
Oakland , CA 94619
(415) 253-1192
*Pat Feldsien, Ed, JoAnn McAllister, Books
Ed. Bimonthly. Spirituality. 8,500 circ, 4
rev/issue, mentions books/authors, na,
interna readership.*

**Critique: A Journal Exposing Consen-
sus Reality**
Box 11368
Santa Rosa, CA 95406
(707) 525-9401
*Bob Banner, Ed.
Carl Fairchild, Books Ed. 3x/year, magazine "critically exposing consensus reality
to prepare for the new paradigms and the
new species." 6,500 circ, 50 rev/issue,
mentions books/authors, interna readership.*

Crystal Congress Newsletter
Box 5442
Mill Valley, CA 94942
(415) 388-8355
Quarterly, New Age. 8,000 circ.

Cupertino Courier
Box 368
Cupertino, CA 95015
(415) 255-7500
Mary Ann Cook, Ed. Weekly, 19,000 circ.

Daily Pacific Builder
2450 17th St.
San Francisco, CA 94110
(415) 495-4200
*Dave McDonald, Ed. Daily. Northern Calif
building industry. 20,000 circ.*

Daily Republic
1250 Texas St.
Fairfield, CA 94533
(707) 425-4646
Bill Buchanan, Ed, Mary Ann Murdoch, Books Ed. Daily newspaper. Upper Solano Co. 19,000 circ, 5 rev/issue.

Daily Review
Box 5050
Hayward, CA 94540
(415) 783-6111
Scott Livingston, Ed. 109,000 combined w/Fremont Argus, Tri-Valley Herald & Alameda Times-Star.

Daly City Record
1331 San Mateo Ave.
South San Francisco, CA 94080
(415) 266-9600
Will Thomas, Ed. 25,000 circ.

DBMS Magazine
501 Galveston Dr.
Redwood City, CA 94063
(415) 366-3600
Kevin Strehlo, Ed. Monthly computer magazine no reviews, interna readership.

Design Book Review
2508 Ridge Rd.
Berkeley, CA 94709
(415) 486-1956
Elizabeth Snowden, Ed. Quarterly, 7,500 circ., reviews interior design & architecture books.

Design News
3031 Tisch Way #100
San Jose, CA 95128-2530
(408) 243-8838
Lyle McCarty, Ed. Bimonthly, business, computer design.

Diablo Business
2520 Camino Diablo, Suite 200
Walnut Creek, CA 94596
10,000 circ.

Diablo Magazine
2520 Camino Diablo, Suite 200
Walnut Creek, CA 94596
(415) 943-1111
Jane Paulsen, Ed. Monthly, lifestyle, East Bay. 60,000 circ, no reviews, mentions East Bay books/authors, East Bay Area readership.

Doctor Dobb's Journal
501 Galveston Dr.
Redwood City, CA 94063
(415) 366-3600
Jonathan Erickson, Ed, Michael Floyd, Books Ed. Monthly. Computer programmers. 65,000 circ, some reviews, mentions books/authors, Grtr Bay Area readership.

Dong; A Daily News
2703 Geary Blvd.
San Francisco, CA 94118
(415) 563-0900
Ji Cheong, Ed. Daily. Korean news, local & interna. 9,500 circ.

East Bay Express
Box 3198
Berkeley, CA 94703
(415) 652-4610
John Raeside, Ed, Robert Hurwitt, Books Ed. Weekly. East Bay, community issues, events, entertainment. 55,000 circ, some reviews, favors Bay Area authors, Grtr Bay Area readership.

East/West News
838 Grant Ave., Suite 302
San Francisco, CA 94108
(415) 781-3194
Serena Chen, Ed. Weekly, Asian-Amer. tabloid, in Chinese & English; Bay Area.17,000 circ, 3 rev/issue, mentions books/authors, na, interna readership.

Ebbtide
c/o Drawer S
Sausalito, CA 94966
(415) 332-3778
Billie L Anderson, Ed. Weekly

EditSpeak
736 Jones St., #31
San Francisco, CA 94109
(415) 474-7429
Pat Soberanis, Ed. Monthly newsletter for magazine editors. 150 circ, occasional reviews of books re magazine editing, No. Cal. readership.

El Bohemio News
3133 22nd St.
San Francisco, CA 94110
(415) 647-1924
Fred Rosado, Ed. Weekly, bilingual tabloid. 71,000 circ.

El Mensajero
345 9th St.
San Francisco, CA 94103
(415) 626-4111
Francisco Garcia, Ed. Weekly, Hispanic. 20,000 circ.

El Mundo, Alameda Publishing Co., Inc.
630 20th St.
Oakland, CA 94612
(415) 763-1120 ext 248
Oscar A Benavides Jr, Ed, Rosario Daigle, Books Ed. Weekly Spanish newspaper. 32,000 circ, some reviews, mentions books/authors, Grtr Bay Area readership.

El Observador
Box 1990
San Jose, CA 95109
(408) 295-4272
Rebecca K Valdez, Ed., Hilbert Morales, Books Ed. Weekly, bilingual news tabloid. 20,000 circ, some reviews, Santa Clara County readership.

El Tecolote
3240 21st St.
San Francisco, CA 94110
(415) 824-7878
Juan Gonzales, Ed. Monthly tabloid, Mission district bilingual newspaper, free. 20,000 circ, some reviews, mentions Bay Area authors, na, interna readership.

Electronic Design
1307 S Mary Ave. #210
Sunnyvale, CA 94087
(408) 736-6667
Steve Orr, Ed. 30x/year. Art, music, computers, science.

Electronic Design Magazine
1625 The Alameda, #900
San Jose, CA 95126
(408) 282-7000
Dave Bursky, Ed. For technicians, engineers, Silicon Valley. Bimonthly.

Estos Tiempos
Building 590-E
Stanford, CA 94305
(415) 723-2089
Carole Hyde, Ed. Twice/year, tabloid; Latino news and cultural commentary, 7,000 circ, no reviews but mentions books/authors, na readership.

Etc
Box 2469
San Francisco, CA 94126
(415) 543-1747
Russell Joyner, Ed, Jeremy Klein, Books Ed. Quarterly review of general semantics. 2,500 circ, 12 rev/issue, mentions books/ authors, interna readership.

Family Life Educator
Box 1830
Santa Cruz , CA 95061-1830
(408) 438-4060
Kay Clark, Ed. Quarterly mag., reviews new books for teachers and health educators who work with adolescents. 4,000 circ, 5 rev/issue, mentions books/authors, Grtr Bay Area readership.

Feminist Bookstore News
Box 882554
San Francisco, CA 94188
(415) 626-1556
Carol Seajay, Ed. Bimonthly trade magazine regarding books about women. 450 circ, 200+ rev/issue, interna readership.

Fiction Network Magazine
Box 5651
San Francisco, CA 94101
(415) 391-6610
Jay Schaefer, Ed. 2x/year. Short fiction by undiscovered & established writers. 6,000 circ, no reviews.

Film Quarterly
UC Press
Berkeley, CA 94720
(415) 642-4247
Ernest Callenbach, Ed.

Film/Tape World
Box 6639
San Mateo, CA 94403
(415) 571-7210
Jennifer Edwards Boone, Ed. Monthly tabloid, film & video business, resources & news. 4,000 circ, no reviews, mentions Bay Area authors, West. U.S. readership.

Fine Print
Box 3394
San Francisco, CA 94119
(415) 543-4455
Sandra Kirshenbaum, Ed. Quarterly review for arts of the book. 3,500 circ, 8 rev/issue, interna readership.

Floating Island
Box 516
Point Reyes Station, CA 94956
(415) 663-1181
Michael Sykes, Ed. Irregular. Poetry, fict., graphics/artwork. 2,000 circ, no reviews, favors Bay Area authors, na, interna readership.

Food Journal
Box 15779
Sacramento, CA 95852
(916) 321-1144
Jan Townsend, Ed. Weekly, reviews cookbooks and other food books. 250,000 circ, 1 rev/issue, No. Cal. readership.

Foster City Progress
969 Edgewater Blvd., Suite N
Foster City, CA 94404
(415) 574-9293
Barbara Vogt, Ed. Weekly, 10,500 circ.

Frank Magazine
Box 59
San Francisco, CA 94117
(415) 387-0292
Rebecca Biggs, Ed. Quarterly. Lifestyle of SF. 16,000 circ.

Generations
833 Market St.
San Francisco, CA 94103
(415) 543-2617
Mary Johnson, Ed, David Shiriboga, Books Ed. Quarterly magazine of Amer. Society on Aging, 10,000 circ, book reviews.

Gesar
2425 Hillside Ave.
Berkeley, CA 94704
(415) 548-5407
Iris Maitland, Ed. Quarterly. Buddhism in the West, includes book reviews.

Gnosis
Box 14217
San Francisco, CA 94114
(415) 255-0400
Jay Kinney, Ed. Quarterly, New Age journal. 10,000 circ, 12 rev/issue, mentions books/authors, na, interna readership.

Golden State Report
444 North 3rd St., #20
Sacramento, CA 95814-0227
(916) 448-2653
Ed Mendel, Ed. Monthly magazine of politics & public policy in Cal. 14,000 circ, no reviews, does not mention books/authors, Cal. readership.

**Golden State,
The Magazine of California**
555 19th St.
San Francisco, CA 94107
(415) 621-0220
Anne Evers, Ed. Quarterly magazine for tourists. 3.5 million circ, no reviews, mentions books/authors, Cal. readership.

Growing Family
70 Skyview Terr.
San Rafael, CA 94903
(415) 492-0720
Mary Jane DeWolf Smith, Ed. Quarterly tabloid, Association for Positive Parenting, Leadership & Education (A.P.P.L.E. Family Center). 7,000 circ, no reviews, mentions books/authors, Grtr Bay Area readership.

Haight Ashbury Literary Journal
Box 15133
San Francisco, CA 94115
1.5x/year. Diverse magazine.1,600 circ, mentions books/authors, na readership.

Haight-Ashbury News
409 Clayton Ave.
San Francisco, CA 94117
(415) 621-9553
Monthly, 8,000 circ.

Half Moon Bay Review
714 Kelly Ave.
Half Moon Bay, CA 94019
(415) 726-4424
Kim Stein, Ed. Weekly, 6,500 circ.

Hard Money Digest
Box 37
Corte Madera, CA 94925
(415) 924-1612
Roderick P Crandall, PhD. Investment newsletter, summarizes 30 other newsletters, stocks, interest rates, economy, bonds, inflation. 1,500 circ, no reviews, mentions books/authors, na, interna readership.

Hayward Daily Review
Box 5050
Hayward, CA 94540-5050
(415) 783-6111
Barry Caine, Ed. Daily. News, features, sports, entertainment. 47,000 circ, 4 rev/issue, mentions books/authors, Grtr Bay Area readership.

Healdsburg Tribune
736 Healdsburg Ave.
Healdsburg, CA 95448
(707) 433-4452
Rollie Atkinson, Ed, Paula Lombardi, Books Ed. 2x/week. Community newspaper. 9,125 circ, some reviews, favors Bay Area authors.

Hillsborough Boutique & Villager
1755 Rollins Rd.
Burlingame, CA 94010
(415) 692-9406
Kimberly Kordick, Ed. Weekly, 12,000 circ.

Hippocrates - The Magazine of Health & Medicine
475 Gate 5 Rd.
Sausalito, CA 94965
(415) 332-5866
Eric Schrier, Ed, Ann Bartz, Books Ed. 6x/year. Consumer magazine on health & medicine. 500,000 circ, some reviews, na readership.

Hokubei Mainichi
Box 3321
San Francisco, CA 94119-3321
(415) 567-7324
Misako Okamura, Ed. Daily Japanese community newspaper, bi-lingual, na & interna. 9,000 circ.

Housewife-Writer's Forum
PO Drawer 1518
Lafayette, CA 94549
Deborah Haeseler, Ed
Humor and literary magazine for those who juggle writing with family responsibilities, housewife's humour.

IABC Communications World
One Hallidie Plaza, Suite 600
San Francisco, CA 94102
(415) 433-3400
Gloria Gordon, Ed, Cliff McGoon, Books Ed. Business communicators. 14,500 circ, 1 rev/issue, interna readership.

Image Magazine
110 Fifth St
San Francisco, CA 94103
(415) 777-27905
*Bruce Adams, Ed, Jim Woods, food & wine
Ed. Sunday magazine of SF Examiner,
707,000 circ, no reviews but mentions
books/authors.*

In Marin
640 Mission
San Rafael, CA 94901
(415) 453-9824
*Delsa Ham, Ed. Bimonthly 4-color glossy
magazine 20,000 circ, no reviews, Grtr
Bay Area readership.*

Independent Coast Observer
Box 1200
Gualala, CA 95445
(707) 884-3501
*J Stephen McLaughlin, Ed. Weekly news-
paper. 3,200 circ, 1 rev/issue, favors
North Coast authors, No. Coast readership.*

Info World
1060 Marsh Rd, Suite C-200
Menlo Park, CA 94025
(415) 328-4602 or (800) 217-8365
*Jonathan Sacks, Ed, Michael McCarthy,
Books Ed. Weekly. News for PC users.
160,000 circ, no reviews, does not mention
books/authors, na readership.*

Information Marketing News
Box 546
El Cajon, CA 92022
(619) 282-5822
*Russ Von Hoelscher, Ed, Cindy Kanne,
Books Ed. Newsletter for information
publishers, reviews of books for information marketers. 3 rev/issue, na readership.*

Institute of Noetic Sciences Newsletter
475 Gate 5 Rd #300
Sausalito, CA 94965
(415) 331-5650
*Barbara McNeill, Ed, Nola Lewis, Books
Ed. Quarterly, magazine re health and
societal well-being through research on the
human mind and consciousness, articles
and book reviews,*

Inter-City Express
Box 30157
Oakland , CA 94604
(415) 465-3121
Nell Fields, Ed. 25,000 circ.

International Monthly
Box 5335
San Jose, CA 95150-5335
(408) 227-0458
*Ute Lorenz, Ed. Monthly newsletter, a
review of the German press and world
affairs, in English and German. Some
reviews, interna readership.*

IO
2800 Woolsey
Berkeley, CA 94705
(415) 653-9177
*Richard Grossinger, Ed. Irregular. Poetry,
essays, translations, interviews, graphics/
artwork, prose. 2,000 circ, no reviews.*

**Japanese American Times/Nichi Bei
Times**
2211 Bush St.
San Francisco, CA 94115
(415) 921-6820
*Michi Onuma, Ed. Tue-Sat. Bilingual
Japanese/Eng newspaper. 8,000 circ.*

Jewish Bulletin
88 1st St.
San Francisco, CA 94105
(415) 957-9340
*Sherwood L Weingarten, Ed. Weekly
newspaper re Bay Area Jewish community, events, issues & personalities.
25,000 circ, 2 rev/issue, favors Bay Area
authors, Grtr Bay Area readership.*

Jewish Star
109 Minna St., #323
San Francisco, CA 94105-3701
(415) 421-4874
*Nevon Stuckey, Ed. Monthly. Jewish
interest book reviews and display ads,
sent to bookstores*

Jump Cut
Box 865
Berkeley, CA
94701
(415) 658-4482
John Hess, Ed. Biannual journal of contemp. media; film. 6,000 circ, 5 rev/ issue, mentions books/authors, interna readership.

Just for Laughs
22 Miller Ave.
Mill Valley, CA 94941
(415) 383-4746
Hut Landon, Ed. Monthly tabloid; comedy & standup comedians, some book reviews; comedy book review special issue. 50,000 circ, na readership.

Katipunan
Box 8477
Berkeley, CA 94707
(415) 428-0438
Rene Ciria-Cruz, Ed, Marie Castillo-Pruden, Books Ed. Monthly Philippine community tabloid. 10,000 circ, 1 rev/ issue, mentions books/authors, na, interna readership.

Korea Times/Hankook Ilbo
274 Shotwell St.
San Francisco, CA 94110
(415) 864-0954
George Kim, Ed, Anna S. Lee, Books Ed. Daily. Local & na news in Korean, 2-3 book reviews/issue, 11,000 circ in Western U.S.

Korean-American Journal
474 West Hamilton Ave.
Campbell, CA 95008
(408) 370-0888
Young Su Yi, Ed. Semiweekly. Korean language. 16,000 circ.

La Bella Figura
Box 411223
San Francisco, CA 94141-1223
Rose Romano, Ed. Quarterly. Italian Amer. women. 200 circ, 1 rev/issue, na readership.

La Oferta
3146 Bilbo Dr.
San Jose, CA 95121
(408) 729-6397
Evelyn Sanchez, Ed. Weekly bilingual newspaper. 40,000 circ, Grtr Bay Area readership.

La Ventana
Box 6327
Santa Rosa, CA 95406
Cristina Briano, Ed. Monthly tabloid newspaper. 4,000 circ, no reviews, Grtr Bay Area readership.

La Voz Hispana
1530 South Novato Blvd.
Novato, CA 94947
(415) 897-2622
Pepe Becerra, Ed. Monthly newspaper. 16,000 circ.

Landscape
Box 7107
Berkeley, CA 94707
(415) 549-3233
Bonnie Loyd, Ed. 2 or 3/year, artistic, image-oriented magazine, includes book reviews.

Latitude 38
Box 1678
Sausalito, CA 94966
(415) 383-8200
Richard Spindler, Ed, John Riise, Books Ed. Monthly. About boats & sailing, 48,000 circ, 6 rev/year, mentions books/ authors, na, interna readership.

Lector Monograph Review Series
16161 Ventura Blvd., Suite 830
Encino, CA 91436
(818) 990-1885
Roberto Cabello-Argandoña. Biannual. Hispanic, Latin Amer. lit. 3,000 circ, 100 rev/issue, na readership.

Lifestyle
419 West MacArthur Blvd.
Oakland, CA 94609
(415) 420-1381
Dave Sawle, Ed. Bimonthly. Art, music, entertainment, regional titles, health, new age. 90,000 circ, 1 rev/issue, mentions books/authors, Grtr Bay Area readership.

Livermore Independent
Box 1198
Livermore, CA 94550
(415) 447-8700
Robert Several, Ed, Janet Armantrout, Books Ed. Weekly, 42,000 circ, no reviews, Livermore-Amador Valley readership.

Local Color
15495 Los Gatos Blvd.,#9
Los Gatos, CA 95030
(408) 356-1313
Grace Parker, Ed. Bimonthly. Regional; upper income residents of Santa Clara Valley.

Los Altos Town Crier
Box Drawer 7
Los Altos, CA 94022
(408) 948-4489
Cheryl Temdick, Ed. Weekly newspaper, community oriented 15,000 circ.

Los Gatos Times Observer
236 North Santa Cruz Ave., #105A
Los Altos, CA 95030
(408) 354-3900
Iver Davidson, Ed. Weekly newspaper, community oriented. 5,000 circ.

Macweek
525 Brannan St.
San Francisco, CA 94107
(415) 882-7370
Dan Ruby, Ed, Becky Waring, Books Ed. Weekly, Macintosh-computer-related news magazine Some reviews, mentions books/ authors, na readership.

Macworld
501 Second St.
San Francisco, CA 94107
(415) 546-7722
Jerry Borrell, Ed. Monthly. Computers (Macintosh). 131,000 circ.

Magical Blend Magazine
Box 11303
San Francisco, CA 94101
(415) 282-9338, 673-1001
M Langevin, Ed, Richard Daab, Silma Smith, Nicole Dalin, Books Eds. Quarterly magazine re metaphysical, lifestyles, New Age. 10 book reviews/issue, 45,000 circ.

Marin Arts Guide
251 North San Pedro Rd.
San Rafael, CA 94903
(415) 499-8350
Monthly tabloid, cultural events including book/author, no reviews, Marin Arts Council.

Marin Independent Journal
Box 330
San Rafael, CA 94915
(415) 883-8600
Jay Silverberg, Ed, Rebecca Larsen, Books Ed. Daily, Gannett chain. 43,000 circ, several rev/week, Marin readership.

Marin Messenger
Box 848
Mill Valley, CA 94942
(415) 388-3211
Peter Sideman, Ed. Weekly newspaper, community oriented, also Mill Valley Record. 24,000 circ.

Marin Scope
Drawer S
Sausalito, CA 94966
(415) 332-3778
Billie L Anderson, Ed. Weekly tabloid. 30,000 circ.

Martinez News Gazette
615 Estudillo St., Box 151
Martinez, CA 94553
(415) 228-6400
Robert Osmond, Ed. Daily, 14,500 circ, some reviews, mentions Bay Area authors, Grtr Bay Area readership.

Mediafile
Building D, Fort Mason Center
San Francisco, CA 94123
(415) 441-2557
*Laura Fraser, Ed. Monthly. Bay Area
media news. 11,000 circ, some reviews,
na readership.*

Medical Self-Care
349 Healdsburg Ave.
Healdsburg, CA 95448
(707) 431-1100
*Carole Pisarcyzk, Ed, Nishama Franklin,
Books Ed. Bimonthly. Hands-on health
info. 100,000 circ, 10 rev/issue, mentions
books/authors, na readership.*

Medical World News
c/o Miller Freeman Publications Inc
500 Howard St.
San Francisco, CA 94105-3002
(415) 397-1881
*Don Gibbons, Ed. Semimonthly medical
mag, no reviews,does not mention books/
authors, na readership.*

Metro Reporter Group
1366 Turk St.
San Francisco, CA 94115
(415) 931-5778
*Greg Brooks, Ed. Weekly, black-oriented
newspapers. 160,000 circ, 1 rev/issue,
Grtr Bay Area readership.*

Microtimes Magazine
5951 Canning St.
Oakland, CA 94609
(415) 652-3810
*Mary Eisenhart, Ed. Monthly computer
magazine 200,000 circ, no reviews,
mentions books/authors, Grtr Bay Area,
L.A. readership.*

Mill Valley Record
438 Miller Ave.
Mill Valley, CA 94941
(415) 388-3211
*Peter Sideman, Ed. Weekly newspaper,
community oriented. 22,000 circ.*

**Millbrae Sun/Millbrae Burlingame
Leader**
205 Broadway
Millbrae, CA 94030
(415) 697-5336
Tim Donahue, Ed. Weekly, 7,700 circ.

Milpitas Post
20 Corning Ave.
Milpitas, CA 95035
(415) 262-2454
Andrew F Hamm, Ed. Weekly, 15,000 circ.

Montclarion
6208 La Salle
Oakland, CA 94611
(415) 339-8777
*Nancy Kieffer, Ed, Barbara Sloane, Books
Ed. Weekly newspaper, 50,000 circ, 2 rev/
issue, Oakland readership.*

Morena
1600 Woolsey
Berkeley, CA 94703
(415) 548-0318
*Gwen Carmen, Ed. Tabloid, women of
color. 20,000 circ, 2 rev/issue, mentions
books/authors, na, interna readership.*

Mother Jones
1663 Mission St.
San Francisco, CA 94103
(415) 558-8881
*Douglas Foster, Ed. 10x/year. Magazine,
liberal political opinion, national & interna
readership. 211,000 circ.*

Motorland
150 Van Ness
San Francisco, CA 94101-1860
(415) 565-2451
*John G. Holmgren, Ed. 6x/year. Travel
magazine, published by Calif Automobile
Association, 1.75 Million circ.*

Mystery Readers International Journal
Box 8116
Berkeley, CA 94707-8116
(415) 548-5799
*Janet Rudolph, Ed. Quarterly, reviews,
interviews, reading lists for mystery
readers, publishers, critics, editors,
writers, worldwide.*

Napa County Record
Box 88
Napa, CA 94559-0088
(707) 252-8877
John Nemes, Ed.Weekly newspaper. 6,500 circ, 3 rev/issue.

Napa Register
Box 150
Napa, CA 94559
(707) 226-3711
Lynn Penny, Ed. Daily newspaper. 23,000 circ.

National Motorist
188 The Embarcadero
San Francisco, CA 94105
(415) 777-4000
Jane M Offers, Ed. Bimonthly. Travel/auto 4-color publication edited for 160,000 National Automobile Club members; distributed in Calif. only. 7 rev/issue.

Needlepoint Plus
Box 6086
Concord, CA 94520
(415) 671-9852
Gerri Eggers, Ed. Bimonthly. Needlecrafts and related needlework, magazine 22,000 circ, 1 rev/issue, na readership.

Network Magazine
310 Blue Ridge Rd.
Boulder Creek, CA 95006
(408) 462-5810
Sara Elena, Ed. Quarterly tabloid for New Age professionals, some book reviews. 75,000 free circ.

New Bayview Newspaper
Box 24477
San Francisco, CA 94124-0477
(415) 822-6123
Muhammad Al-Kareem, Ed. Weekly, black-oriented newspaper. 16,000 circ, 2 rev/issue, na readership.

New Bernal Journal
515 Courtland Ave.
San Francisco, CA 94110
(415) 648-0330
Fred Allingham, Ed. Monthly. Neighborhood. 8,000 circ,

New Options Newsletter
131 Camino Alto, Suite D
Mill Valley, CA 94941
(415) 381-0553
Monthly newsletter on health care, community organizing. 8,500 circ.

New York Times (Na. Edition)
One Embarcadero Center, #1310
San Francisco, CA 94111
(415) 362-3912
Robert Lindsey, Bureau Chief. Daily, 26,000 circ.

Newspointer
Box T
San Rafael, CA 94912
(415) 332-3778
Billie L Anderson, Ed. Weekly

Newsweek Magazine
Bay Area Bureau, 505 Sansome St., #501
San Francisco, CA 94111
(415) 788-2651
Tony Clifton, Bureau Chief.

Nob Hill Gazette
The Hearst Bldg, Suite #222, 5 Third St.
San Francisco, CA 94103
(415) 227-0190
Judith Rich, Ed. Monthly tabloid, upscale SF neighborhood; art, culture, entertain, personalities. 55,000 circ, no reviews, mentions books/authors, Grtr Bay Area readership.

Noe Valley Voice
1021 Sanchez St
San Francisco, CA 94114
(415) 821-3324
Sally Smith, Ed, Jane Underwood, Books Ed. Monthly tabloid, SF neighborhood. 10,000 circ, favors Noe Valley authors.

Nolo News c/o Nolo Press
950 Parker Street.
Berkeley, CA 94710
(415) 549-1976
Mary Randolph, Ed, Ralph Warner, Books Ed. Quarterly. Book reviews on legal, consumer & small business issues. 5 rev/issue.

North Beach Now
210 Columbus Ave./Box 122
San Francisco, CA 94133
(415) 391-1043
Joan Dahlgren, Ed. 10x/year. Tabloid re North Beach neighborhood area of SF. 25,000 circ, no reviews.

Northern California Jewish Bulletin
88 First St., Suite 300
San Francisco, CA 94105
(415) 957-9340
Marc Klein, Ed. Weekly. World and local news for Jews. 25,000 circ, some reviews, mentions Bay Area authors, Grtr Bay Area readership.

Novato Advance
Box 8
Novato, CA 94948
(415) 892-1516
John Jackson, Ed, Shelley Sheperd, Books Ed. Weekly newspaper. 10,500 circ, no reviews.

Oakland Press (see Berkeley Press)

Observer, Alameda County
Box 817
San Leandro, CA 94577
(415) 483-7119
Ad Fried, Ed, Michael Roberts, R.A. Burrell, Books Eds. Weekly newspapers (also Hayward Observer, Oakland Observer, San Leandro Observer), community, regional & na news, 100 book reviews/year, favor Bay Area authors,135,000 combined circ.

On Our Backs
526 Castro St.
San Francisco, CA 94114
(415) 861-4723
Suzy Bright, Ed. Monthly magazine, lesbianism, photos, fiction, features, book reviews, 10,000 circ.

Our Animals
c/o San Francisco SPCA
2500 16th St.
San Francisco, CA 94103
(415) 554-3000
Paul Glassner, Ed. Quarterly. Animals, no reviews.

Pacific Discovery
c/o California Academy of Sciences
Golden Gate Park
San Francisco, CA 94118
(415) 221-5100
Janet Cox, Ed, Chris Cunningham, Books Ed. (415) 750-7116. Quarterly, 4-color magazine, articles on nature, ecology, including reviews, reading lists, regional interests.

Pacific Historical Review c/o The University of California
2120 Berkeley Way
Berkeley, CA 94720
(415) 642-7485
Norris Hundley, Ed. Quarterly. Book reviews.

Pacific Horticulture
Box 485
Berkeley, CA 94701
(415) 524-1914
W George Waters, Ed. Quarterly. For gardeners who read. 16,000 circ, 6 rev/issue, interna readership.

Pacific Sun
Box 5553
Mill Valley, CA 94942
(415) 383-4500
Linda Xiques, Ed. Weekly tabloid newspaper, Marin County issues, events. 33,000 circ.

Pacifica Tribune
59 Aura Vista
Pacifica, CA 94044
(415) 359-6666
Renee Deal, Ed. Weekly. 1,900 circ.

Palo Alto Times Tribune
245 Lytton Ave.
Palo Alto, CA 94302
(415) 853-1200
Mike Kidder, Ed, Meg Morris, Books Ed. Daily newspaper, 60,000 circ.

Palo Alto Weekly
Box 1610
Palo Alto, CA 94302
(415) 326-8210
Becky Martindale, Ed. Weekly newspaper. 45,000 circ.

Parenting
501 2nd St.
San Francisco, CA 94107
(415) 546-7575
David Markus, Ed. Monthly magazine,
national circ, parents, kids 0-10 years.
200,000 circ., national readership.

Parents Press
1454 6th
Berkeley, CA 94710
(415) 524-1602
Dixie Jordan, Ed, Margot Rapoport, Books
Ed. Monthly paper for parents of children
from birth to adolescence. 75,000 circ,10
rev/issue, Grtr Bay Area readership.

PC World
501 2nd St.
San Francisco, CA 94107
(415) 243-0500
Robert Luhn, Ed. Monthly magazine for
computer users. 315,000 circ.

Pedantic Monthly
1383 Idaho St.
Santa Clara, CA 95050
(408) 985-9208
Erik A Johnson, Ed, Lydia Renay, Books
Ed. Monthly. Humor, poetry, politics,
satire, fict. 1,000 circ, no reviews, men-
tions books/authors, na readership.

Peninsula Magazine
2317 Broadway
Redwood City, CA 94063
(415) 368-8800
Lifestyle, South Bay Area

Peninsula Parent/San Francisco Parent
Box 89
Millbrae, CA 94030
(415) 342-9203
Lisa Rosenthal, Ed. Monthly tabloid;
resources, articles of interest to parents,
kids, Bay Area schedule of family events.
42,000 circ, 3 rev/issue.

Peninsula Progress
440 San Mateo Ave.
San Bruno, CA 94066
(415) 588-3392
Margie O'Clair, Ed. Weekly. 65,000 circ.

Philippine News
Box 2767
San Francisco, CA 94083-2767
(415) 872-3000
Nick Benoza, Ed. Weekly newspaper,
Philippine community nationally. 89,000
circ.

Photo Metro
6 Rodgers #207C
San Francisco, CA 94103
(415) 861-6453
Henry Brimmer, Ed, Bernadette Powell,
Books Ed. 10x/year. Tabloid: articles, ads
of interest to photographers. 15,000 circ, 5
rev/issue, mentions books/authors, na,
interna readership.

Piedmont Press (see Berkeley Press)

Piedmont/Oakland Bulletin
131 41st St.
Oakland , CA 94611
(415) 658-2441
Weekly, local newspaper. 10,000 circ.

Poetics Journal
2639 Russell St.
Berkeley, CA 94705
(415) 548-1817
Lyn Hejinian, Ed. Criticism, essays,
reviews. 600 circ.

Poetry Flash
Box 4172
Berkeley, CA 94704
(415) 548-6871
Poetry, reviews, calendar.

Poets On
29 Loring Ave
Mill Valley, CA 94941
Quarterly poetry journal.

Point Reyes Light
Box 210, Point Reyes Station
Point Reyes , CA 94956
(415) 663-8404
David Mitchell, Ed. Weekly newspaper,
community oriented. 3,600 circ.

Popular Woodworking
1300 Galaxy Way
Concord, CA 94520
(415) 671-9852
*David Camp, Ed, Hugh Foster, Books Ed.
Bimonthly woodworking mag., full-color.
65,000 circ, 5 rev/issue, mentions books/
authors, na readership.*

Portalwood Press
329 West Portal Ave.
San Francisco, CA 94127
(415) 681-6397
*Robert S O'Brien, Ed, Charlotte Callis,
Books Ed. Monthly. Community newspaper. 30,000 circ, 1 rev/issue.*

Portuguese Journal
1912 Church Lane
San Francisco, CA 94806
(415) 237-0888
Alberto Lemos, Ed. Weekly newspaper.

Portuguese Tribune
1617B East Santa Clara St.
San Jose, CA 95116
(408) 251-7300
Arthur Oliver, Ed. 16,000 circ.

Post Dispatch
515 Railroad Ave.
Pittsburg, CA 94565
(415) 432-7336
Robert Weaver, Man. Ed. 7,000 circ.

Post-Record
76 West Saint John St.
San Jose, CA 95113
(408) 287-4866
*Opal McLean, Ed. Legal newspaper. 600
circ, no reviews, South Bay Area readership.*

Potrero View
953 DeHaro
San Francisco, CA 94107
(415) 826-8080
*Ruth Passen, Ed. Monthly, neighborhood.
10,000 circ.*

Power Points Newsletter
Box 67-8000
Placerville, CA 95667
(916) 622-7777
*E. Hamilton Hensley, Ed. 8x/year. Ex-
cerpts, reviews of books re business,
sales, mktg. 20 rev/issue, na, interna
readership.*

Publish
501 2nd St.
San Francisco, CA 94107
(415) 243-0600
*Jim Felici, Ed. Monthly magazine, how-to
desktop publishing*

Publishing Poynters
Box 4232-841
Santa Barbara, CA 93140-04232
(805) 968-7277, FAX (805) 968-1379
*Dan Poynter, Ed. Monthly newsletter re
book marketing for small publishers. 2
rev/issue, mentions books/authors,
interna readership. Send news releases,
mail list offers.*

Quarry West
c/o Porter College, Univ. of Cal. @ Santa
Cruz
Santa Cruz, CA 95064
(408) 429-2155
*Kenneth Weisner, Ed. 2x/year. Poetry,
fict., essays, graphics. 1,000 circ.*

Quilt
1446 Sixth St., Suite D
Berkeley, CA 94710
(415) 527-1586
*Ishmael Reed, Ed. 1x/year. Poetry, fict.,
criticism, essays, graphics. 1,000 circ.*

Radiance
Box 31703
Oakland, CA 94604
(415) 482-0680
*Alice Ansfield, Ed. Quarterly, 4-color mag.,
for large women. 40,000 circ, 15/year,
mentions books/authors, na, interna
readership.*

Rainbo Electronic Reviews
8 Duran Ct.
Pacifica, CA 94044
(415) 993-8029
Maggie Ramirez, Ed. 30x/month. Book review service seen on electronic media. 600,000 circ, 30 rev/issue, interna readership.

Recorder Progress
1331 San Mateo Ave.
South San Francisco, CA 94080
(415) 266-9600
Will Thomas, Ed. Bimonthly newspaper.16,000 circ.

Release Print
346 9th St, 2nd Fl
San Francisco, CA 94103
(415) 552-8760
Robert Anbian, Ed. 10/yr. Newsletter of Film Arts Foundation, Northern Calif organization of independent film & video makers.

Representations
English Department, Univ. of Cal.
Berkeley, CA 94720
(415) 642-9044
Stephen Greenblatt, Svetlana Alpers, Ed. 4x/year. Criticism, essays, translations. 2,200 circ, no reviews, mentions books/ authors.

Research
2201 Third St.
San Francisco, CA 94107
(415) 621-0220
Thomas A Elliott, Ed. Monthly. Stockbrokers, financial analysts.

Rohnert Park/Cotati Clarion
211 Southwest Blvd.
Rohnert Park, CA 94928
(707) 795-5451
Jud Snyder, Ed. 2/week, newspaper, community oriented. 15,000 circ.

Ross Valley Reporter
Box B
San Anselmo, CA 94953
(415) 332-3778
Cinda Becker, Ed. Weekly. Community news.12,000 circ.

Rossmoor News
Box 2109
Walnut Creek, CA 94595
(415) 939-0622
Maureen O'Rourke, Ed. Weekly. Rossmoor & local news. 8,500 circ, reviews only about Rossmoor, Walnut Creek. Rarely mentions books/authors.

Russian Life Daily
2460 Sutter St.
San Francisco, CA 94115
(415) 921-5380
N Petlin, Ed. 3,000 circ.

Russian River News
14065 Armstrong Woods Rd.
Guerneville, CA 95446
(707) 869-3520
John DeSalvio, Ed. Weekly newspaper, community oriented.

RV West
2019 Clement St.
San Francisco, CA 94501
(415) 769-8338
David Johnson, Ed. Monthly magazine of RV travel in Western states. 76,000 circ.

Sacramento Bee
2100 Q St
Sacramento, CA 95852
(916) 321-1001
Gregory Favre, Ed, Paul Craig, Books Ed. Daily metropolitan newspaper. 225,000 circ.

Sacramento Bee Magazine
Box 15779
Sacramento, CA 95852
(916) 446-9211
Terry Dvorik, Ed. Sunday magazine of Sacto Bee. 261,000 circ.

Sacramento Magazine
1021 Second St.
Sacramento, CA 95814
(916) 446-7548
Nancy Curley, Ed, Ann McCully Sisemore, Books Ed. Monthly magazine, travel & lifestyle featuring Sacto area. 4 rev/issue, mentions books/authors.

Sacramento Union
301 Capitol Mall, Box 2711
Sacramento, CA 95812-2711
(916) 442-7811
Jim Vesily, Ed, Jerry Cox, Books Ed. Daily metropolitan newspaper.93,000 circ.

Sagewoman Magazine
Box 5130
Santa Cruz, CA 95063
(408) 429-8637
Lunaea Weatherstone, Ed. Quarterly. Women's spirituality, religion, women and New Age only. 1,400 circ, 5 rev/issue, Santa Cruz readership.

San Francisco Bay Guardian
2700 19th St.
San Francisco, CA 94110
(415) 824-7660
Tim Fields, Ed, Eileen Ecklund, Books Ed. Arts, entertainment, news weekly. 65,000 circ, 10 rev/issue, favors Bay Area authors, Grtr Bay Area readership.

San Francisco Business
456 California St, 9th Floor
San Francisco, CA 94104
(415) 392-4511
Evangeline Tolleson, Ed. Monthly. 9,000 circ.

San Francisco Business Times
325 5th St.
San Francisco, CA 94107
(415) 777-9355
Michael Mazec, Ed. Weekly. Bus news in Alameda, Contra Costa, Marin, SF & San Mateo counties. 33,000 circ, no reviews, mentions books/authors.

San Francisco Catholic
441 Church St.
San Francisco, CA 94114-1793
(415) 565-3630
Charlotte Pace, Ed. Monthly. Features, news for Bay Area Catholic community. 49,000 circ, some reviews, mentions books/authors.

San Francisco Chronicle
901 Mission St.
San Francisco, CA 94103
(415) 777-1111
William German, Ed, Patricia Holt, Books Ed. 553,000 Daily, 709,000 Sunday Book Review magazine, 1000 reviews/yr. Favor Calif authors/publishers and Calif subjects. Grtr Bay Area readership.

San Francisco Examiner
110 5th
San Francisco, CA 94103
(415) 777-2424
William R Hearst III, Ed, Tom Dowling, Books Ed. Daily metropolitan newspaper, Wine & food: Jim Wood. Media Watch: David Armstrong. 150,000 Daily, 707,000 Sunday circ, Sunday edition combined with SF Chronicle. Book review section is SF Chronicle.

San Francisco Focus Magazine
680 8th St.
San Francisco, CA 94111
(415) 553-2800
Mark Powelson, Ed. Monthly magazine, city & regional issues, personalities, arts, entertainment, KQED radio & TV schedule. 200,000 circ.

San Francisco Independent
21 West Portal Ave.
San Francisco, CA 94127
(415) 731-1140
John Moses, Ed. Weekly newspaper. 50,000 circ.

San Francisco Magazine
680 Eighth St.
San Francisco, CA 94111
(415) 982-3232
Warren Sharpe, Ed, Katharine Fong, Books Ed. Monthly, upscale magazine covering SF Bay Area issues, arts, enter-taiment, personalities. 75,000 circ.

San Francisco Post
Box 1350
Oakland, CA 94604-1350
(415) 763-1120
Gail Berkeley, Ed. Biweekly,100,000 circ.

San Francisco Progress
851 Howard St.
San Francisco, CA 94103
(415) 982-8022
William Rentschler, Ed. 3x/week. Temporarily suspended publication, January 1989, San Francisco's "Hometown Newspaper," local, neighborhood, City Hall, school sports. 275,000 circ.

San Francisco Review of Books
1117 Geary
San Francisco, CA 94109
(415) 771-1252
Peter Caroll, Ed. Quarterly. "Always on the look-out for Bay Area writers," the most important literary review periodical in SF Bay Area. Also film reviews, interviews, articles, news re publishers. 5,000 circ, 25 rev/issue.

San Francisco Sentinel
500 Hayes St.
San Francisco, CA 94102
(415) 861-8100
Tom Murray, Ed, Michael Gunsaulus, Books Ed. Weekly tabloid, gay lifestyle, news, entertain, sports, diet. 93,000 circ, 2 rev/issue, na readership.

San Francisco Times
329 West Portal Ave.
San Francisco, CA 94127
(415) 681-6397
Robert S O'Brien, Ed, Charlotte Callis, Books Ed. Monthly. Community. 30,000 circ, 1 rev/issue, mentions Bay Area authors, Grtr Bay Area readership.

San Jose Business Journal
152 North Third St., Suite 100
San Jose, CA 95112
(408) 295-3800
Scott Smith, Ed. Weekly tabloid, local business news in Santa Clara county. 13,000 circ.

San Jose Magazine
1778 Technology Dr.
San Jose, CA 95110
(408) 452-0380
Paula Munier Lee, Ed. Monthly, 4-color city regional. 15,000 circ, 1 rev/issue, favors Bay Area authors.

San Jose Mercury News
750 Ridder Park Dr.
San Jose , CA 95190
(408) 920-5000
Robert Ingle, Ed, Connie Casey, Books Ed. Daily, Knight Ridder chain newspaper. 267,000 circ, 10 rev/issue.

San Mateo Times
1080 South Amphlett Blvd.
San Mateo, CA 94402
(415) 348-4321
Michelle Carter, Ed, Jack Russell, Books Ed. Daily, newspaper. 47,000 circ, 3 rev/issue, favors San Mateo County authors.

Santa Clara American
Box 755
Santa Clara, CA 95052
(408) 243-2000
Newspaper.

Santa Cruz Sentinel
207 Church St., Box 638
Santa Cruz, CA 95061-0638
(408) 423-4242
Bruce McPherson, Ed, Christine Watson, Books Ed. 31,600 circ, 4 rev/issue.

Santa Rosa Business Journal
5577 Skylane Blvd. #1A
Santa Rosa, CA 95403
(707) 579-2900
Ken Clark & Randy Sloan, Eds. Monthly tabloid newspaper re business news in Sonoma County. 9,000 circ.

Santa Rosa Press Democrat
472 Mendocino Ave., Box 569
Santa Rosa, CA 95402-0569
(707) 546-2020
Mike Parman, Ed, Dan Taylor, Books Ed. Daily newspaper, Sonoma County and na news. 90,000 circ.

Sea Letter
National Maritime Museum Assoc.,
Presidio of San Francisco, Bldg. #275
San Francisco, CA 94129
(415) 929-0202
Steve Haller, Ed. Semiannual. National Maritime Museum Association, articles on West coast maritime-related subjects. 1,200 circ, no reviews, mentions books/authors, na readership.

Sebastopol Times & News
Box 521
Sebastopol, CA 95473-0521
(707) 823-7845
*John H K Riley, Ed, Lawrence McDonald,
Tom McKay, Books Eds. Weekly newspaper, community oriented. 3,000 circ, some
reviews, favors Bay Area authors.*

Second Coming
Box 31249
San Francisco, CA 94131
(415) 647-3679
*A D Winans, Ed, Wilfred Castano, Books
Ed. 2x/year. Poetry, fiction, criticism,
reviews, graphics. 1,000 circ, no reviews,
na, interna readership.*

Senior News & Views
Box 750097
Petaluma, CA 94975-0097
(707) 585-8551
*Verna Mays, Ed. Monthly tabloid: articles,
ads, & calendar of events of interest to
seniors. 26,000 circ, no reviews, mentions
books/authors, Grtr Bay Area readership.*

Senior Spectrum
9261 Folsom Blvd. #401
Sacramento, CA 95826
(415) 398-3303
*Steve Chanecka, Ed. Newspaper for
seniors, monthlies & weeklies, 18 editions
in greater No. Cal. Favor authors/publishers 55 yrs & older. 257,000 combined circ.*

Senior Times
2780 Aiello Dr.
San Jose, CA 95111
(408) 629-4977
*Mary E Roach, Ed. Monthly magazine
53,439 circ, some reviews, mentions
books/authors, Grtr Bay Area readership.*

Sequoia
Storke Publications Bldg.
Stanford, CA 94305
(415) 497-9282
*Anne M. Gulliskan, Ed. Journal of poetry,
fiction, criticism, art, 2/year, 450 circ.
books/authors mentioned as criticism
rather than reviews.*

SF Magazine
1045 Sansome, #110
San Francisco, CA 94111
(415) 986-5196
*Sarah Lee Ryder, Ed. Monthly, "Matters of
style," design, food, art, architecture,
fashion, interiors, published by California
magazine, 75,000 free circ, mentions
books/authors, greater Bay Area readership.*

Shaman's Drum
Box 2636
Berkeley, CA 94702
(415) 525-5122
*Timothy White, Ed, Arianna Siegel, Books
Ed. Quarterly journal of experimental
shamanism. 20,000 circ, 10 rev/issue, na
readership.*

Shareware Magazine
1030 D East Duane Ave.
Sunnyvale, CA 94086
(408) 730-9291
*Mark Barnes, Ed, Michelle Ramage, Books
Ed. Bimonthly software marketing magazine 100,000 circ, 2 rev/issue, mentions
books/authors, interna readership.*

SHMATE
Box 4228
Berkeley, CA 94704
*Steve Fankuchen, Ed. Quarterly political
and cultural review with emphasis on
issues relevant to Jews and the Jewish
community. 2,500 circ, 2 rev/issue,
interna readership.*

Sierra
730 Polk
San Francisco, CA 94109
(415) 776-2211
*Jonathon King, Ed, Jim Cohee, Books Ed.
6x/year, conservation, environment,
magazine of the Sierra Club. 320,000 circ,
na readership.*

Silicon Valley
Box 60145
Sunnyvale, CA 94088-0145
(408) 249-8020
*Norbert Stein, Ed. Bimonthly, 4-color
magazine, business oriented, "people &
products of Silicon Valley," 16,000 circ.*

Silicon Valley Tech News
199 1st St.
Los Altos, CA 94022
(408) 941-1663
*Frank Burkhard, Ed. Monthly, Tech.
community. 56,000 circ, no reviews, does
not mention books/authors, na readership.*

Single Again
Box 384
Union City, CA 94587
(415) 793-6315
*Len Harris, Ed. 9x/year, lifestyle of the
divorced, separated, widowed. 7,500 circ,
5 rev/issue, Grtr Bay Area readership.*

Sinister Wisdom
Box 3252
Berkeley, CA 94703
*Elana Dykewomon, Ed. 4x/year. Poetry,
fict., reviews, interviews, plays, graphics,
lesbian, feminist. 3,000 circ, 5 rev/issue,
mentions books/authors, interna readership.*

Sipapu
Route 1, Box 216
Winters, CA 95694
(916) 752-1032
*Noel Peattie, Ed. 2x/year. Newsletter for
librarians, editors, collectors interested in
dissent literature, reviews, interviews,
conference news. 450 circ, 20 rev/issue,
interna readership.*

Small Business Exchange
Box 11305
San Francisco, CA 94101
(415) 695-0505
*Gerald Johnson, Ed. Weekly newspaper,
business oriented.*

Small Business Reports
203 Calle del Oaks
Monterey, CA
(408) 899-7221
*Thomas Owens, Ed. Monthly. For manag-
ers of small to mid-sized businesses.
30,000 circ, 1 rev/issue, mentions books/
authors, na readership.*

Small Press Review
Box 100
Paradise, CA 95967
*Len Fulton, Ed. Monthly. Many reviews of
literary titles; misc news of small presses;
tabloid. 10 rev/issue, interna readership.*

Socialist Review
3202 Adeline St.
Berkeley, CA 94703
(415) 547-3732
*Ron Silliman, Ed. Quarterly magazine,
politics, history, economic. 4,500 circ.*

Sonoma Business Magazine
3559 Airway Dr.
Santa Rosa, CA 95403
(707) 575-8282
*Carol Caldwell-Ewart, Ed. Monthly. Local,
4-color business magazine. 7,500 circ, no
reviews, mentions Sonoma County authors.*

Sonoma Index Tribune
117 West Napa St.
Sonoma, CA 95476
(707) 938-2111
*William Lynch, Ed.10,500 circ, no reviews,
Sonoma Valley readership.*

Sonoma Sports Digest
1415B North Dutton Ave.
Santa Rosa, CA 95401
(707) 578-6146
*Andrew Hidas, Ed. Quarterly, 4-color
magazine 10,000 circ, no reviews, mentions books/authors, Grtr Bay Area
readership.*

South Bay Accent
4320 Stevens Creek Blvd.,#230
San Jose, CA 95129
(408) 244-5102
*Debbe Klosowski, Ed. 6/year, magazine
on South Bay Area interests. 41,000 circ.*

South Valley Times
5725 Winfield Blvd., Suite 6
San Jose, CA 95123
(408) 365-1245
*Bob Shibley, Ed. Monthly tabloid newspa-
per, community oriented.*

Spectrum Review
Box 1030
Lower Lake, CA 95457
(707) 928-5751
Georg Feuerstein, Ed. Quarterly. Religion, spirituality, philosophy, psych. & art; book reviews. 2,000 circ, 40 rev/issue, interna readership.

SPEX
#9 Channel Landing
Tiburon, CA 94920
(415) 381-4601
Karen Misuraca, Ed, Dick Murdock, Jayne Murdock, Books Eds. Bimonthly newsletter for small publishers; reviews local books & books on publishing.

Sports Unlimited
3310 Beacon #1
San Jose, CA 95118
(408) 723-2233
Dick Degan, Ed. Bimonthly tabloid, young adult, sports and recreation. 36,000 circ.

Stone Soup
Box 83
Santa Cruz, CA 95063
(408) 426-5557
Gerry Mandel, Ed. 5x/year. Fiction, poetry, book reviews and art by children ages 6-13. 10,000 circ, 2 rev/issue, na readership.

Sun Yat-Sen News
1109 Powell St.
San Francisco, CA 94108
(415) 391-3691
Lilly Tsau, Ed. Monthly, 2,000 circ.

Sun-Reporter/Metro Papers
1366 Turk St.
San Francisco, CA 94115
(415) 931-5778
Amelia Ashley Ward, Ed, Thomas Fleming, Books Ed. Weekly black oriented newspaper. 150,000 circ, favors Bay Area authors.

Sunset
80 Willow Rd.
Menlo Park, CA 94025-3691
(415) 321-3600
William Marken, Ed. Monthly. Cook, craft, family, house, garden. 1,500,000 circ., Western States readership.

Tenderloin Times
25 Taylor St.
San Francisco, CA 94102
(415) 776-0700
Sara Colm, Ed. Monthly newspaper, in Vietnamese, Laotian, Cambodian & Eng, SF neighborhood. 30,000 circ.

The Antioch Daily Ledger
1700 Cavallo Rd., Box 2299
Antioch, CA 94509
(415) 757-2525
Robert Wearr, Ed. Daily, 15,000 circ.

The Apartment Owners News
2329 Eagle Ave.
Alameda, CA 94501
(415) 769-7523
Dianna Hoffman, Ed. Monthly. 26,000 circ.

The Argus
37427 Centralmont Pl., Box 5100
Fremont, CA 94537
(415) 794-0111
Phyliss Argent, Man. Ed, Diane Dawson, Lifestyle Ed. Daily newspaper. 30,000 circ, no reviews.

The Ark
Box 1054
Tiburon, CA 94920
(415) 435-2652
*Marilyn Kessler, Barbara Gnoss, Eds, Rita Fink, Books Ed.
Weekly. Southern Marin county news, regular book reviews. 4,000 circ.*

The Berkeley Monthly
1301 59th St.
Emeryville, CA 94608
(415) 658-9811
Paul Shaffer, Ed. Monthly. General interest. 95,000 circ, 1 rev/issue, mentions books/authors, Grtr Bay Area readership.

The Berkeley Voice
2936 Domingo Ave.
Oakland, CA 94705
(415) 644-8208
Chip Brown, Ed. Weekly. 27,000 circ.

The Black Scholar
Box 2869
Oakland, CA 94609-0869
(415) 547-6633
Robert Chrisman, Ed, Jonina Abron, Books Ed. Bimonthly journal of black studies. 10,500 circ,

The Californians
5720 Ross Branch Rd.
Sebastopol, CA 95472
(415) 587-2240
Jean Sherrell, Ed, Dr Abraham Hoffman, Books Ed. Semimonthly, Alta & Baja Cal. hist. 17,000 circ, 25 rev/issue, mentions books/authors, na, interna readership.

The Catholic Voice
2918 Lakeshore Ave.
Oakland, CA 94610-3697
(415) 893-4711
Monica Clark, Ed. Semimonthly. Local & world news. 101,000 circ, no reviews, Grtr Bay Area readership.

The Christian Communicator
c/o Joy Publishing,
26131 Avenida Aeropuerto
San Juan Capistrano, CA 92675
(714) 493-8161
Woody Young, Ed. Monthly newsletter for writers and speakers, 1-3 book reviews/issue, 3000 circ, mostly Bay Area.

The Daily Californian
2150 Dwight Way
Berkeley, CA 94704
(415) 548-8080
Liz Moore, Ed, Jim Herron, Carolyn Jones, Books Ed. Newspaper produced by & for UC students, also Berkeley city & some na & interna news. 26,000 circ, 7 rev/issue.

The Daily Review
116 W Winton Ave., Box 5050
Hayward, CA 94544
(415) 783-6111
David Halvorsen, Ed. Daily, 48,000 circ.

The Galley Sail Review
1630 University Ave., #42
Berkeley, CA 94703
(415) 486-0187 *
Stanley McNail, Ed. 3x/year. "A Journal of New Poetry," reviews. 400 circ, 2 rev/issue, na, interna readership.

The Grito Del Sol Collection
Box 9275
Berkeley, CA 94709
(415) 655-8036
Octavio Romano, Ed. Quarterly. Four newsletters, "eclectic Chicano thought", no reviews, mentions books/authors, na, interna readership.

The Gull
1550 Shattuck Ave., #2044
Berkeley, CA 94709
(415) 843-2222
Don Sanford, Ed. Monthly newsletter. Golden Gate Audubon Society; book reviews.

The Herald
6207 Sierra Ct., Box 3000
Dublin, CA 94568
(415) 829-9111
Bob Wynne, Ed. Daily newspaper. 30,000 circ, 2 rev/week, Alameda, Contra Costa readership.

The Irishman
Box 11278
San Francisco, CA 94101
(415) 665-2838
Thomas McDonagh, Ed, Joe Hession, Books Ed. Monthly, Irish & Irish-Amer., tabloid newspaper. 6,000 circ, 1 rev/issue, mentions books/authors, West. U.S. readership.

The Kobrin Letter
732 Greer Rd.
Palo Alto, CA 94303-3022
(415) 856-6658
Dr. Beverly Kobrin, Ed. 7x/year. Children/young adults. 20 rev/issue, interna readership.

The Library Bookseller
Box 9544
Berkeley, CA 94709-0544
(415) 340-6951
Scott Saifer, Ed, Dorothy Hoover, Books Ed. Semimonthly. Books wanted by libraries, free listing service. 100 libraries, 100 book dealers, no reviews, interna readership.

The Marina Newspaper
3235 Fillmore
San Francisco, CA 94123
(415) 929-8430
Maggie McCall, Ed. Bimonthly newspaper, neighborhood news, specializes in SF Bay sailing events plus general interest. 11,000 circ.

The Monthly Planet
Box 8463
Santa Cruz, CA 95061
(408) 429-8755
John Govsky, Ed. Monthly. Pacifist, nuclear freeze. 15,000 circ, 1 rev/issue, mentions books/authors, na readership.

The Node
547 Frederick St.
San Francisco, CA 94117
(415) 759-1407
Eve Furchgott, Ed. Quarterly magazine re computers, graphics, no reviews, 36,000 circ.

The Northwesterner
Box 1346
Ross, CA 94957
(415) 454-1771
Dick Murdock, Ed. 2x/year. Railroads, especially the Old Northwestern Pacific Railroad, history, photos. 1,000 circ, 1 rev/issue, No. Cal. readership.

The Opera Companion
40 Museum Way
San Francisco, CA 94114
(415) 626-2741
Dr James Keolker, Ed.15x/year. Music, opera magazine 8,000 circ, 2 rev/issue, na, interna readership.

The Owner Builder
c/o The Owner Builder Center
1250 Addison #209
Berkeley, CA 94702
(415) 848-6860
Annette Gill, Ed. Quarterly. Home bldg., repair, remodeling. 15,000 circ, 1 rev/ issue, mentions books/authors, Grtr Bay Area readership.

The Paper
Box 1250
Forestville, CA 95436
(707) 887-1564
Tom Roth, Ed. Weekly tabloid newspaper, West Sonoma County regional. 5,000 circ, no reviews.

The Piedmonter
131 41st St., Box 11095
Oakland , CA 94611
(415) 658-2441
Loraine Strain, Ed. Weekly newspaper. 9,000+ circ.

The Reaper
403 Continental St.
Santa Cruz, CA 95060
(408) 426-5539
Robert McDowell and Mark Jarman, Ed's. Yearly. Poetry, fict., criticism, essays, reviews, graphics. 700 circ, 2 rev/issue, mentions books/authors, na, interna readership.

The Review
Box 92
El Verano, CA 95433
(707) 938-0780
Julie Tapia, Ed. Weekly. Tourist, wine country, No. Cal. tabloid. 2.2 Million circ.

The San Matean
1700 Hillsdale Blvd
San Mateo, CA 94402
(415) 574-6330
Peter Schubert, Ed. Weekly. 4,000 circ.

The Shapers
Box 32386
Oakland, CA 94604
(415) 843-3088
Ade Y Aro, Ed, Oluremo Omodele, Books Ed. Free newspaper, "to address the potential contributions of individuals & groups in their evolutions and their environment." 10,000 circ, bimonthly reviews, Grtr Bay Area readership.

The Threepenny Review
Box 9131
Berkeley, CA 94709
(415) 849-4545
Wendy Lesser, Ed. Quarterly literary arts magazine, liberal, sent to bookstores, 8,000 circ.

The Tribune
409 13th St., Box 24424
Oakland, CA 94623-1424
(415) 645-2000
Robert C Maynerd, Ed. Daily, 158,000 circ.

The Wine Spectator
601 Van Ness Ave.
San Francisco, CA 94102
(415) 673-2040
Marvin Schanken, Ed. Monthly, articles, wine news for consumers, book reviews.

The Wise Woman
2441 Cordova St.
Oakland, CA 94602
(415) 536-3174
Ann Forfreedom, Ed. Quarterly. Feminist issues, witchcraft, goddess lore, women's hist. Some reviews, na, interna readership.

The Wormwood Review
Box 8840
Stockton, CA 95208-0840
(209) 466-8231
Marvin Malone, Ed. 4x/year. Poetry, reviews, translation, graphics. 700 circ, 20 rev/issue, interna readership.

Third World Resources
464 19th St.
Oakland, CA 94612
(415) 835-4692
Tom Fenton, Ed, Mary Heffron, Books Ed. Quarterly newsletter, reviews, listings on Third World areas and issues. 1,500 circ, 25 rev/issue, na, interna readership.

Tiempo Latino
870 Market St., #952
San Francisco, CA 94102
(415) 982-6592
Fernando Pachece, Ed. Weekly. Spanish lang. 31,000 circ.

Tikkun, Institute for Labor and Mental Health
5100 Leona St.
Oakland, CA 94619
(415) 482-0805
Michael Lerner, Ed, Michael Kazin, Books Ed. Bimonthly critique of politics, culture and society.

Time Magazine
Bay Area Bureau Office,
#2 Embarcadero, #1900
San Francisco, CA 94111
(415) 982-5000
Paul Wittman, Ed. Weekly. 4,600,000 circ.

Times Tribune
245 Lytton Ave.
Palo Alto, CA 94301
(415) 853-1200
Michael Kidder, Ed, Jean Griffin, Books Ed. Daily newspaper, Peninsula area, 56,000 circ, 6 rev/issue.

Tole World
Box 6086
Concord, CA 94524
(415) 671-9852
Zach Shatz, Ed. Bimonthly. Tole and decorative painters, full-color magazine 33,000 circ, 1 rev/issue, na readership.

Tradeswomen
Box 40664
San Francisco, CA 94140
(415) 821-7334
Molly Martin, Ed. Quarterly. Women in blue collar work. 900 circ, 2 rev/issue, mentions books/authors, na, interna readership.

Travel Publishing News
Box 7548
Berkeley, CA 94707
(415) 527-9885
Elaine O'Gara, Ed. Quarterly newsletter regarding travel periodicals, publishers. 20 rev/issue, mentions books/authors, interna readership.

Travelage West
100 Grant Ave.
San Francisco, CA 94108
(415) 781-8353
Donald Langley, Ed. Weekly. Retail travel agents magazine 36,000 circ, brief mentions of travel guides, West. U.S. readership.

Twin Cities Times
Box 1864
Corte Madera, CA 94925
(415) 924-8552
Billie L Anderson, Ed. Weekly. 5,200 circ,

U.S. News & World Report
601 California St, #204
San Francisco , CA 94108
(415) 392-8593
Peter Dworkin, Bureau Chief. Na & interna distributed news magazine.

Update
2120 Green Hill Rd.
Sebastopol, CA 95472-9306
(707) 823-2867
Bill McMillan, Ed. Quarterly. Alternative travel. 500 circ, 1 rev/issue, mentions books/authors, na, interna readership.

Vallejo Times Herald
440 Curtola Parkway
Vallejo, CA 94590
(707) 644-1141
Coleen Truelsen, Ed. Daily newspaper, East Bay. 25,000 circ.

Valley Journal
298 Sunnyvale Ave., #104
Sunnyvale , CA 94086
(408) 739-3093
Anne Chappell, Ed. Weekly newspaper. 31,000 circ.

Valley Times
127 Spring St., Box 607
Pleasanton, CA 94566
(415) 462-4160
Robert Goll, Ed. Daily. 46,000 circ.

Vestkusten
435 Duboce Ave.
San Francisco, CA 94117
(415) 621-4851
Karin W Person, Ed. Biweekly newspaper in Swedish/English.

Voices of Youth
Box JJ
Sonoma, CA 95476
(707) 938-8314
Alvin J Gordon, Ed, Diana Haigwood, Catherine Jones, Books Eds. Twice/year. Education, self-development, civic values, "intergenerational dialogue." 2,000 circ, 3 reviews/issue, na readership.

Voz De Portugal
370 A St.
Hayward, CA 94541
(415) 537-9503
Laurence Costa Aguilar, Ed. Bimonthly.

Wall Street Journal
220 Battery St.
San Francisco , CA 94111
(415) 986-6886
Greg HIll, Bureau Chief. 426,000 circ.

West
750 Ridder Park Dr.
San Jose, CA 95190
(408) 920-5000
Jeffrey Klein, Ed. Magazine in Sunday San Jose Mercury News. 327,000 circ, no reviews, mentions books/authors.

West Coast Review Of Books
5265 Fountain Ave., Upper Terrace - Six
Los Angeles, CA 90029
(213) 660-0433
D David Dreis, Ed. 200 rev/issue, mentions books/authors, na readership.

West County Times
1660 San Pablo Ave., Box 128
Pinole, CA 94564
(415) 741-7171
Albert C Pacciorini, Ed, Carol Fowler, Books Ed. Daily, 45,000 circ, 4 rev/issue. Grtr Bay Area readership.

Western Banker
1110 Main St
St Helena, CA 94574
(415) 362-5452
Greg Sadfell, Ed. Monthly magazine of financial management, for bankers. 9,000 circ.

Western Real Estate News
3057 17th St.
San Francisco, CA 94110
(415) 861-7200
Bill Jenkins, Ed. Semimonthly magazine regarding real estate. 25,000 circ, 2 rev/issue, West. U.S. readership.

Whole Earth Review
27 Gate Five Rd.
Sausalito, CA 94965
(415) 332-1716
Kevin Kelly, Ed, Richard Nilsen, Books Ed. Quarterly, New Age, tools, books, crafts, self-help. 50,000 circ, 30 rev/issue, mentions books/authors, interna readership.

Wine Country Magazine
985 Lincoln Ave.
Benecia, CA 94558
(707) 746-0741
Shirley G Ray, Ed. Semimonthly. World food, wine, travel, fine living. 46,000 circ.

Wines & Vines
1800 Lincoln Ave.
San Rafael, CA 94901-1298
(415) 453- 9700 FAX (415) 453-2517
Philip E> Hiaring, Ed. monthly trade magazine for wineries, na readship. 5000 circ.

Yellow Silk: Journal of Erotic Arts
Box 6374
Albany, CA 94706
(415) 841-6500
Lily Pond, Ed. Quarterly. Erotic lit., arts, please don't send queries. 14,000 circ, 2 rev/issue, mentions books/authors, interna readership.

Yoga Journal
2054 University Ave., #604
Berkeley, CA 94704
(415) 841-9200
Stephan Bodian, Ed, Gary Doore, Books Ed. Bimonthly mag., hatha yoga, meditation, holistic healing, health, psych. 58,000 circ, 12 rev/issue, mentions books/ authors, interna readership.

Young China Daily
49 Hang Ah St.
San Francisco, CA 94108
(415) 982-6161
Peter Xsu, Ed.19,000 circ.

ZYZZYVA
41 Sutter,#1400
San Francisco, CA 94104
(415) 982-3440
Howard Junker, Ed. Quarterly. West coast writers & artists. 3,500 circ, no reviews, favors Bay Area authors, na readership.

Periodicals Published Elsewhere:
Newspapers, Magazines, Newsletters and Journals

Periodicals Published Elsewhere:
Newspapers, Magazines, Newsletters and Journals

**Alaska Assoc of Small Presses
Newsletter**
Box 821
Cordova, AK 99574
*Constance Taylor, Ed. News, events,
reviews for small publishers, regional or-
ganization.*

Albuquerque Journal
PO Drawer J
Albuquerque, NM 87103
*Tom Mayer, Books Ed. Journal of litera-
ture, fiction, poetry.*

American Bookseller
122 East 42nd St. #1410
New York, NY 10168-0034
(212) 867-9060
*Ginger Curwen, Ed. Trade journal for
bookstores.*

American Historical Review
914 Atwater
Bloomington, IN 47405
(812) 855-7609
*David L. Ransel, Ed. Book reviews; query
first, 5x/year, 7,000 circ, 200 reviews/
issue, na., interna. readership.*

Asian Literary Market Review
Jaffe Publishing Management Serv.,
Kunnuparambil Bldgs
Kurichy, Kottayam 686549
India 04826-470
*Kunnuparambil P Punnoose, Ed.,Nigy K
Punnoose, Books Ed. Helps publishers to
sell books and foreign rights in Asia.
Quarterly, 3,200 circ, 30 reviews/issue,
Asian readership.*

**Association for Authors, Inc.
Newsletter**
4189 Bellaire Blvd., #222
Houston, TX 77025
(713) 666-9711
*Electronic buletin board system, nights
after 5 pm & weekends 24 hrs. Reviews
books on writing/publishing/book, distributing. New magazine for writers to
debut in June 1989: "The Real World
Writer Magazine.", na, interna. readership.*

Aunt Edna's Reading List
2022 H Hunnewell St.
Honolulu, HA 96822
*Monthly newsletter to "connect feminist
readers w/authors & publishers which
haven't received mainstream publicity."
Many reviews.*

AWB News
Box 6133
Albuquerque, NM 87197
(505) 821-1393
*Jane Duval, Ed. Mary Morrell, Reviewer
Women in business, 1 review/issue.
Mentions books/authors, Albuquerque
readership.*

Bay Area Consumers' Checkbook
806 15th St., North West
Washington, DC 20005
(202) 347-7283
Robert M Krughoff, Ed.

BC Bookworld
940 Station St.
Vancouver, BC, Canada V6A 2X4
*Alan Twigg, Ed. News re writers, publish-
ers, libraries in BC. 50,000 circ.*

Bloomsbury Review
2933 Wyandot St.
Denver, CO 80211-3820
(303) 455-0593
*Tom Auer, Ed. Many literary reviews, fic &
nonfic, poetry; request editorial sched.
Tabloid, literary essays. Bimonthly.*

Book Forum
38 East 76th St.
New York, NY 10021-2714
(212) 861-8328
*Marilyn Wood, Ed. Contemporary litera-
ture, art, foreign affairs, for professionals,
academics, writers, written for the "highly
literate."Quarterly.*

Book Marketing Update
51 North Fifth St., Box 1102
Fairfield, IA 52556-1102
(515) 472-6617
*John Kremer, Ed. Newsletter for publishers
and writers, news and reviews, all aspects
book marketing, small press and self-publishers. Bimonthly, 3,000 circ, 10 rev/
issue. Na. readership.*

Book News
5600 NE Hassalo St.
Portland, OR 97213
(503) 281-9230
*Jane Erstine, Books Ed. Reviews of re-
search and reference books or librarians.
Bimonthly, 1,700 circ, 600 reviews/issue,
na., interna. readership.*

Book Research Quarterly
Transaction Periodical Consortium
Rutgers University, Dept. 4010
New Brunswick, NJ 08903
*Beth Luey, Ed. Magazine, articles by
experts in publishing, scholarly. Book
reviews re books on publishing.*

Bookbuilders West/South Newsletter
c/o Unisource
2600 South Commerce Way
Commerce, CA 90040
(213) 725-3700
*Helen Hawekotte Organization for produc-
ers of books, printers, publishers, typogra-
phers, etc.*

Booklist
50 East Huron St.
Chicago, IL 60611-2729
(312) 244-6780
*Bill Ott, Ed., Martin Brady, Books Ed.
Book review magazine published by the
American Library Assoc. 6,000 reviews
annually. Submit galley proof 15 weeks
pre-pub. Non-print also. 12/yr, 32,000
circ, 250 rev/issue, na. readership.*

Bookman's Weekly
Box AB
Clifton, NJ 07015
(201) 772-0020
*Jacob Chernofsky, Ed. Magazine for the
specialist in book trade.*

Bookwomen
9342 Big River Run
Columbia, MD 21045
(301) 730-8744
*Brenda Brienza, Ed. Newsletter of
Women's Na Book Assoc, reviews "books
of interest to working women."*

Boston Review
33 Harrison Ave.
Boston, MA 02111
(617) 350-5353
*Margaret Ann Roth, Ed. Bimonthly literary
tabloid, 5 reviews/issue, na readership.*

Business Book Review
615 W Kirby
Champaign, IL 61820
(217) 398-2077
Elaine Oldham, Ed.

Business Library Newsletter
427-3 Amberst St..
Nashua, NH 03063
(603) 672-0705
*Raymond Hubbard Ed. Reviews of busi-
ness books for libraries. 12 reviews/
month, interna readership.*

Campus Market Report
528 E Lorain St.
Oberlin, OH 44074-1298
(216) 775-7777
*Mavis Clark, Ed., Ronnie Hughes, Books
Ed. Newsletter, Na. Assoc of College
Stores. Monthly, 1,000 circ, no reviews.
Mentions books/authors, na. readership.*

Canadian Author & Bookman
25 Farmview Cir.
Willowdale, Ontario M2J 1G5
(416) 493-3111
*Diane Kerner, Ed. Trade journal, writers,
publishers.*

Canadian Printer and Publisher
481 University Ave.
Toronto M5W 1A7 ON Canada
(416) 596-5000
Jack Homer, Ed. Trade journal for publishers, business.

Changing Men Magazine
306 North Brooks #BY
Madison, WI 53715
Michael Biernbaum, Ed. Na. journal exploring issues of masculinity, including fiction. 3x/year, 3,500 circ, 6 pgs of reviews/issue. Mentions books/authors, na., interna. readership.

Chicago Tribune
435 N Michigan Ave., #400
Chicago, IL 66011-4022
(312) 222-3232
Diane Donovan, Books Ed. Major metro. newspaper.

Childrens' Book Council Newsletter
67 Irving Pl.
New York, NY 10003
(212) 254-2666

Choice Magazine
100 Riverview Center
Middletown, CT 06457
(203) 347-6933
Academic library book reviews, magazine & reviews on card deck. Monthly, 600 reviews/issue, na., interna. readership.

Clockwatch Review
Dept. of English, Illinois Wesleyan
Univ.Bloomington, IL 61702
James Plath, Ed. Literary journalism, reviews.

Columba: Midwest Review of Books
101 E Wilson Bridge Rd.
Columbus, OH 43085-2303
(614) 885-1031
Jeanne Bonham, Ed. Non-fic, fic, children's, mystery, young adult. 25-40 reviews/issue, national readership.

Columbia Journalism Review
700 Journalism Bldg., Columbia Univ.
New York, NY 10027-6937
(212) 280-5595
Gloria Cooper, Ed.Media issues, book reviews.

Computer Book Review
735 Ekekela Pl.
Honolulu, HI 96817-1633
Carlene Char, Ed. 60 reviews/issue, na. readership.

Crafts Magazine
PJS Publications News Plaza, Box 1790
Peoria, IL 61656
(309) 682-6626
Judith Brossart, Ed. Reviews craft & small business books.

Denver Post
Box 1709
Denver, CO 80201
Glenn Giffin, Books Ed. Metropolitan newspaper, 6 reviews/issue, Western U.S. readership.

Editor & Publisher
11 West 19th St.
New York, NY 10011-4234
(212) 752-7050
John Consoli, Ed. Weekly trade journal for newspaper publishers, editors, communications professionals.

EPB Electronic Publishing & Bookselling
2214 N Central #103
Phoenix, AZ 85004-1483
(602) 254-6156
Sandra Paul, Ed.

Fact Sheet Five
6 Arizona Ave.
Renselaer, NY 12144
Mike Gunderloy, Ed. Reviews books, magazines & tapes by independent publishers, reviews amateur periodicals. Quarterly, 40 reviews/issue, na., interna. readership.

Feminist Bookstore News
3639 Hidalgo
Dallas, TX 75220-1714
B Ruth Rinehart, Ed. Reviews of books re children, young adults, women, news and events re feminist bookstores.

Fessenden Review
Box 7272
San Diego, CA 92107-0272
(415) 327- 6121
Douglas Cruickshank, Ed. Literary journal, poetry, criticism, reviews, some non-fiction. 100 reviews/issue. Poetry Ed. A.W. Allworthy, interna. readership 20,000 circ, quarterly.

FORECAST
6 Kirby Ave.
Somerville, NJ 08876
(201) 526-8000
Vicki L Hanson, Ed. Reviews & news, published by Baker & Taylor, largest book wholesaler.

Frontiers
CB 246, Univ. of Colorado
Boulder, CO 80309-0246
Charlotta Hensley, Ed. Journal of womens' studies, 5 reviews/issue.

Gifted Child Today
350 Weinacker Ave., Box 6448
Mobile, AL 36660-0448
(205) 478-4700
Marvin Gold, Ed., Charlie Beck, Books Ed. Education, gifted children. Bimonthly, 20 reviews/issue, na., interna. readership.

Health News & Review
Box 876
New Canaan, CT 06840
DJ Arneson, Ed. Bimonthly newspaper, health books.

Hellas : The Journal of Neo-Classicism
304 South Tyson Ave.
Glenside, PA 19038
Gerry Harnett, Ed. Quarterly poetry journal, essays, scholarship, first issue Dec. 1989. 4 reviews/issue.

Hispanic
111 Mass Ave., NW, #410
Washington, D.C. 20001
(800) 338-2590
Monthly magazine of the contemp Hispanic; book review column, 2 reviews/issue, na. readership.

Holistic Health Network News
3275 West Hillsboro Blvd., #204-B
Deerfield Beach, FL 33442
(800) 332-2257
Hank Hudson, Ed. Some reviews.

Horn Book Magazine
31 St. James Ave.
Boston, MA 02116-4167
(617) 482-5198
Anita Silvey, Ed. Reviews books for kids and young adults, literary magazine for libraries, bookstores, academics. Bimonthly. 22,000 circ, 500 reviews/year.

Hotline
15 Arbutus Lane
Stony Brook, NY 11790
(516) 751-7840
John Gill, Ed. Quarterly newsletter, fic, nonfic reviews of books re kids in divorce, Children's Rights of New York, Teenagers, suicide, step-parenting, safety, etc. 20 reviews/issue, na. readership.

Houston Post
Box 4747
Houston, TX 77210-4747
(713) 972-1373
Elizabeth Bennett, Books Ed. Metropolitan newspaper, 10 reviews/issue, Texas readership.

Hudson Review
684 Park Ave.
New York, NY 10021
Paula Dietz, Ed. Literary fiction & nonfiction, short stories, poetry, literary journal, articles, translations, reviews.

Huenefield Report
Box U
Bedford, MA 01730
(617) 861-9650
*John Huenefeld, Ed. Bimonthly newsletter
for small publishers, marketing and promo
info. 850 circ, no reviews but mentions
books/authors, na., interna. readership.*

Hungry Mind Review
1648 Grand Ave.
St Paul, MN 55105-1896
(612) 699-0587
Bart Schneider, Ed.

Independent Publishers Trade Report
Box 176-B
Southport, CT 06490
(203) 268-4878
*Henry Berry, Ed. Monthly newsletter for
growing independent publishers, well-
known experts in the field, trends, news,
articles, reviews of books re publishing. 3
reviews/issue, na. readership.*

Innkeeping
1333 Bath St.
Santa Barbara, CA 93101
(805) 965-0707
*Pat Hardy, Ed. Monthly, 3 reviews/issue,
mentions books/authors, na. readership.*

Inside Books
5555 Biscayne Blvd.
Miami, FL 33137
*Howard Barbanel, Ed. Magazine for
consumers, 75 reviews/issue of books on
entertainment, fun, bestsellers, na.
readership.*

International Publishing Newsletter
1133 Broadway, #1301
New York, NY 10010-7903
(212) 645-5150
*K S Giniger, Ed. Business of book publish-
ing for interna. audience. 8 reviews/issue.*

Interracial Books For Children Bulletin
1841 Broadway
New York, NY 10023
(212) 757-5339
*Ruth Charnes, Ed. Articles, 8x/year, 5,000
circ, reviews.*

Interstate
Box 7068
Univ. Station
Austin, TX 78713
*Loris Essary, Ed. Journal for writers,
reviews.*

Jeffrey Lant Associates
50 Follen St., Ste 507
Cambridge, MA 02138
(617) 547-6372
*Dr Jeffrey Lant Business devel., profit-
making, entrepreneurial, reviews. Monthly,
1.5 million circ, interna. readership.*

Kansas City Star
1729 Grand Ave.
Kansas City, MO 64108-1413
(810) 234-4380
*Steve Paul, Books Ed. Daily metropolitan
newspaper, 10 reviews/issue.*

Kirkus Reviews
200 Park Ave.
New York, NY 10003-1543
(212) 777-4554
*Anne Larsen, Ed. Prepublication reviews
for bookstores, libraries. Send galleys 2-3
mo in advance. Fiction, nonfic, no poetry.
Biweekly, 5,400 circ, 4,500 reviews/year.*

**Kliatt Young Adult Paperback Book
Guide**
425 Watertown St.
Newton, MA 02158
(617) 965-4666
*Doris Hiatt, Ed., Claire Russer, Books Ed.
Young adult. 325 rev/issue, interna.
readership.*

LA Times
Times Mirror Sq.
Los Angeles, CA 90053
(313) 965-4570
*Jack Miles, Books Ed. Daily metropolitan
newspaper. 2,000 rev/year.*

LA Times Book Review
Times Mirror Sq.
Los Angeles, CA 90053
(213) 972-5000
*Elizabeth Mehren, Ed.
Weekly magazine.*

LA Times Magazine
Times Mirror Sq.
Los Angeles, CA 90053
*Linda French, Copy Ed. "Previews" column;
write for guidelines. Articles re upscale So.
Calif people & lifestyle, some pre-pub book
excerpts. Weekly, no reviews, but mentions
books/authors, Western U.S. readership.*

Library Journal
249 West 17th St.
New York, NY 10011
(212) 645-0067
*Nora Rawlinson, Ed. Professional trade
journal for librarians, contact 3-4 mo in
advance. 20x/year, 250 reviews/issue,
na. readership.*

Literary Center Quarterly
Box 85116
Seattle, WA 98145-1116
(206) 523-5529
*Marilyn Stalbein, Bks. Ed. Contemp.
writing/publications. NW emphasis.*

**Los Angeles Review of
Literature & Current Affairs**
1005 Pruitt Dr.
Redondo Beach, CA 90278-4520
(213) 376-1630
*Articles, reviews, literary, some nonfiction,
prominent writers.*

Magazine & Bookseller
322 Eighth Ave.
New York, NY 10001
(212) 620-7330
*Mark Hinckley, Ed. Business of selling
books & magazines. 23,105 circ, no reviews, na. readership.*

**Magill Book Reviews for Dow Jones
News/Retrieval**
150 S Los Robles Ave. #720
Pasadena, CA 91101
(818) 584-0106
*Karen Cleveland, Ed. Brief reviews cover-
ing fiction and nonfiction trade books. 10
reviews/issue, na. readership.*

Magnifying Glass
1767 Juliet Ave.
St. Paul, MN 55105
*Laura Sobalvarro, Ed. Bimonthly newslet-
ter reviews mystery books, sent to bookstores.*

Mail Order Book Report
Dept Z, 830 SW Grove, #3
Corvallis, OR 97333
*Mike Jones, Ed. Newsletter for writers/
publishers/mail order booksellers, articles,
news, reviews of books re self-publishing,
writing, marketing.*

Markets Abroad, c/o Strawberry Media
2460 Lexington Dr
Owosso, MI 48867
(517) 725-9027
*Michael H. Sedge Quarterly newsletter,
marketing opportunities worldwide for
writers and photographers. Mentions
travel books.*

Meditation Magazine
Box 1449
Goleta, CA 93116
*David Alan Ramsdale, Books Ed.
Quarterly magazine; yoga & meditation,
new age, spirituality. 10 reviews/issue,
na. readership.*

MGW (Mom Guess What)
1725 L St
Sacramento, CA 94814
(916) 441-6397
*Linda Birner, Ed Joyce Bright, Books Ed.
Monthly tabloid for men, 7-8 book reviews
/issue, 21,000 circ, favors No. Calif.*

Midwest Book Review
278 Orchard Dr.
Oregon, WI 53575-1129
(608) 835-7937
*James Cox, Ed.,Diane Donovan, Books Ed.
Newsletter of reviews for libraries. Large
and small presses, also syndicated on TV,
radio. 70,000 circ, 75 reviews/issue, na.
readership.*

Nashville's Book Talk
3823 Green Hills Village Dr.
Nashville, TN 37215-2610
(615) 298-3357
Roger Bishop, Ed.

New Age Book Review
Four Park Ave.
New York, NY 10016-5339
Douglas Aronson, Ed.

New Age Journal
342 Western Ave.
Brighton, MA 02135
*Lisa Tane, Books Ed. Bimonthly magazine,
New Age, articles, book reviews, how-to,
personal experience, body/mind, more.
150,000 circ.*

New Age Retailer
Box 224
Greenbank, WA 98253
(206) 678-7772
*Duane Sweeney, Ed. Monthly trade
journal sent to 3,000 New Age book and
music retailers; reviews, articles. (AKA
Report to Booksellers). 3,200+ circ, 5
reviews/issue, na. readership.*

New Age Marketing Newsletter
Box 2478
Sedona, AZ 86336
(602) 282-9574
*Newsletter re New Age marketing, co-op
opportunities, news, info, reviews.*

New Pages
4426 S Belsay Rd.
Grand Blanc, MI 48439
(313) 743-8055
*Casey Hill, Ed., Grant Burns, Books Ed.
Book rev. journal for alternative press,
news & info, resource columns, interviews.
3x/year, 50 reviews/issue, na. readership.*

New York Daily News
220 West 42nd St.
New York, NY 10017
(212) 210-2100
*Sheryl Connelly, Books Ed. Metropolitan
daily newspaper.*

New York Post
210 South St.
New York, NY 10002-7807
(212) 815-8000
*Steve Cuozzo, Books Ed. Metropolitan
daily newspaper.*

New York Review of Books
250 West 57th
New York, NY 10107
(212) 757-8070
*Robert Silvers, Ed., Barbara Epstein,
Books Ed. Biweekly tabloid, 25 reviews/
issue, interna. readership.*

New York Times
229 W 43rd St.
New York, NY 10036
(313) 961-7858
*Rebecca Sinkler, Books Ed. Weekly book
review magazine (3000 reviews/year) and
daily reviews in Living Arts Section: "Bk
Notes": Edwin McDowell. Philip Boffey
(science & health ed), Nancy Newhouse
(travel ed), Claudia Payne (Living Homes
ed).*

Newsday
235 Pinelawn Rd.
Melville, NY 11747
(212) 303-2930
*Jack Schwartz, Books Ed. Daily metropoli-
tan newspaper.*

North Atlantic Review
15 Arbutus Lane
Stony Brook, NY 11790-1408
(516) 751-7886
*Literary journal, new in '89. Book reviews,
fic, poetry, essays, criticism, art.*

Overland Journal
Box 42
Gerald, MO 63037
(314) 764-2801
*Gregory Franzwa, Ed. Oregon/Calif. Trails
Association, articles, reviews re western
migration.*

Paper Bag
1839 W. Touhy
Chicago, IL 60626
(312) 285-7972
Michael H. Brownstein, Ed., Deborah Brownstein, Books Ed. Literary magazine, some reviews, na. readership.

Philadelphia Inquirer
Box 8263
Philadelphia, PA 19101
(215) 854-5616
Rebecca Klock, Books Ed. Daily metropolitan newspaper.

PMA Newsletter
2401 Pacific Coast Highway, Suite #206
Hermosa Beach, CA 90254
(213) 372-2732
Jan Nathan, Ed. Publishers Marketing Assoc monthly newsletter. (see Sec. 10, 7 & Calendar). Na, interna. readership. For independent publishers.

Poetic Liberty
3301 John Muir Ct.
Plano, TX 75023
Charles Corry, Ed. Publishes poetry, fic, 1 review/issue, na. readership.

Poets & Writers Magazine
(a.k.a. CODA)
72 Spring St.
New York, NY 10012
(212) 226-3586
Darlyn Brewer, Ed. For literary writers, news & info re: publication, grants, awards, deadlines, submission. Bi-monthly, 12,500 circ, no reviews, na., interna. readership.

Preview
Box 8330
Ann Arbor, MI 48107
(313) 662-3925 *Christy Havens, Ed. Monthly magazine, book reviews of reference materials & publications in library & information science. 20 reviews/issue, Canadian readership.*

Publishers Report
72 Elsham Road, London
W148HH, England
Interna. publishing newsletter, information re selling foreign rights.

Publishers Weekly
249 West 17th St.
New York, NY 10011
(212) 645-0067
John F. Baker, Ed., Sybil Steinberg, Books Ed. THE trade magazine for bookstores, libraries & publishers. Contact 3-4 mo in advance. New books only, subjects w/ broad general appeal. 500 reviews/year.

Rave Reviews
163 Joralemon St.
Brooklyn Heights, NY 11201
(718) 237-1097
Marc Cerasini, Ed. Reviews of bestsellers, for consumers. Bimonthly, 90,000 circ, 150 reviews/issue, na., interna. readership.

Rocky Mountain News
Box 719
Denver, CO 80201
Margaret Carlin, Books Ed. Metropolitan newspaper.

Scholarly Publishing
Univ. of Toronto Press
Toronto, Canada M5S 1A6
Mark Carroll, Ed. Publishing. 4 rev/issue, interna. readership.

School Library Journal
249 W 17th St.
New York, NY 10011
(212) 645-9700
Trevelyn Jones, Ed.Articles and reviews, public libraries, elem-high school libraries; send book info 90 days pre-pub. 5000 reviews/year.

Science Books & Films
1333 H St. NW
Washington, DC 20005-4792
(202) 326-6454
Kathleen Johnston, Ed. Computers, education, reference, science. 200 rev/issue, interna. readership.

Seybold Report on Publishing
Box 644
Media, PA 19063-0644
(215) 565-2480
Newsletter re business of publishing.

Small Press
11 Ferry Lane West
Westport, CT 06880
(203) 226-6967, FAX (203) 454-5840
*Brenda Mitchell-Powell, Ed. Bimonthly
magazine for small press, articles, news,
events, 90 reviews/issue.*

Small Press News
Box 780, Weeks Mills
New Sharon, ME 04955
*Diane Kruchkow, Ed. Newsletter for small
press, reviews, news, events.*

Spectrum Review
Box 1030
Lower Lake, CA 95457
*Georg Feuerstein, Ed. Articles, reviews;
spiritual.*

Success Magazine
342 Madison Ave.
New York, NY 10173
*Scott DeGarmo, Ed. Reviews inspirational
books on business. 3 reviews/issue,
interna. readership.*

The American Poetry Review
1704 Walnut St.
Philadelphia, PA 19103
(215) 732-6770
*David Bonnano, Ed. Poetry reviews.
30,000 circ, 3 reviews/issue, na, interna.
readership.*

The Christian Science Monitor
1 Norway St.
Boston, MA 02115-3195
(617) 450-2000
*Richard Cattani, Ed., Jim Bencivenga,
Books Ed. Daily newspaper,180,000 circ,
1 book review/issue, interna readership.*

The Nation
72 5th Ave.
New York, NY 10011
*Stuart Klawans, Ed. Magazine re liberal/
left, politics, society, consumer affairs,
foreign affairs, labor, etc. Includes review
column of small press literary titles, "The
Small Time."*

the new renaissance
9 Heath Rd.
Arlington, MA 02174
*Louise Reynolds, Ed. Book reviews and
excerpts, short stories, novels, essays,
memoirs, poetry, art, bio; annual paperback book; send news releases not review
copies. 4 reviews/issue, interna. readership.*

The New Republic
1220 19th St., NW
Washington, DC 20036
(202) 331-7494
*Michael Kinsley, Ed., Leon Wieseltier,
Books Ed. Journal of political, social
opinion, excerpts. 3 reviews/issue, mentions books/authors, interna. readership.*

The Plowman
Box 414
Whitby ON LIN 5S4 Canada
(416) 668-7803
*Tony Scavetta, Ed., C F Kennedy, Books
Ed. Monthly magazine re poetry. 5,000
circ, several reviews, interna. readership.*

The Small Press Book Review
Box 176
Southport, CT 06490
(203) 268-4878
*Henry Berry, Ed. Bimonthly reviews of
small press & independent press books,
also tapes, periodicals, videos. 100
reviews/issue, na. readership.*

The Writer
120 Boylston St.
Boston, MA 02116-4611
(617) 423-3157
*Sylvia K Burack, Ed., Anne Drowns, Books
Ed. Articles on writing for publication.
4 reviews/issue, interna. readership.*

Times Literary Supplement
Priory House, St John's Lane
London EC1M 4BX England
(01) 253-3000
Alan Hollinghurst, Ed.

1801 9th Street, Sacramento, CA 95814

(916) 448-3511 or (800) 448-3511.

Spilman Printing is the
West Coast short-run book
and directory specialist,
with over 80 years of printing experience. Now we're
adding larger, more mod-
ern equipment, providing
you with higher quality
books, manuals, directo-
ries, mailers, and news-
letters. For all your book
manufacturing needs.

*b
o
o
k

m
a
n
u
f
a
c
t
u
r
e
r
s*

SPILMAN
PRINTING

Towers Club Newsletter
9107 NW 11th Ave., Box 2038
Vancouver, WA 98668-2038
(206) 574—3084
Jerry Buchanan, Ed. Newsletter: "The Original Writer's Entrepreneurial Research Service." Writing, publishing, direct response advertising, mktg. Monthly, 1 review/issue, interna. readership.

Utne Reader
2732 West 43 St.
Minneapolis, MN 55410
(612) 338-5040
Eric Utne Ed., Helen Cordes, Books Ed. Excerpts from alternative press. 20 reviews/issue, na., interna. readership.

Voice Literary Supplement
842 Broadway
New York, NY 10003
M. Mark, Ed., Ralph Sassone, Books Ed. Monthly magazine., part of Village Voice, literature, 25 reviews/issue, na. readership.

Wall Street Review Of Books
380 Adams St.
Bedford Hills, NY 10507-2024
(914) 241-7100
David O'Whitten, Ed.

Washington Monthly
1611 Connecticut Ave., NW
Washington, DC 20009
(202) 462-0128
Charles Peters, Ed., Matt Cooper, Books Ed. Monthly national magazine; politics, government, the press. 6 reviews/issue, mentions books/authors, na. readership.

Washington Post Book World
1150 15th St. NW
Washington, D.C. 20005
(202) 334-6000
Nina King, Books Ed. Sunday magazine in metropolitan daily newspaper, 200 reviews/year.

Woman
1115 Broadway
New York, NY 10010
Sherry Amatenstein, Ed. Monthly magazine; womens' interests, book excerpts.

Womens' Review of Books
Wellesley College
Wellesley, MA 02181
(617) 431-1453
Linda Gardiner, Ed. Womens,' politics, literary, feminist. Monthly, 11,500 circ,15 reviews/issue, na., interna. readership.

World Monitor
321 Columbus Ave.
Boston, MA 02116
(617)536-4000
Clayton Collins, Ed. Monthly magazine, interna. subjects, politics, diplomacy, trade, arts, sciences, travel; pre-pub. galleys & news releases.

World of Cookbooks
1645 S Vineyard Ave.
Los Angeles, CA 90019
(213) 933-1645
Grace Kirschenbaum, Ed., Cookbooks.

Writer's Digest
1507 Dana Avenue
Cincinnati, OH 45207
(513) 531-2222
William Brohaugh, Ed., Bill Strickland, Books Ed. Monthly magazine, articles re writing for publication, publishing, how-to, fiction, nonfic, poetry, screenwriting. 250,000 circ, 5 reviews/issue, na., interna. readership.

Writer's N.W. Newsletter
Route 3, Box 376
Hillsboro, OR 97124
(503) 621-3911
Linny Stovall, Ed., Mac Swan, Books Ed. Free within NW, news, articles, events for writers, publishers, 2 reviews/issue. Quarterly, 50,000 circ. ID, MN, WA, BC, OR, AR readership.

Writers Journal
Box 9148
St Paul, MN 55109
(612) 433-3626
Valerie Hockert, Ed. Bimonthly magazine for writers, articles on all phases of how-to. 10,000 circ, 5 reviews/issue, na., interna. readership.

3 Bay Area Libraries

Selling To Libraries

By Tom Drewes, President, Quality Books Inc., a nation-wide distributor to libraries, specializing in small and independent publishers. Quality Books, 918 Sherwood Drive, Lake Bluff, IL 60044-2204, (312) 295-2010.

There are over 103,000 libraries in the U.S., spending about one billion dollars a year on books. This enormous size is illusory, however, as the market is fragmented into different types and sub-types of libraries with varying needs and book selection procedures.

The key, as with all marketing efforts, is to have a specific customer in mind for your books.

The library market should not be the primary target of your publishing efforts. At the same time, there are a few elements that can be incorporated into the initial publishing plan that will, at little or no expense, enhance the book's chances in the library market without harming its acceptability to other markets.

Here are some suggestions for non-fiction, academic, school, special, armed forces and public libraries:

Format: Libraries provide information, education and/or recreation, and librarians arrange books and materials to ensure rapid retrieval of the information. A book's format can affect its usefulness to the library user. For example, an oblong or hexagonal book may be an eye-catcher in the corner drug store, or a book with a die-cut hole may hang on a spinner rack at K-Mart. In the library, however, these irregularities make it difficult to prepare the book for the shelves. There should be space to accommodate a library card pocket without obscuring too much text. Don't get too creative with the shape of the book.

Imagine a library with thousands of volumes, all with blank spines. It's important to put the title on the spine; the lower 3/4" of the spine is usually going to be covered by a spine label with the call number.

Place your title and your carefully designed logo so that all of it is visible when the book is on the library shelf.

And, be sure the correct title is on the spine and on the title page; a librarian's pet peeve is when the titles on spine, front and title page are all different.

What's this book about?

Probably one of the most common reasons for a book to be relegated to the remainder heap is an inappropriate title. With 50,000 titles published each year, most librarians are barraged with more new books than they could ever hope to buy, and they don't have time to decipher a clever title. Oftentimes, the sub-title of a book should have been the title. Don't be cutsie. Let the title describe the book right up front.

Along with the layout and design features which can help your book fit into a library easily, there is also CIP data.

CIP (Cataloguing in Publication) is a program run by the Library of Congress. The LIC, using galley proofs and information you supply, will catalogue your book and return to you camera ready copy, which is generally printed on the verso of the title page.

The benefit is that once a library owns a book, it can make it available to readers quickly.

Application forms can be obtained by writing: Library of Congress, CIP division, Washington, D.C., 20540.

A good table of contents and index are appreciated by all users of the library, and their absence might negatively influence the reviewer.

All of this just echoes the need for easy access to the information. Build a book that's user-friendly.

Because many library books are available for general circulation, lots of invitations to "fill-in-the blanks," multiple choice or essay questions, are generally not acceptable. Once written in, the book quickly loses its value to the next person who checks it out.

A book doesn't have to be a hardcover to work for a library. Nor must a publisher do a separate run in hardcover just to get a book reviewed.

A decade ago, only 6% of library book purchased were paperbound. Today, over 35% are paperbound, the primary reason being the increase in hardcover prices. (Trade paperbacks have gone from an average of $5.95 to $13.86 in just ten years.)

Stapled books are often treated as pamphlets and placed in vertical files.

Reviews: Only about one in eight new titles gets reviewed in the library review media, so the best chance for a small/independent publisher to be reviewed is to build a good book, unique in its field, and

submit review copies or galley proofs to the library review media 90 days before publication.

Review media most commonly used are ALA Booklist, Library Journal and Choice.

A favorable review, ideally one that ends with those melodious words "highly recommended," may yield additional orders for 500 to 1500 copies.

Many publishers think all of this represents far too much work for such limited results. For most publishers, library sales should be thought of as "plus," rather than primary.

My advice is to weigh priorities and spend time and money in markets that appear most cost beneficial.

Bay Area Libraries

Purchases for branch libraries are usually made through the main city or county library, however, the branches usually submit their own orders and/or requests to the main library.

Alameda City Library
Main Branch, 2264 Santa Clara Ave.
Alameda, CA 94501
(415) 748-4660
Public.

Alameda County Library Administration
3121 Diablo Ave.
Hayward, CA 94540
(415) 670-6270
Purchases for all Alameda Co libraries. Nancy Boca, Acquisitions, Ext. #234.

Albany Library
1216 Solano Ave.
Albany, CA 94706
(415) 526-3720
Bonnie Davis, head librarian. Public.

Alliance Francaise
1345 Bush
San Francisco, CA 94104
(415) 775-7755
Xavier Dumange. French books only, few purchases.

Archives for the Performing Arts
301 Van Ness Ave.
San Francisco, CA 94102
(415) 431-0717
Rick Sprague, Acquisitions. Institutional.

Belvedere-Tiburon Library
Beach Rd.
Belvedere, CA 94920
(415) 435-1361
Public.

Benecia Public Library
114 East G St.
Benecia, CA 94510
(707) 745-2265
Carol Starr, head librarian. Public. 49,000 volumes. B & T. 2% budget for audio, 8% budget for reference, 10% budget for periodicals.

Berkeley Public Library
Main Branch, Shattuck Ave. & Kittredge
Berkeley, CA 94704
(415) 644-6095
June Nash, Acquisitions. Public, purchases for city system.

Biblioteca Latino Americana
690 Locust
San Jose, CA 95150
(408) 294-1237
Public. Purchases made by main library.

Bolinas Library
Wharf Rd.
Bolinas, CA 94924
(415) 868-1171
Linn Murray, head librarian.

Burlingame City Library
1800 Easton Dr.
Burlingame, CA 94010
(415) 343-1794
Public.

California Genealogical Society
300 Brannan
San Francisco, CA 94107
(415) 777-9936
Betty Kot, head librarian. Institutional, books, microfilm, fiche, 35,000 volumes. Open to the public.

California Medical Facility Library
Box 2000
Vacaville, CA 95688
(707) 448-6841
Cam Jansak, head librarian. 22,000 volumes, general, including religion, Calif hist, classic literature.

Calistoga Public Library
1108 Myrtle
Calistoga, CA 94515
(707) 942-4833
Nan Vaaler, head librarian. Public. Calif. collection. 18,000 volumes, audio, video.

Marin County Library, Civic Center Branch
Civic Center Dr.
San Rafael, CA 94903
(415) 499-6065
Barbara Hughes, Administrative Librarian. Fiction: Margaret Galvin, kids: Sylvia Gallego, 000-700: Doreen Emery, 700-000: Sylvia Gallego. Public. 80,000 volumes, 260 periodicals, 450 audios, 60 videos. B & T, Midwest, Walden Books, Anne Kent California collection, California/Marin County collection, special interest in art, biography, business. 11% budget for audio/video, 32 % budget for reference, 22% budget for periodicals.

Cloverdale Regional Library
401 North Cloverdale Blvd.
Cloverdale, CA 95425
(707) 894-5271

Community Hospital Medical Library
3325 Chanate Rd.
Santa Rosa, CA 95404
(707) 576-4675
Joan Chilton, head librarian. Open to public. Medical, nursing, family medicine. 8,000 volumes.

Community Resource Library
Peninsula Comm. Foundation,
1204 Burlingame Ave.
Burlingame, CA 94010
(415) 342-2505
Bill Somerville, Director. Public, corporate & gov't supported, for non-profit organizations. Specialize in management, business, fund raising, education, etc.

Contra Costa County Library
6510 Stockton Ave.
El Cerrito, CA 94530
(415) 526-7512
Public.

Corte Madera Library
707 Meadowsweet Dr.
Corte Madera, CA 94925
(415) 924-4844
Harriet Goldfluss, head librarian. Adult fiction, non-fic: Harriet Goldfluss, Adult non-fic, reference: Jim Sullivan, Juvenile: Nancy Davis, Marilyn Wronsky. Public. 60,000 volumes, 285 periodicals, 250 audios, 50 videos. Books purchased by main library. B & T. 10% budget for audio, 10% budget for reference.

Dominican College Library
1520 Grand Ave.
San Rafael, CA 94901
(415) 457-4440
Humanities, art, music, Amer. lit., English lit. 84,000 volumes, 223 periodicals.

Erik H Erikson Library, San Francisco Psychoanalytic Institute Inc
2420 Sutter
San Francisco, CA 94115
(415) 563-4477
Marc Brewer, director, book buyer. Institutional, open to public. 5000 books, psychoanalytic-related. 5,005 volumes, 3,900 periodicals. 50% budget for books, 50% budget for periodicals.

Fairfax Library
2097 Sir Francis Drake Blvd.
Fairfax, CA 94930
(415) 453-8092
Virginia L. Bowen, head librarian. Public. Specializes in foreign language. Buys for all West Marin libraries.

Fashion Institute of Design and Merchandising Library
55 Stockton
San Francisco, CA 94108
(415) 433-6691
Carol Block, director. Fashion, architecture, interior design, merchandising, 4,000 books and periodicals, videotapes.

Feminist Audio Books
52-54 Featherstone Street
London, England ECIY 8RT UK
01-291-2908/0713
Library of feminist, lesbian and women-oriented books on tape for blind, partially sighted. 150 books, 100 audio.

Fremont Main Library
39770 Paseo Padre Parkway
Fremont, CA 94537
(415) 796-9749
Public.

Goethe Institute Library and German Culture Center
530 Bush
San Francisco, CA 94104
(415) 391-0428
Barbara Bernhart, director. Institutional, open to public. German culture related, 20th century, after 1945. 5500 books.

Golden Gate Baptist Theological Seminary Library
Strawberry Pt.
Mill Valley, CA 94941
(415) 388-8080
William B Hair III, head librarian. Pastoral care/counseling: Lisa Lepeltak, Theology: Bill Hair. Bible, religious, music, sociology, history.100,000 volumes, 763 periodicals, 5300 audios. Midwest Library Service, 2% budget for audio/visual, 5% for periodicals.

Graduate Theological Union Library
2400 Ridge Rd.
Berkeley, CA 94709
(415) 649-2400
John David Baker-Batsel, director. Open to public, theology, religion. 350,000 volumes.

Guerneville Regional Library
14107 Armstrong Woods Rd.
Guerneville, CA 95446
(707) 869-9004
Barbara Paulson, head librarian. Public.

Harding Lawson Association
Box 578
Novato, CA 94948
(415) 892-0821
Sharon Hotz, director. Private, not open to public. Environment, geology, engineering, earthquake, maps. 7,000 volumes.

Healdsburg Regional Library
221 Matheson
Healdsburg, CA 95448
(707) 433-3772
Helen Hinterader, hd lib. Hispanic collection, Sonoma Co Wine Library. 40,000 vol.

Held-Poage Memorial Home & Research Library
603 West Perkins
Ukiah, CA 95482
(707) 462-6969
Norman Hallam, head librarian. Mendocino County history, California, U.S., Amer. Indian history, books purchased by main library. 5,000 volumes. Calif & local history purchased only; donations accepted of U.S. history.

Holocaust Center of Northern Calforina
601 14th
San Francisco, CA 94118
(415) 751-6040
Joel Newberg, director. Institutional, open to public. 8,000 volumes, 250 video, 250 audio.

Institute for Health & Aging, UCSF
201 Filbert, Suite 555
San Francisco, CA 94133
(415) 362-3620
Not open to public. Health, aging, health policy. 10,000 books, documents.

Institute of Transpersonal Psychology Library
250 Oak Grove Ave.
Menlo Park, CA 94025
(415) 326-1960
Elizabeth Thacker, head librarian. Psychology and spirituality. 6500 books, 1% audio, 14% reference, 7% periodicals, 50 journal titles, Midwest Library Service.

J W Mailliard, Library
Cal. Acad. of Sciences, Golden Gate Park
San Francisco, CA 94118
(415) 750-7102
Thomas Moritz, director. Open to public, plants, animals, taxonomy, bio-geography. 160,000 volumes, audio.

Japanese American Library
1619 Sutter St., mail: Box 590598
San Francisco, CA 94159-0598
(415) 567-5006
Karl Matsushita, head librarian. Institutional. 6,000 volumes, 700 periodicals, 100 audios,10 videos. Japanese in America collection.10% budget for audio, 60% budget for reference, 30% for periodicals.

Jewish Community Library
601 14th Ave.
San Francisco, CA 94118
(415) 751-6983
Nanette Sahl, director. Open to public.
Jewish subjects and Jewish authors.
24,000 volumes, audio.

Lake County Library
1425 N High Street
Lakeport, CA 95453
(707) 263-8816
Kathleen Jansen, head librarian. Public.
70,000 in 3 branches.
60,000 volumes,1,200 audios.

Lincoln Memorial Library
Veterans Home of Calif
Yountville, CA 94599
(707) 944-4916
Cynthis Heggedus, director. General,
large-type, mysteries, Western,World
Wars, biography. 20,000 volumes.

Mechanics' Institute
57 Post
San Francisco, CA 94103
(415) 421-1750
Kathleen T. Pabst, director. Institutional,
open to public membership. General
library, specialize in business. 150,000
volumes.

Mendocino Community College Library
105 North Main St.
Ukiah, CA 95482
(707) 463-4491
General, geneology, Amer. Indian, forestry.
143,000 volumes.

Menlo Park City Library
100 Terminal Ave.
Menlo Park, CA 94025
(415) 858-3460
Karen Fredrickson, head librarian. Public.

Mill Valley City Library
375 Throckmorton Ave.
Mill Valley, CA 94941
(415) 388-2190
Public. 115,000 volumes.

Millbrae City Library
1 Library Ave.
Millbrae, CA 94030
(415) 697-7607
Ruth Stout, head librarian. Public. 62,000
volumes.

Napa College Library
2277 Napa-Vallejo Highway
Napa, CA 94558
(707) 253-3011
Bonnie Thoreen, head librarian, Carolyn
Freuchtenicht, buyer. 42,000 volumes, 250
periodicals, 3,000 audios, 1,300 videos.
B & T, Midwest.

Napa County Library
Main Branch
Napa, CA 94558
(707) 253-4072
Nan Vaaler, Director. 190,000 volumes,
including Calif history collection.

Napa Valley Genealogical and
Biographical Society
2977 Solano Ave.
Napa, CA 94559-0385
(707) 252-9829
Gloria Scarloss, director. Open to public,
geneology and history.

National Library of Sports
180 West San Carlos
San Jose, CA 95150
(408) 287-0993
Public.

National Marine Fisheries Service
Library
3150 Paradise Dr.
Tiburon, CA 94920
(415) 447-3489
Maureen H. Woods, head librarian.
Commercial fisheries, marine biology,
aquaculture.10,000 volumes, 60% periodi-
cals, 20% reference. Ballan. Collections:
shark taxonomy, aquaculture.

Northern Calif Center for African-
American History & Life
5606 San Pablo Ave.
Oakland, CA 94612
(415) 658-3158
L. P. Crouchett, director. Open to public.

Northwest Santa Rosa Regional Library
150 Coddingtown Center
Santa Rosa, CA 95401
(707) 546-2265

Novato Regional Branch Library
1720 Novato Blvd.
Novato, CA 94947
(415) 897-1141
Barbara Rauhala, head librarian. Public. Specializes in easy-to-read books for new adult readers, environment, history. 82,000 volumes.

Oakland Business Library
2201 Broadway
Oakland, CA 94612
(415) 271-4292
Joan Galvez, head librarian. Public.

Oakland City Library
Main Branch, 125 14th
Oakland, CA 94612
(415) 273-3134
Lelia White, head librarian. Public. Special collections: Oakland history, Pacific Rim countries and business, large print. 800,000 volumes.

Oakland City Library, Asian Branch
449 9th
Oakland, CA 94612
(415) 273-3400
Public.

Oakland Latin American Library
1900 Fruitvale Ave.
Oakland, CA 94601
(415) 532-7882
Elisa Miller, head librarian. Public. Volumes in English & Spanish. Ordered by main branch.

Occidental Library
73 Main
Occidental, CA 95465
(707) 874-3080
Doris Klingelhofer, head librarian.

Oliver Professional Library
Napa St. Hospital, 2100 Napa-Vallejo Highway
Napa, CA 94558
(707) 253-5477
Barbara Fetesoff, director. Social services, psycotherapy, medical. Not open to public. 7,000 volumes, audio.

Pacific Union College Library
Pacific Union College
Angwin, CA 94508
(707) 965-6242
Religion, theology, science, human, Napa Valley history, music, Pitcairn Island, Seventh-Day Adventist studies. 113,000 volumes.

Palo Alto City Library
Main Branch, 1213 Newell Road
Palo Alto, CA 94303
(415) 329-2436
Mary Joe Levy, head librarian. Public.

Petaluma Regional Library
100 Fairgrounds Dr.
Petaluma, CA 94952
(707) 763-9801
Kiyo Okazaki, head librarian. 98,000 volumes.

Planetree Health Resource Center
2040 Webster
San Francisco, CA 94115
(415) 923-3680
Tracey Cosgrove, head librarian. Ann Lazarus, director. Public, medical, health books for layperson. 2,000 volumes.

Point Reyes Bird Observatory
4990 Shoreline Highway
Stinson Beach, CA 94970
(415) 868-1221
Karen Hamilton. Marine mammals, ornithology, natural hist. 2,500 volumes, 100 periodicals. Blackwell No. Amer. 33% budget for reference, 67% budget for periodicals.

Point Reyes Library
4th & A
Point Reyes, CA 94956
(415) 663-8375
Public.

Redwood City Library
Main Branch, 881 Jefferson Ave.
Redwood City, CA 94064
(415) 780-7018
Jane Light, head librarian. Public. 175,000 volumes. Technology collection.

Rohnert Park-Cotati Regional Library
6600 Hunter Dr.
Rohnert Park, CA 94928
(707) 584-9121
Don Gass, head librarian. 45,000 volumes.

Saint Helena City Library
1492 Library Lane
Saint Helena, CA 94574
(707) 963-5244
Head librarian: Clayla Davis. Public, general library, large wine-related collection. 50,000 volumes.

San Francisco Public Library
Civic Center
San Francisco, CA 94102
(415) 558-3471
Glenda Goldwater. 1.2 million volumes. Call for acquisitions person for your category, Faun McInnis.

San Geronimo Valley Library
Meadows Lane
San Geronimo, CA 94963
(415) 488-0430
Mary Wick, head librarian. Public. 6000 childrens' books, 3000 adults.

San Jose Bible College Library
790 South 12th
San Jose, CA 95150
(408) 293-6651
Kay Llovio, head librarian. Religious books, special collection: Disciples, history of Christ Church. 33,000, 94 periodicals, 1876 audios, 7 videos. Spring Arbor.

San Jose City Library
Main Branch, 180 West San Carlos
San Jose, CA 95150
(408) 277-5700
Public, purchases for San Jose city libraries, Charlotte Sakai, Acquisitions, (408) 277-4831.

San Leandro City Library
Main Branch, 300 Estudillo Ave.
San Leandro, CA 94577
(415) 577-3490
David Bohne, Director, purchases for San Leandro city libraries. Nancy Fong, senior librarian. Public. 150,000 volumes. B & T, Gaylord California collection.

San Lorenzo Library
395 Paseo Grande
San Lorenzo, CA 94580
(415) 670-6283
Public.

San Mateo County Library
Main Branch, 55 W 3rd St
San Mateo, CA 94402
(415) 377-4680
Chris Robinson, head librarian. Public, 200,000 combined branches. Specialize in business reference.

San Rafael Public Library
1100 E St.
San Rafael, CA 94901
(415) 485-3323
Vaughn Stratford, Director. Children: Holly Stanaland, adult fiction: Gail Lockman, art, sciences, business: Gwen Davis, medicine, bio, history: Catherine Wright, social sciences, foreign lang, literature: Teri Gonzales. Public. 130,000 volumes. 280 periodicals, some audios. B & T, direct order.

Santa Clara County Libraries
1095 North 7th
Santa Clara, CA 95112
(408) 293-2326
Susan Fuller, head librarian. Adult: Carol Jaech, young adult: Judy Susges, childrens: Janice Yee, recordings: Linda Lubovich. 1 million volumes, purchases made centrally for Alum Rock, Campbell, Cupertino, Gilroy, Los Altos, Milpitas, Morgan Hill, Saratoga. B & T, Qualiy, Yankee Peddlar, 10% audio, 670 periodicals.

Santa Clara County Library
Main Branch, 13 South San Antonio Rd.
Los Altos, CA 94022
(415) 948-2751
*Carol Tefft, head librarian. Public. Special-
izes in classics, travel, mysteries, videos.
125,000 volumes. Buys for Woodland br.*

Sausalito Public Library
420 Litho St.
Sausalito, CA 94965
(415) 332-2325
*Mary Richardson, head librarian. General,
specialize in boat building, sailing. Juvenile, young adult: Lois Anderson, adult fic
& no-fic: Mary Richardson. 46,000 volumes, 169 periodicals, 2,100 audios, 200
videos.*

**Schubert Library of the California
Historical Society**
2099 Pacific
San Francisco, CA 94122
(415) 567-1848
*Barbara Lekisch, director. Open to public,
SF history, California and U.S. history.*

Science Education Library
Lawrence Hall of Science, UC Berkeley
Berkeley, CA 94720
(415) 642-1334
*Ann Jensen, director. Teaching materials,
books, periodicals, software, video, 9,000
volumes.*

Sebastopol Regional Library
7140 Bodega Ave.
Sebastopol, CA 95472
(707) 823-7691
General and California collection.

Shields Library
Univ. of Calif.
Davis, CA 95616
(916) 752-2251
*General, agriculture, medical, engineering,
veterinary medicine, viticulture, social
science. 1,900,000 volumes, 48,000
periodicals.*

Solano County Library
1150 Kentucky St.
Fairfield, CA 94533
(707) 429-6601

*Collection development librarian, Linda
Schade. 515,000 volumes in five branches.
Info: Ann Cousineau, 429-6625. McCune
collection: Californiana.*

Sonoma County Library
3rd & E St.'s
Santa Rosa, CA 95404
(707) 545-0831
*David Sabsay, Director. Coordinator of
childrens' services: Gail Sage, Coordinator
of adult services, Winifred Swanson.
Public. Books selected by branches but
centrally ordered. 660,000 volumes, 671
periodicals, 18,400 audios. B & T, Midwest. Sonoma Co. history collection, wine
library.*

Sonoma Regional Library
755 West Napa
Sonoma, CA 95476
(707) 996-5217
*Joanne Hockett, head librarian. 43,000
volumes.*

Sonoma State Univ. Library
1801 East Cotati Ave.
Rohnert Park, CA 94928
(707) 664-2397
*Academic, Susan C. Harris, head librarian.
Tim Huston, collection development
librarian. 330,000 volumes, 63,000
periodicals, 20,000 audios, 900 videos.*

Stinson Beach Library
3470 Shoreline Highway
Stinson Beach, CA 94970
(415) 868-0252
Public.

World Affairs Council Library
312 Sutter, Room 310
San Francisco, CA 94108
(415) 982-0430
*Lone C. Beeson, head librarian. Mostly
review copies requested from publishers.
International issues, foreign countries.
6,500 volumes, 40 periodicals, 400 audios.*

Yountville Public Library
6550 Yount
Yountville, CA 94599
(707) 944-1888
Public.

# Bay Area Bookstores

Bay Area Bookstores

*Abbreviations for distributors/wholesalers
preferred by bookstores:
B & T: Baker & Taylor
PGW: Publishers Group West
Ing.: Ingram
Bkpple: Bookpeople
Gldn-Lee : Golden Lee
Cnsrtium: Consortium*

A Book Garden
1281 East Calaveras Blvd.
Milpitas, CA 95035
(408) 262-9003
*Barbara Williams-Sheng, buyer. General.
12,000 books, 2% audio, 5% gifts, 10%
periodicals, Ing., Bkpple.*

A Clean Well-Lighted Place For Books
2417 Larkspur Landing Circle
Larkspur, CA 94939-1804
(415) 461-0171
*Jude Sales, Martha Jackson, buyers.
General, specializes in literature, kids.
64,000 books, 5% audio, 15% gifts, 2%
periodicals. Ing., B & T, L & S, Bkpple,
PGW.*

A Clean Well-Lighted Place For Books
21271 Stevens Creek Blvd.
Cupertino, CA 95014
(408) 255-7600
General, specializes in literature.

A Clean Well-Lighted Place For Books
601 Van Ness Ave.
San Francisco, CA 94102
(415) 441-6670
*General, specializes in music, opera,
literature.*

Aardvark Books
2075 Market
San Francisco, CA 94114
(415) 558-0420
*Alan Walker, buyer. General, sci-fi, psych.,
occult, children's, travel. 38,200 books,
20% audio, periodicals. L & S, Bkpple,
Ing., B & T.*

Acorn Books
740 Polk
San Francisco, CA 94109
(415) 563-1736
New, used, rare.

Adventure in Reading
Box 826
San Anselmo, CA 94960
(415) 492-9583
*Robin Levy, buyer. Book fairs, children's
literature. Books direct from publishers.*

Albatross Book Stores
166 Eddy
San Francisco, CA 94102
(415) 885-6501
General.

Albatross III Book Shop
143 Clement
San Francisco, CA 94118
(415) 752-8611
*Jennifer Flannigan, buyer. General,
women's, philosophy, West. Americana,
search service. 20,000 books, 10%
periodicals.*

Armstrong Business College
2222 Harold Way
Berkeley, CA 94704
(415) 848-2500
Business texts.

Asian Center for Theology and Strategy
1798 Scenic Ave.
Berkeley, CA 94709
(415) 848-0173
*Asian Amer books, 15% audio, 30% gifts,
20% periodicals.*

ASUC Store General Book Department
UC Campus
Berkeley, CA 94720
(415) 642-7294
General books & textbooks.

Avenue Books
2904 College Ave.
Berkeley, CA 94705
(415) 549-3532
Elise White, buyer. General.

B Dalton Bookseller: *purchases made through NY headquarters, call for name of buyer in your category. B. Dalton Bookseller, 104 Fifth Ave, NY, NY, 10003, (212) 633-3300*

Other Locations:

10560 Rampart Ave.
Cupertino, CA 95014

Sun Valley Mall, #357
Concord, CA 94520
(415) 825-0111
Michael Davis, Store Mgr. General, 100,000+ books, 3% audio, 1% gifts, 2% periodicals. B & T, Ing., Gordon's, Bkpple, L & S, PGW.

Serramonte Center
Daly City, CA 94015
(415) 994-1177
General. 5% audio, % gifts, 5% periodicals. Ing., B & T, Bkpple.

Valley Fair Shopping Center
Santa Clara, CA 95051
(408) 246-6760
General. 80,000 books.

1346 Town Center Lane
Sunnyvale, CA 94086
(408) 739-8160

200 Kearny
San Francisco, CA 94108
(415) 956-2850

20510 Stevens Creek Blvd.
Cupertino, CA 95014
(408) 257-5530

248 Bay Fair Mall
San Leandro, CA 94578
(415) 278-0890

446 Santa Rosa Plaza
Santa Rosa, CA 95401
(707) 526-9670

63 Town & Country Village
Palo Alto, CA 94301
(415) 321-8502

Eastridge Shopping Center
San Jose, CA 95122
(408) 270-1070

Embarcadero Center
San Francisco, CA 94111
(415) 982-4278

Oakridge Mall
San Jose, CA 95123
(408) 226-0387

Broadway Shopping Center
Walnut Creek, CA 94598
(415) 944-0212

Bay Book & Tobacco Co
80 N Cabrillo Highway, Suite F
Half Moon Bay, CA 94019
(415) 726-3488
Kevin McGee, buyer. General.

Bay Books
1830 Salvio
Concord, CA 94520
(415) 671-2245
Donna Davison, buyer. New, used, & rare. 50,000 books.

Bay Tree Books
116 Throckmorton Ave.
Mill Valley, CA 94941
(415) 388-1229
Dorothy Weiss, buyer. General. 1% audio. B & T, Ing., Bkpple, L & S.

Bell's Book Store
536 Emerson
Palo Alto, CA 94301
(415) 323-7822
General, specializes in horticulture, history, out-of-print, kids.

Ben Franklin Books
1600 Shattuck Ave
Berkeley, CA 94709
(415) 845-6666
Audrey M Berger, buyer. General . 15,000 books. L & S, Bkpple, B & T.

Berkeley Book Store
2476 Bancroft Way
Berkeley, CA 94704
(415) 848-7906
Ed Hunolt, buyer. Textbooks, general.

Bibal Press
2606 Dwight Way
Berkeley, CA 94704
(415) 841-1905
*Religious nonprofit institute, bible, archae-
ology, law.*

Black Oak Books
1491 Shattuck Ave.
Berkeley, CA 94709
(415) 486-0698
*Bob Brown, buyer. General, new & used.
110,000 books, 250 audio, 100 periodicals. Ing., L & S, B & T, Pac. Pipeline.*

Black Oak Books
1633 Portland Ave.
Berkeley, CA 94707
*Bob Baldock, Bob Brown, buyers. General,
specializes in psych, literature, classics.
100,000 books, 1% audio, 1% gifts, 1%
periodicals. Ing., B & T, L & S, Bkpple,
Gordon's.*

Bonanza Street Books
1546 Bonanza
Walnut Creek, CA 94598
(415) 932-2466
*Jackie Miskel, buyer. Used, rare, out-of-
print. 15,000 books.*

Book Arbour
10 West 5th
Gilroy, CA 95020
(408) 842-2665
*Elaine Long, buyer. General. 10,000
books, 1% audio, 5% gifts. Bkpple, Ing.*

Book Center
883 B-1 Island Dr.
Alameda, CA 94501
(415) 523-0474
Audrey Sutton, buyer. General.

Book Exchange
7824 Covert Lane
Sebastopol, CA 95472
(707) 829-0819
Used.

Book Galley
228 Tennant Station
Morgan Hill, CA 95037
(408) 779-0444
Scott Phillips, buyer. General.

Book Mark
1281 East Calaveras Blvd.
Milpitas, CA 95035
(408) 262-9003
*Barbara Williams-Sheng, buyer. General.
12,000 books, 2% audio, 55 gifts, 10%
periodicals. Ing., B & T.*

Book Passage
51 Tamal Vista Blvd.
Corte Madera, CA 94925
(415) 927-0960
*Elaine Petrocelli & Victor Jones buyers.
General, specializes in travel.*

Book Place
2710 Middlefield Rd.
Palo Alto, CA 94306
(415) 324-1471
Used.

Book Rack
5892 Santa Teresa Blvd.
San Jose, CA 95123
(408) 225-1844
Used.

Book Revue
536 East Perkins St.
Ukiah, CA 95482
(707) 462-3577
*General. 15,000 books, 6% audio, 6% gifts.
Ing., Bkpple.*

Book Shelf
1555 Washington Ave.
San Leandro, CA 94578
(415) 483-0991
*Barbara Keenan, buyer. General, special-
izes in romance, fiction, sci-fi, mystery. 100,000+ books, 2% audio, 2% gifts,
2% comics. Cal-West, Ing., B & T.*

Book Shop
982 B
Hayward, CA 94541
(415) 538-3943
General.

Book Store Of San Mateo
132 East 3rd Ave.
San Mateo, CA 94401
(415) 343-2751
Fred Krupp, buyer. General.

Book Tree
1828 Salvio
Concord, CA 94520
(415) 687-7343
General, discount.

Book Tree
6123 La Salle Ave.
Oakland, CA 94611
(415) 339-0513
General.

Book Works
667 Lighthouse Ave.
Pacific Grove, CA 93950
(408) 372-2242
General.
Kathy Palermo, Jean Thurmond, buyers.

Book World
1141 B South Saratoga-Sunnyvale Rd.
San Jose, CA 95129
(408) 996-2384
General used.

Bookends
1014 Coombs St.
Napa, CA 94559
(707) 224-7455
Tom Pieper, buyer. 75,000 books, 200 audios, 400 periodicals. Ing., B & T, Bkpple, L & S, Gordon's, PGW.

Bookplate
2080 Chestnut
San Francisco, CA 94133
(415) 563-0888
General bookstore & restaurant.

Books & Bookshelves
99 Sanchez Street
San Francisco, CA 94114
(415) 863-5864
David Highsmith, buyer. General, specializes in poetry, fiction, literary biography, used & new, 30,000 books. Small Press, Bkpple.

Books Inc
120 Park Lane
San Mateo, CA 94005-1374
(415) 486-6111
Mike Grant, buyer. **Books Inc. stores:** *purchases made through headquarters.*

Books Inc
210 Coddingtown Center
Santa Rosa, CA 95401
General, Nancy Curdts, buyer, 90,000 books, L & S, Ing., B & T, PGW

Other locations:

140 Powell
San Francisco, CA 94102
(415) 397-1555

3515 California
San Francisco, CA 94118
(415) 221-3666

420 Town & Country Village
San Jose, CA 95128
(415) 243-6262

Stanford Shopping Center
Palo Alto, CA 94304
(415) 321-0600

California at Olympic
Contra Costa, CA
(415) 934-7211

Booksellers
1875 South Bascom Ave.
Campbell, CA 95008
(408) 879-9300
Grady Lawyer, buyer. all stores General.

Other locations:

210 El Paseo Shopping Center
San Jose, CA 95120
(408) 378-7633

No. 740, Pruneyard Shopping Center
Campbell, CA 95008

Bookshop Santa Cruz
1547 Pacific Garden Mall
Santa Cruz, CA 95060
(408) 423-0900
Judith Milton, buyer. General, children's, women's. 200,000 books, 3% audio, 6% gifts, 3% periodicals. Ing., Bkpple, L-S.

Booksmith
1644 Haight
San Francisco, CA 94117
(415) 863-8688
Gary Frank, buyer. General. 30,000 books, 400 audio, gifts, 400 periodicals. L & S, Ing., Bkpple, B & T.

Booksmith Inc
615 San Anselmo Ave.
San Anselmo, CA 94960
(415) 459-7323
Michael White, buyer. General.

Bookworks of San Francisco
2848 Mission
San Francisco, CA 94110
(415) 648-3324
Ed Woasa, buyer. General.

Bound Together Book Collective
1369 Haight
San Francisco, CA 94117
(415) 431-8355
*General, specializes in small press books,
no big publishers.*

Brentano's
Valley Fair Plaza
San Jose, CA 95128
(408) 249-1728
*Kathleen Boyd, local buyer. Purchases
mostly through headquarters.*

Brentano's
3251 20th Ave.
San Francisco, CA 94132
(415) 664-6981
*Kevin Johnson, local buyer. Purchases
mostly through headquarters.*

Browser Books
2239 Fillmore
San Francisco, CA 94115
(415) 567-8027
General.

Califia Books
2266 Union
San Francisco, CA 94123
(415) 346-9740
*Rich Innerst, buyer. General, specializes in
art books.*

California College of Arts and Crafts
Broadway & College Ave.
Oakland, CA 94618
(415) 658-2787
Cari Vellos, buyer.

**California Graduate School of Marital &
Family Therapy**
4340 Redwood Highway
San Rafael, CA 94903
(415) 472-5511
Carmen Diaz, buyer.

California School of Prof. Psychology
1900 Addison
Berkeley, CA 94704
(415) 523-2300
Judy Inouye, buyer.

Calistoga Bookstore
1343 Lincoln Ave.
Calistoga, CA 94515
(707) 942-4123
General.

Canterbury Corner Book Store
5301 Geary Blvd.
San Francisco, CA 94121
(415) 751-7770
Laurie Hughes, buyer. General.

Capitola Book Cafe
1475 41st Ave.
Capitola, CA 95010
(408) 462-4415
Ron Lang, buyer. General.

Carlmont Village Book & Tobacco Co.
1025 Alameda De Las Pulgas
Belmont, CA 94002
(415) 593-6333
General.

Cartesian Bookstore
2445 Dwight Way
Berkeley, CA 94704
(415) 549-3973
General, used.

Central Park Bookstore Express
32 East Fourth Ave.
San Mateo, CA 94401
(415) 579-4900
*Coleen LIndsay, buyer. General, special-
izes in alcohol, poetry, occult.*

Chabot College Bookstore
25555 Hesperian Blvd.
Hayward, CA 94545
(415) 783-9800
General books and textbooks.

Chapter One Bookstore
4620 Meridian Ave.
San Jose, CA 95124
(408) 448-6498
Ann Whalen, buyer. General new & used, specializes in art, military, children's classics. 40,000 books, 5% gifts.

City College of San Francisco
50 Phelan Ave.
San Francisco, CA 94112
(415) 239-3000
David Hunter, buyer. Text & reference books.

City Lights Bookstore
261 Columbus Ave.
San Francisco, CA 94133
(415) 362-8193
General, specializes in art, literature.

City University
3333 Bowers Ave.
Santa Clara, CA 98008
(800) 543-5476
Pat Kieswetter, buyer. Textbooks, business, public service manuals.

Civic Center Books
360 Golden Gate Ave.
San Francisco, CA 94102
(415) 885-5072
John Weidner, buyer. General & civil service, test-prep, SF city codes. 30,000 books, 2% audio,1% gifts, 20% periodicals. L & S, Ing.

Coastside Books
521 Main
Half Moon Bay, CA 94019
(415) 726-5889
Inge Sofer, buyer. General, specializes in metaphysics, kids.

Cody's Books
2454 Telegraph Ave.
Berkeley, CA 94007
(415) 845-7852
Nicholas Setka, buyer. General, "interna famous, since 1956," 90,000 books, 3% audio, 5% periodicals. Ing., Bkpple, Cnsrtium, SPD, B & T.

College of Alameda
555 Atlantic Ave.
Alameda, CA 94501
(415) 522-7221
Tom Martinez, buyer. Textbooks, general.

College of Notre Dame
1500 Ralston Ave.
Belmont, CA 94002
(415) 593-1601
Teresa Housen, buyer. Textbooks.

College of San Mateo
1700 West Hillsdale Blvd.
San Mateo, CA 94402
(415) 574-6161
Ms. Worster, buyer. Textbooks & general.

Columbia Pacific University
1415 3rd
San Rafael, CA 94901
(415) 459-1650
Paula Stout, buyer.

Copperfield's Annex
Fourth & D
Santa Rosa, CA 95405
(707) 545-5326

Copperfield's Books
138 North Main
Sebastopol, CA 95472
(707) 823-8991
Copperfield's stores: *Paul Jaffe, new books, Michael Merritt, backlists. General, specializes in psych, children's, substance abuse, metaphysical. 20,000 books,10% audio,1% gifts,1% periodicals. Ing., B & T, Bkpple, PGW, Grt. Tradition.*

Othe locations:

153 Kentucky
Petaluma, CA 94952
(707) 762-0563

2402 Magowan Dr.
Santa Rosa, CA 95405
(707) 578-8938

540 Raley's Town Centre
Rohnert Park, CA 94928
(707) 584-4240

Corrick's
637 4th
Santa Rosa, CA 95404
(707) 546-2423
*Rick Burmester, buyer. General.10,000
books,1% audio, 5% gifts. Ing., B & T,
Bkpple.*

Cottage Bookshop
1225 4th
San Rafael, CA 94901
(415) 453-2010
*Dan Druckerman, buyer. General. 30,000
books, 200 audios, gifts. Ing., B & T,
Bkpple, L & S.*

Cover to Cover Booksellers
3910 24th St.
San Francisco, CA 94114
(415) 282-8080
*Nicky Salan, buyer. Children's, fiction.
22,000 books. B & T, Ing., L & S, Bkpple.*

Crown Books
3300 75th Ave.
Landover, MD 20785
(301) 731-1200
**Buying headquarters for all Crown
bookstores,** *discount chain, call for buyer
in your category, Jeanne Herrick.*

Other locations:

1017 4th
San Rafael, CA 94901
(415) 456-3123

102 University Ave.
Palo Alto, CA 94301
(415) 328-1525

121 East 4th Ave.
San Mateo, CA 94401
(415) 579-1184

1236 West El Camino Real
Sunnyvale, CA 94087
(408) 732-8007

1245 Sutter
San Francisco, CA 94109
(415) 441-7479

1600 Saratoga Ave.
San Jose, CA 95129
(408) 374-9283

182 Northgate One
San Rafael, CA 94901
(415) 472-3205

19720 Stevens Creek Blvd.
Cupertino, CA 95014
(408) 973-8100

2504 Telegraph Avenue
Berkeley, CA 94704
(415) 548-8247

332 Gellert Blvd.
San Francisco, CA 94132
(415) 994-7990

3705 El Camino Real
Santa Clara, CA 95051
(408) 244-1573

4500 El Camino Real
Los Altos, CA 94022
(415) 949-1044

518 Castro
San Francisco, CA 94114
(415) 552-5213

5353 Almaden Expressway
San Jose, CA 95118
(408) 266-2015

57 El Camino Real
San Carlos, CA 94070
(415) 595-2811

740 Clement
San Francisco, CA 94118
(415) 221-5840
*Robert L Merjano, buyer. 10,000
books,125 audios, 250 periodicals. Ing.,
Bkpple.*

75 Murchison Dr.
Millbrae, CA 94030
(415) 697-3224

851 Cherry Ave.
San Bruno, CA 94096
(415) 589-2622

Crum's Bookmark
866 Grant Ave.
Novato, CA 94947
(415) 897-1183
General, used.

De Anza College
21250 Stevens Creek Blvd.
Cupertino, CA 95014
(408) 739-2616
College, reference, nursing. 6,000 titles,
10% audio, 10% gifts, 10% periodicals. Ing.

Depot Bookstore
87 Throckmorton Ave.
Mill Valley, CA 94941
(415) 383-2665
Korje Guttormsen, buyer. General, special-
izes in literature, philosophy, religion,
psych. 25,000 books.

Discount Books
114 Eddy
San Francisco, CA 94102
(415) 928-9111

Dominican College of San Rafael
Grand Ave. & Acacia
San Rafael, CA 94901
(415) 457-4440
David Mount, buyer. Texts and general.

Doubleday Book Shop
140 California
San Francisco, CA 94111
(415) 421-7822
Victor Belt, local buyer. **Doubleday chain**
books purchased by NY headquarters,
limited amount ordered locally. Doubleday
Bookshops, 673 Fifth Ave, New York, NY
10022-4297, (212) 223-6550.

Other locations:

265 Sutter
San Francisco, CA 94108
(415) 989-3420
General.

6170 Northgate Mall
San Rafael, CA 94901
(415) 479-3232
Cheryl Zainfield, buyer. General. Ing.,
Bkpple, L & S , PGW, B & T, Gldn Lee.

Eeyore Books
554 E Cotati Ave.
Cotati, CA 94928
(707) 795-8301
Lote Thistlewaite, buyer. General, litera-
ture, children's, nature, baseball, cooking.
1% audio, 5% gifts, 1% periodicals. Ing.,
Bkpple, L & S.

Elmwood Bookshop
2924 College Ave.
Berkeley, CA 94705
(415) 848-4582
Charles Baskett, buyer. General.

Empire College
3033 Cleveland Ave.
Santa Rosa, CA 95403
(707) 546-4000
Judy Moneymaker, buyer. Business, legal.

ESL Institute, New College of California
450 Chadbourne Ave.
Millbrae, CA 94030
(415) 697-6313
Paul Masaoka, buyer. ESL books.

Evergreen Valley College
3095 Yerba Buena Rd.
San Jose, CA 95135
(408) 274-7900
Michelle Fuqua, buyer. Texts, general.

First Street Books
850 College Ave.
Kentfield, CA 94904
(415) 456-8770
Woodie Leary, buyer. General.

Florey's Book Company
2316 Palmetto Ave.
Pacifica, CA 94044
(415) 355-8811
Mary Florey, buyer. 40,000 books, 1% gifts.
L-S, Bkpple, B & T, Ing.

Foghorn Books & Gifts
913 Highway One
Bodega Bay, CA 94923
(707) 875-3787
General & regional travel.

Foley Books Inc
71 Spear St.
San Francisco, CA 94105
(415) 982-7766
Carol Foley, buyer. General, 20% discount.
5,000 books, 1% audio. Ing.

Foothill College
12345 South El Monte Rd.
Los Altos Hills, CA 94022
(415) 960-4600
Roberto Sias, buyer.

Franciscan Shops
1650 Holloway Ave.
San Francisco, CA 94132
(415) 338-2023
Bill McMullen, buyer. Fiction, psych.,
education, ethnic studies. 75,000
books, 1% audio, 5% periodicals. L & S, Ing.

Free Forum Books
1800 Market
San Francisco, CA 94102
(415) 864-0952
Economics.

Gavilan College
5055 Santa Teresa Blvd.
Gilroy, CA 95020
(408) 847-1400
Dale Cadile, buyer. Textbooks & general.

Gay Lee's Bookshop
815 Main
Martinez, CA 94553
(415) 228-6660
General.

Genny's Book Nook
5678 Thornton Ave.
Newark, CA 94560
(415) 791-9190
Genny & Ken Smith, buyers. General, new
& used. 65,000 books, 1% audio, 1%
gifts, 1% periodicals. Pblshrs, Ing.

George's News Stand
27 7th
San Francisco, CA 94103
(415) 861-3250

Glen Park Books
654 Chenery
San Francisco, CA 94131
(415) 586-2424
Used.

Golden Gate Books
1905 San Pablo Ave.
El Cerrito, CA 94530
(415) 832-9194
General.

Golden Gate University
5050 El Camino Real
Los Altos, CA 94022
(408) 749-1699
Robert Henderson, buyer. Textbooks.

Graduate Theological Union Bookstore
2465 Le Conte
Berkeley, CA 94709
(415) 649-2470
Debra Farrington, buyer. For seminaries &
affiliates of GTU, open to the public,
theology, spirit, psych, bible, Judaica.
20,000 titles, cards, icon prints. Direct
from publishers.

Gray's Book Company
1821 Solano Ave.
Berkeley, CA 94707
(415) 527-9677
Lynn Gray, buyer. General, children's,
disabled. 17,000 books, 2% audio. Bkpple,
L & S, Gldn-Lee.

Great Expectations Bookstore
1512 Haight
San Francisco, CA 94117
(415) 863-5515
General.

Green Apple Books
506 Clement
San Francisco, CA 94118
(415) 387-2272
General, new & used. 150,000 books, 2%
audio, 2% gifts, 1% periodicals.

Guild Bookshop
648 Santa Cruz Ave.
Menlo Park, CA 94025
(415) 322-4763
Sally Conley, buyer. General.

Gull Book & Print Gallery
1551 San Pablo Ave.
Oakland, CA 94612
(415) 836-9142
40,000 books.

Half-Price Books
2525 Telegraph Ave.
Berkeley, CA 94704
(415) 843-6412
Used.

Heald Business College
684 El Paseo De Saratoga
San Jose, CA 95103
(408) 370-2400
Karen Graul, buyer. Business texts.

Other locations:

100 Professional Center Dr.
Rohnert Park, CA 94928
(707) 584-5900
Doreen Anderson, buyer. Business texts.

505 14th
Oakland, CA 94612
(415) 444-0201
Berdel Smith, buyer. Business texts.

Heald Institute of Technology
150 4th
San Francisco, CA 94103
(415) 441-5555
Ed Smeill, buyer. Technical texts.

Richard Hilkert Bookseller
333 Hayes
San Francisco, CA 94102
(415) 863-3339
Richard Hilkert, buyer, General.

Holmes Book Company
274 14th St.
Oakland, CA 94612
(415) 893-6860
David N Hurlbut, buyer. General, with specialties in West. Americana, Californiana, railroads. 500,000 books. Bkpple, L & L, Ing.

Holy Names College
3500 Mountain Blvd.
Oakland, CA 94619
(415) 436-1000
Ann Ardel, buyer. Texts, trade journals.

Hooked On Books
1854 Tice Valley Blvd.
Walnut Creek, CA 94595
(415) 933-1025
Rosemary McVey, buyer. General new, used, specializes in romance, mystery, sci–fi. 60,000 books, 500 used mags. L & S, Ing., Bkpple.

Hunter's Bargain Bookstore
151 Powell
San Francisco, CA 94102
(415) 397-5955
Remainders.

In and Out of Print Books
443 Clement
San Francisco, CA 94118
(415) 668-5070
Used.

Indian Valley Colleges
1800 Ignacio Blvd.
Novato, CA 94947
(415) 883-2211
Kathy Gold, buyer. Texts only.

Infinity Store
1982 Concord Ave.
Concord, CA 94520
(415) 827-4345
Todd Brewer, buyer. New Age, music, healing stones, superior quality books only. 50,000 books, 10% audio, 10% gifts, 2% periodicals. Bkpple, New Leaf.

Infoport
524 La Copita Ct.
San Ramon, CA 94583
(415) 831-9908
General, mail order. Ing, B & T.

JFK University
12 Atlarinda Rd.
Orinda, CA 94563
(415) 254-0200
Debbie Dedrick, buyer. Texts, general.

J K Gill Stationers
10123 North Wolf Rd.
Cupertino, CA 95014
(408) 255-1164
Linda Klein, buyer. General.

J K Gill Stationers
168 Eastridge Center
San Jose, CA 95122
(408) 238-1774
Phil Garrett, buyer. General.

JJ Perry's Pacific
2822 F St.
Eureka, CA 95501
(707) 445-1928
*P Bradford Wilson, buyer. General,
periodicals, software, video. 50,000 books,
300 audio, gifts, 200 periodicals. Ing.,
B & T, Bkpple, PGW.*

John Zubal, Inc.
2969 W 25th St.
Cleveland, OH 44113
(216) 241-7640
*Most titles of any bookstore in the world;
1.1 million books.*

Kepler's Books & Magazines
821 El Camino
Menlo Park, CA 94025
(415) 324-4321
Trade books, magazines & newspapers.

Lafayette Book Store
3579 Mount Diablo Blvd.
Lafayette , CA 94549
(415) 284-1233
*Sue Whalen, buyer. General, 10,000
books, specializes in kids & cookbooks,
Ing., L & S.*

Land of Counterpane
3610 Sacramento
San Francisco, CA 94118
(415) 346-4047
Stephanie Hardgrave, buyer. General,10,000 books, 30% gifts. L & S, B & T.

Landon Books
Strawberry Town & Country Village
Mill Valley, CA 94941
(415) 388-7929
*Hut Landon, buyer. General, 6,000 books,
1% audio, 5% gifts, 5% periodicals.
L & S, B & T, Ing.*

Landon Books
1553-C South Novato Blvd.
Novato, CA 94947
(415) 897-9395
*Hut Landon, buyer. General, specializes in
mysteries. 5,000 books,1% audio, 5% gifts,
5% periodicals. L & S, B & T, Ing.*

Lane's Books
1900 Park Blvd.
Oakland, CA 94606
(415) 465-9231
Tom Lane, buyer. General.

Laney College
900 Fallon
Oakland, CA 94607
(415) 834-5740
Dale Chung, buyer. Texts, study guides.

Language Resource Institute
1336 Polk
San Francisco, CA
(415) 441-8145
Tony Marlen, buyer.

Larkspur Office Supplies & Books
242 Magnolia Ave.
Larkspur, CA 94934
(415) 924-6939
*10,000 books, 2% audio, 5% gifts. Ing.,
L & S .*

Larry's Book Nook
730A Bancroft Rd.
Walnut Creek, CA 94598
(415) 933-2665
Larry Sydes, buyer. General.

Leaves of Grass
630 South Main St.
Willits, CA 95430
(707) 459-3744
Mark Komer, buyer. General.

Little Professor Book Center
5400 Ygnacio Valley Rd.
Concord, CA 94521
(415) 672-9300
Michael Wall, buyer. General.

Little Professor Book Center
3125 Meridian Ave.
San Jose, CA 95124
(408) 269-7323
Tim Pratt, buyer. General

Los Altos Book Store
205 State
Los Altos, CA 94022
(415) 941-0550
Barbara Bryson, buyer. General, specializes in French. 7,000 books, 5% audio, 1% gifts. B & T, Bkpple.

Manna - The Family Book Store
1950 Grant
Concord, CA 94520
(415) 686-1507
Hal Hougey, buyer. General & Christian books.

Marcus Book Stores
3900 Martin Luther King Way
Berkeley, CA 94703
(415) 652-2344
Julian Richardson, buyer. Books for black readers.

Marcus Books
1712 Fillmore St.
San Francisco, CA 94115
(415) 751-9211
Julian Richardson, buyer. Books for black readers.

Marin Community College District
College Ave.
Kentfield, CA 94904
(415) 485-9411
Kathy Gold, buyer. Texts only.

Menlo College
1000 El Camino Real
Atherton, CA 94025-4185
(415) 323-6141
Patricia Moore, buyer. Texts mostly.

Merritt College
12500 Campus Dr.
Oakland, CA 94619
(415) 436-2438
Jack Roos, buyer. 30,000 books, 5% gifts.

Mills College Bookstore
5000 Mac Arthur Blvd.
Oakland, CA 94613
(415) 430-2234
Suzanne Barton, buyer. Textbooks & general, women's, education, current affairs. 3,500 books, 1% audio, 40% gifts, 3% periodicals. Nacscorp.

Mission College
3000 Mission College Blvd.
Santa Clara, CA 95052
(408) 988-2200
Texts & general.

Moe's Books
2476 Telegraph Ave.
Berkeley, CA 94704
(415) 849-2087
Laura Tibbals, buyer. General.

Moraga Book Company
1460C Moraga Rd.
Moraga, CA 94556
(415) 376-1030
Myrtis Johnson, buyer. General.

My Favorite Bookstore
920 West College Ave.
Santa Rosa, CA 95401
(707) 575-5227
Liz Barnes, buyer. General.

Napa Valley College
Napa-Vallejo Highway
Napa, CA 94558
(707) 253-3000
Jerry Duncan, buyer. Texts & general.
.
Natural Instincts
600 Sycamore Valley Rd. West
Danville, CA 94526
(415) 820-8654
Chris Farris, buyer. General, specializes in nature, science.

New Albion Bookshop
1820 Sir Francis Drake Blvd.
Fairfax, CA 94930
(415) 456-1464
Hal Bertram, buyer. 100,000 books, many periodicals. Diamond.

Newstand
37 Caledonia St.
Sausalito, CA 94965
(415) 332-3640
Newstand with trade books.

Ninth Avenue Book Store
1348 9th Ave.
San Francisco, CA 94122
(415) 665-2938
Kathy Zickler, buyer. General, new, used.

Nut Tree Store
Nut Tree, CA 95698
(707) 448-6411
Roy Moehrke, buyer. Travel, aviation, garden, cooking, Calif travel & history, kids. 800 books, audios, gifts. Direct from publishers, Bkpple.

Orinda Books
276 Village Sq.
Orinda, CA 94563
(415) 254-7606
James H Boreta, buyer. General, 70,000 books, 5% audio, 1% gifts. Ingr., B & T, Bkpple.

Pacific Union College Bookstore
Box B
Angwin, CA 94508
(707) 965-6271
Sandra Rice Stauffer, buyer. General, no New Age, no gay, no general fiction, 1,000 titles, 15% gifts, 2% periodicals. Ingram.

Paperback Traffic
1501 Polk
San Francisco, CA 94109
(415) 771-8848
General.

Pathfinder Bookstore
3702 Telegraph Ave.
Berkeley, CA 94705
(415) 420-1165
Henry Scheer, buyer. Political, international.

Patten College
2433 Coolidge Ave.
Oakland, CA 94606
(415) 533-8300
Bertha Suitor, buyer.

Pendragon Books
5560 College Ave. North
Oakland, CA 94618
(415) 652-6259
Shelley Jackson, buyer. Mostly used, general.

Phoenix Books & Espresso Cafe
17 North San Pedro
San Jose, CA 95113
(408) 292-9277
Don Dawson, buyer. General. 5,000 books, 200 periodicals, B & T, Ing., L & S, Bkpple, Small Press Dist.

Phoenix Books & Records
3850 24th
San Francisco, CA 94107
(415) 821-3477
Christine Roger, buyer. General, new, used.

Piedmont Book Company
4048 Piedmont Ave.
Oakland, CA 94611
(415) 654-7278
Kitty Locke, buyer. General.

Pioneer Bookstore, Cal State Univ.
25976 Carlos Bee Blvd.
Hayward, CA 94542
(415) 881-3507
Judy Reed, buyer. General.

Plaza Books/Paper Vision
1111 Pacific Ave.
Santa Cruz, CA 95060
(408) 425-1111
Elizabeth Cupp, buyer. General, art, short fiction, 100,000 books, 1% audio, 25% gifts, 10% periodicals. Ing., Bkpple, L & S.

Printers Inc Bookstore
301 Castro
Mountain View, CA 94041
(415) 961-8500
Gerry Masteller, buyer.

Printers Inc.
310 California Ave.
Palo Alto, CA 94306
(415) 327-6500
Gerry Masteller, buyer. General, specializes in literary, 50,000 books, some audio, gifts, periodicals. Ing., B & T, L & S, Bkpple.

Rafael Book & News
1114 4th
San Rafael, CA 94901
(415) 454-5553
Lindon Gainey, buyer. General.

Rakestraw Books
Danville Livery & Mercantile
Danville, CA 94526
(415) 837-7337
Mary Harvey, buyer. General.10,000+ books, 100+ audios. Ing., B & T, Bkpple.

Redwood Bookstore
328 Center
Healdsburg, CA 95448
(707) 433-3410
Mary Zanderino, buyer. General.

Robbins Book Shop
6 Petaluma Blvd North
Petaluma, CA 94952
(707) 763-9122
Gray Robbins, buyer. General.

Ross Valley Book Company Inc
1407 Solano Ave.
Albany, CA 94706
(415) 526-6400
Specializess in the American Far West.

Safari Enterprises
2518 Lafayette Dr.
Davis , CA 95616-1548
(916) 753-5838
General.

**San Francisco College
of Mortuary Science**
1363 Divisadero
San Francisco, CA
(415) 567-0674
Michael Hawkins, buyer. Texts, mortuary science, accounting, business science.

San Francisco Conservatory of Music
1201 Ortega
San Francisco, CA 94122
(415) 564-8086
Patricia B Reardon, buyer. Music history, biography, theory. Direct from publishers.

San Francisco Theological Seminary
2 Kensington Rd.
San Anselmo, CA 94960
(415) 258-6500
Priscilla Peterson, buyer.

San Jose City College
2100 Moorpark Ave.
San Jose, CA 95128
(408) 298-2182
Ruth Lossted, buyer.

San Jose State University
1 Washington Sq.
San Jose, CA 95192
(408) 924-1000
Jeanette Grant, buyer. Texts & general.

Santa Clara University
The Alameda and Market St.'s
Santa Clara, CA 95053
(408) 554-4000
Stephanie Powell, buyer. Textbooks, general. 10,000+ titles, 5% audio, 35% gifts, 5% periodicals. Ing., Bkpple, Nacscorp, B & T.

Santa Rosa Junior College
1501 Mendocino Ave.
Santa Rosa, CA 95401
(707) 527-4011
Maryanne Hylande, buyer. Texts, reference, general.

Sawyer's News
733 4th St.
Santa Rosa, CA 95404
(707) 542-1311
General paperbacks, many periodicals.

Saybrook Institute
1550 Sutter St.
San Francisco, CA 94109
(415) 441-5034
Psych, human sciences. 500 books, 60 audios. Small publishers.

Simpson College
801 Silver Ave.
San Francisco, CA 94134
(415) 334-7400
Rob Wallace, buyer.

Skyline College
3300 College Dr.
San Bruno, CA 94066
(415) 355-7000
Chris Cuffin, buyer. Texts, general.

Small Press Traffic
3599 24th St
San Francisco, CA 94110
(415) 285-8394
*Largest collection of poetry on West Coast.
Publishes a quarterly newsletter w/
reviews. Workshops, reading series,
events. Katharine Harer, Director.
Nonprofit, specializess in literary work
from noncommercial publishers, 10,000
small press books and magazines.*

Solar Light Books
2068 Union
San Francisco, CA 94123
(415) 567-6082
*David Hughes, buyer. General. 20,000
books, 5% audio, 2% gifts, 4% periodicals.
Ing., Bkpple, PGW, Small Press Dist.*

Stacey's
383 Sacramento
San Francisco, CA 94111
(415) 397-7935
Susan Shaw, buyer. General.

Stacey's
581 Market
San Francisco, CA 94104
(415) 421-4687
*Susan Shaw, buyer. General. 120,000
books, 1.5% audio, 2% periodicals. Ing.,
B & T, Bkpple, PGW, L & S.*

Stacey's Book Store of Palo Alto
219 University Ave.
Palo Alto, CA 94301
(415) 326-0681
General.

Stacy's Books & Things
615 West 2nd
Antioch, CA 94509
(415) 757-7141
Used.

St Mary's College of California
Moraga, CA 94575
(415) 376-4411
*MaryLou Beeler, buyer. Texts, some
religious.*

Stanford University
Stanford, CA 94305
(415) 329-1217
Mark Ouimet, buyer. General.

Stinson Beach Books
State Route #1
Stinson Beach, CA 94970
(415) 868-0700
*Annie Rand, buyer. General, nature.
10,000 books, 1% audio, 25% gifts. Ing.,
Bkpple.*

Thunder Bird Book Shop (and Thunderbird for Kids)
3600 the Barnyard
Carmel, CA 93923
(408) 624-1803
*May S Waldroup, buyer. General. 40,000
books, 5% audio, 15% gifts, 2% periodicals.
Ing., B & T, Bkpple.*

Tillman Place Bookshop
8 Tillman Pl.
San Francisco, CA 94108
(415) 392-4668
General.

Tower Books
630 San Antonio Rd.
Mountain View, CA 94040
(415) 941-7300
Jeanine Sartore, buyer. General.

Tower Books
2727 South El Camino Real
San Mateo, CA 94403
(415) 570-7444
*Ken Krieg, buyer. General, specializes in
kids, music, travel, sci-fi. 100,000 books,
1% audio, 8% periodicals.*

Tower Books
2538 Watt Ave.
Sacramento, CA 95821-6392
(916) 481-6600
Albert Chow, buyer. General. 160,000 books,1% audio, .5% gifts, 8% periodicals. Ing., L & S, Gldn-Lee.

Toyon Books
104 Matheson
Healdsburg, CA 95448
(707) 433-9270
Martha Dwyer, buyer. General. 10,000 books, 2% audio, 2% gifts, .5% periodicals. Ing., B & T, Bkpple.

University of California - Santa Cruz
5201 Great American Parkway
Santa Clara, CA 95053
(408) 562-5799
Dan Doernberg, buyer. Texts, general.

University of San Francisco
2130 Fulton St.
San Francisco, CA 94117
(415) 666-688
Craig Hill, buyer. Law, nursing. 3,000 books, gifts, periodicals. Nacscorp.

Vacaville Book Co
315 Main St.
Vacaville, CA 95688
(707) 448-5040
Kristen Loomis, buyer. New & used, general, gay/lesbian. 10,000 books, 80 audio, some gifts, 1% periodicals. Ing., Bkpple, B & T, PGW.

Waldenbooks
122 Serramonte Shopping Center
Daly City, CA 94015
(415) 755-3373
***Waldenbooks stores**: Call for buyer in your category. Walden Book Co, 201 High Ridge Rd, Stamford, CT 06904, (203) 352-2500.*

Waldenbooks
Embarcadero Center
San Francisco, CA 94111
(415) 397-8181
Steve Kimball, buyer. 350 audios, gifts, 250 periodicals.

Waldenbooks
San Antonio Shopping Center
Mountain View , CA 94040
(415) 948-0645
25,000 books, 5% audio,10% gifts, 5% periodicals. Gldn-Lee, Ing., Pac. Pipeline.

Waldenbooks
West Portal Ave.
San Francisco, CA 94127
(415) 664-7596
15,000 books, 20% gifts, 5% periodicals, Ing., B & T.

Other locations:

2754 Town Center Lane
Sunnyvale, CA 94086
(408) 739-9000

129 Geary
San Francisco, CA 94108
(415) 421-6580

1824 Redwood Highway
Corte Madera, CA 94941
(415) 924-6278

201 High Ridge Rd.
Stamford, CT 06904-3417
(203) 356-7500
Paul Kolker, buyer.

2150 Shattuck Ave.
Berkeley, CA 94704
(415) 644-1360

2169 Chestnut
San Francisco, CA 94123
(415) 563-1658

2242 South Shore Center
Alameda, CA 94501
(415) 523-4463

3238 Lake Shore Ave.
Oakland, CA 94610
(415) 268-1602

538 Coddingtown Center
Santa Rosa, CA 95401
(707) 542-7065

Almaden Plaza
San Jose, CA 95118
(408) 264-3616

Waldenbooks (continued)
Eastridge Center
San Jose, CA 95122
(408) 274-1301

El Cerrito Plaza
El Cerrito, CA 94530
(415) 525-5727

Newpark Mall
Newark, CA 94560
(415) 794-4433

Northgate Mall
San Rafael, CA 94901
(415) 479-4474

Oakridge Mall
San Jose, CA 95123
(408) 226-3645

Santa Rosa Plaza
Santa Rosa, CA 95401
(707) 528-1955

Vallco Fashion Park
Cupertino, CA 95014
(408) 996-9431

Westgate Shopping Center
San Jose, CA 95125
(408) 866-8568

Sun Valley Mall
Concord, CA 94520
(415) 689-1342

Watermark at Tiburon
13 Main
Tiburon, CA 94920
(415) 435-4960
General.

Whole Earth Access
*Whole Earth Access stores, books
purchased through headquarters: Jeannie
Fanning, buyer. (415) 428-1600.*

Whole Earth Access locations:

401 Bayshore Blvd.
San Francisco, CA 94124
(415) 285-5244

Concord, CA 94519
(415) 686-2270*General.*

2990 7th & Ashby
Berkeley, CA 94710
(415) 845-3000

863 East Francisco Blvd.
San Rafael, CA 94901
(412) 459-3533

Willis Books
1307 Evans Ave.
San Francisco, CA 94188
(415) 648-7950
General. Ing., Bkpple, B & T, L & S.

Willow Glen Tattler
1318 Lincoln Ave.
San Jose, CA 95125
(408) 286-3981
Nadine Cassarino, buyer. General.

Wordsworth Books
281 North McDowell Blvd.
Petaluma, CA 94952
(707) 762-5665
Michael White, buyer. General.

Writer's Bookstore
2848 Webster
San Francisco, CA 94123
(415) 921-2620
New, used, all discount.

PICK A PROJECT...
ANY PROJECT

When you see the energy Delta Lithograph puts into your specific project and the superior printing that results, you'll probably wonder if we're playing tricks on you. After all, how can one printer meet the needs of so many different types of publishers? The answer is simple. With our expanded facilities, equipment and personnel, we're able to handle a much wider variety of customers than ever before. Whether you publish trade books, catalogues, directories or educational materials... need sizes from 3 × 5 to 11 × 17... desire one, two or multiple colors... or require run lengths from 1,000 to 1 million, we're the right plant for you.

Customer Service? At Delta you'll never have to worry about getting lost in the shuffle; keeping our customers happy has been a top priority since the day we opened more than 30 years ago, and we aim to keep it that way.

So the next time you're called upon to pick a printing company, pick the one who'll meet your specific needs best. Delta Lithograph Company—where magical things do happen.

In California call (800) 223-1478
Nationwide (800) 32DELTA
FAX: 805/257-3867

Book Manufacturers

delta
lithograph co

a Bertelsmann company

Please see BPMC ad in section 5-A.

Specialty Bookstores

*Abbreviations for distributors/wholesalers
preferred by bookstores:*
B & T: Baker & Taylor
PGW: Publishers Group West
Ing.: Ingram
Bkpple: Bookpeople
Gldn-Lee : Golden Lee
Cnsrtium: Consortium

A Different Light Bookstore
489 Castro
San Francisco, CA 94114
(415) 431-0891
*Richard La Bonte, buyer. Gay, lesbian,
feminist. 11,000 bks, 3% audio, 2% gifts,
4% periodicals. Ing., B & T, Bkpple, LS,
Gldn-Lee, Small Press Dist.*

A Learning Exchange
15 West 41st Ave.
San Mateo, CA 94403
(415) 349-0275
*Barbara Block, buyer. Instructional &
games books for kids, schools.*

A Sense of Wonder Bookstore
32302 Camino Capistrano, Suite 107
San Juan Capistrano, CA 92675
(714) 661-1422
*Mark & Jane Siet, buyers. New Age/
metaphysical, women's, sci-fi, astrology.
1,500 books, 10% audio, 20% gifts, 1%
periodicals. Ing., New Leaf, Bkpple, DVrss,
Mus. Design*

A World of Fantasy
979 South Bascom Ave.
San Jose, CA 95128
(408) 279-8070
*Dan Vado, buyer. Comic books, graphic
novels.*

About Music
Box 31415
San Francisco, CA 94131-0415
(415) 647-3343
*Used, music, dance, literature.
Susan Albrecht, buyer. 6,000 books,1%
gifts, 5% periodicals.*

Academy of Sciences Golden Gate Park
Golden Gate Park
San Francisco, CA 94115
(415) 750-7330
*Linda Chalmers, buyer. General interest,
natural history, aquarium.*

Accession Books
Fort Mason Center
San Francisco, CA 94123
(415) 861-5480
*Lynn Stelmah, buyer. Museum, art, crafts,
quilts, children's, international.*

Adventure Book Store
618 El Camino Real
San Carlos, CA 94070
(415) 593-0873
*Ted Cannon, buyer. Used. 65,000 books,
25% audio, 35% gifts, 500 periodicals.*

Alta Book Center Downtown
84 4th
San Francisco, CA 94103
(415) 541-9470
Michael Behrens, buyer. ESL, textbooks.

Altan Metaphysical Music & Books
16593 Ferris Ave.
Los Gatos, CA 95030
(408) 356-4963
*Jeton Holland, buyer. Arts, health, New
Age, psych.*

**America's Legal & Professional Book-
stores**
725 J
Sacramento, CA 95814
(916) 441-0410
*Kathy Ewing, buyer. Legal & professional,
law. 40,000 books. Ing.*

American Carousel Museum
633 Beach St.
San Francisco, CA 94109
(415) 928-0550
*Eric Olsen, buyer. Carousels, restoration,
carving. 20 titles.*

**American Museum
of Quilts and Textiles**
766 South 2nd
San Jose, CA 95112
(408) 971-0323
*Mary L Breithaupt, buyer. Museum, quilts,
needlework, loomed textiles. 250 titles,
40% gifts, 10% periodicals.*

American Opinion Bookstore
3000 Citrus Cir.
Walnut Creek, CA 94598
(415) 937-1404
*Jerry Denham, buyer. Americanist,
biblical, Constitution of U.S. 500 titles.*

other locations:

2314 4th St.
Santa Rosa, CA 95404
(707) 544-3600
*Americanist, biblical, Constitution of U.S.
2,000 books.*

420 South Bascom Ave.
San Jose, CA 95128
(408) 292-9343
Americanist, biblical, Constitution of U.S.

Amron Metaphysical Center
2254 Van Ness Ave.
San Francisco, CA 94109
(415) 775-0227
*James Roeser, buyer. Metaphysical, self-
awareness. 750 books, 20% audio,15%
gifts, 5% periodicals. Bkpple, DVrss,
Weiser, Llewellyn, Great Way*

Applied Science of Mind Bookstore
2115 Mission Blvd.
Hayward, CA 94541
(415) 538-8633
*Culver Wold, buyer. New Age/ Science of
Mind.100 titles. Bkpple, DVrss*

Aquarian Tapes & Books
53 North Santa Cruz Ave.
Los Gatos, CA 95030
(408) 395-5533
*New Age, music. 35,000 books, 50%
audio,10% gifts. Bkpple, DVrss, Bckrds,
Mus. Design*

Arabic Book Center
791 Valencia St.
San Francisco, CA 94110
(415) 864-1585
*Fadya Salfitti, buyer. Arabic, English,
Middle East. 3,000 books,10% audio, 30%
gifts, 3% periodicals. Medialink*

**Armchair Sailor Bookstore & Naviga-
tion Center**
42 Caledonia
Sausalito, CA 94965
(415) 332-7505
*Tamara Kennedy, buyer. Sailing, boats,
marine history, travel, navigational equip.
3,000 books, Ing., Robt. Hale Co.*

Art Store
216 East Mount Hermon
Scotts Valley, CA 95066-4030
(408) 438-0830
Neil Sandow, buyer. Arts.

Artist's Proof
460 Magnolia
Larkspur, CA
94939-2094
(415) 924-3801
*Maryjane Dunstan, buyer. General, Arts,
alter. issues, cookbooks, health, sci-fi.*

As You Like It Books
2556 Telegraph Ave.
Berkeley, CA 94704
(415) 848-2291
*Claudette Hoover, buyer. Women's,
progressive, soc. science, ethnic.*

Asia Printing & Bookstore
341 10th
Oakland, CA 94607
(415) 444-5889
*Nguyen Huynh, buyer. Chinese language
only.*

Asian Art Museum of San Francisco
Golden Gate Park
San Francisco, CA 94115
(415) 750-3642
Valerie Hogan, buyer. Art books.

Austen Books
1687 Haight
San Francisco, CA 94117
(415) 552-4122
Dover design & children's, mostly used.
20,000 bks. Dover, L & S, B & T, Bkpple.

Auto-Bound Inc
2313 Santa Clara Ave.
Alameda, CA
94501
(415) 521-8630
Andrew DeFrancesco, buyer. Auto &
motorcycle repair. 5% gifts,1% periodicals.

Automobilia
2300 16th
San Francisco, CA 94103
(415) 626-2300
Mike Martin, buyer. Historical autos,
manuals, models.

Ava Maria Community Book Center
12900 South Saratoga-Sunnyvale Rd.
Saratoga, CA 95070
(408) 741-1511
Robert Hughes, buyer. Religious. 5%
audio, 35% gifts. Bkpple, Ing., DVrss

Azteca Mexican Imports
1504 East Santa Clara
San Jose, CA 95116
(408) 259-0169
Erma Morgia, buyer. Books from and
about Mexico, in Spanish. Some periodi-
cals.

Baptist Book Store
Seminary Dr.
Mill Valley, CA 94941
(415) 388-1133
Liz Ngan, buyer. Religious, general.

Basic Living Products
2990 7th St. at Ashby
Berkeley, CA 94710
(415) 848-3600
Jeanne Fanning, buyer. Crafts, health,
house/garden, how-to, cooking, construc-
tion, computers, decorating, children's.
56,000 bks, 2% audio, 2% gifts,1% peri-
odicals. Bkpple, L & S, Ing., Gldn-Lee

Bay Area Discovery Museum
1036 Sir Francis Drake Blvd.
Kentfield, CA 94914
(415) 456-8797
Pam Cordingley, buyer. Museum,
children's books.

Beard's Books
637 Irving
San Francisco, CA 94122
(415) 566-0507
Mr Beard, buyer. Near UC Med Center,
technical, science. 20,000 books, .01%
audio, 1% gifts, 1% periodicals. L & S, Cal-
West, Bkpple

Berean Christian Store
2841 Meridian Ave.
San Jose, CA 95124
(408) 265-1833
Dennis Burnett, buyer. Religious.

Berkelouw Books
830 North Highland Ave.
Los Angeles, CA 90038
(213) 466-3321
Mr Berkelouw, buyer. Fine & rare.

Birth Place Resource Center
750 North California #K-1
Palo Alto, CA 94303
(415) 321-2229
Phyllis Ramey, buyer. Pregnancy, parent-
ing, birth. 50 books,Ing.

Black Scholar
Box 7106
San Francisco, CA 94120-7106
(415) 541-0311
Larry Loebig, buyer. Minorities.

Bob & Bob Fine Jewish Gifts, Crafts,
and Books
151 Forest Ave.
Palo Alto, CA 94301
(415) 329-9050
Ellen Bob, buyer. Jewish. 15,000 bks, 5%
audio, 40% gifts, 1% periodicals. B & T,
Bkple.

Book Passage
51 Tamal Vista Dr.
Corte Madera, CA 94925-1145
(415) 927-0960
Victor Jones, buyer. Specialize in travel books, maps, also a general bookstore. 60,000 books,1,000 audios, gifts, periodicals. L & S, Ing., B & T.

Books Etc
538 Castro
San Francisco, CA 94114
(415) 621-8631
Used & rare, art, gay, lesbian.

Books of Harmony
408 Broad St.
Nevada City, CA 95959
(916) 265-9564
Joan Stover, buyer. New Age. 6,000 bks, 9% audio, 4% gifts, 1% periodicals. Bkpple.

Books-By-Phone-Retail
Box 522
Berkeley, CA 94701
(415) 540-2124
Sebastian Orfali, buyer. Controversial, by phone. 500 bks,10% audio. PGW, Bkpple, Ing.

Buddhist Bookstore
1710 Octavia
San Francisco, CA 94109
(415) 776-7877
Sarah Grayson, buyer. Buddhist. 5,500 bks,1% audio, 33% gifts. Tutle.

Builder's Booksource
1817 Fourth St.
Berkeley, CA 94710
(415) 845-6874
George Kiskaddon, buyer. Architecture, construction. 3,600 books,15% gifts,15% periodicals. Bkpple, B & T, Ing.

C O H Christian Book Store
8411 Mac Arthur Blvd.
Oakland, CA 94605
(415) 632-3348
Herma Ross, buyer. Religious. 450 bks, 30% audio,10% gifts. Arbor Dist.

Cable Car Museum
1201 Mason
San Francisco, CA 94108
(415) 474-1887
Sharron Alegria, buyer. Museum, primarily cable cars.

California Book Company Limited
11 Phelan Ave.
San Francisco, CA 94112
(415) 586-1585
College textbooks, pbacks.

California Crafts Museum
900 North Point
San Francisco, CA 94109
(415) 771-1919
Museum, contemp. craft/art periodicals. 100% periodicals.

California Historical Society
2090 Jackson St.
San Francisco, CA 94109-2896
(415) 567-1848
Claire Barosi, buyer. History. 200 books.

Campus Textbook Exchange
2470 Bancroft Way
Berkeley, CA 94704
(415) 848-7700
George Speetzen, buyer. College textbooks.

Camron-Stanford House
1418 Lakeside Dr.
Oakland, CA 94612
(415) 836-1976
Mary Louise Weaver, buyer. Museum, Victorian times, Californiana, Oakland history.

Cavalli Italian Book Store
1441 Stockton
San Francisco, CA 94133
(415) 421-4219
John Valentini, buyer. Books in Italian & English, cookbooks, etc.

Chanticleer: Books For The Young
23 East Main St.
Los Gatos, CA 95030
(408) 354-3331
Harriet Zander, buyer. Arts, animals, children's, language, folklore. 100,000+ books, 200+ audio, gifts. B & T.

Charlotte's Web
1207 Bridgeway
Sausalito, CA 94965
(415) 332-2244
*Beth Urquhart, buyer. Kids & young
adults, literature, foreign lang. 800 books.
B & T, Beyda.*

Children's Book Depot
1340 Sixth Ave.
San Francisco, CA 94122
(415) 731-3417
*Carol Fuerth, buyer. Book parties, fairs,
children's. 300 books,10% audio. L & S,
Bkpple, B & T, Ing.*

Chimera Books
405 Kipling
Palo Alto, CA 94301
(415) 327-1122
*Walter Martin, buyer. Classics.100,000
books.*

China Books & Periodicals
2929 24th
San Francisco, CA 94110
(415) 282-2994
Books, magazines about China.

Chinese Culture & Arts Bookstore
241 Columbus Ave.
San Francisco, CA 94133-4508
(415) 397-4850
K Chiang, buyer. Minority studies.

Chinese Historical Society of America
17 Kerouac Pl.
San Francisco, CA 94133
(415) 391-1188
*E Chann, buyer. Museum, Chinese-
American history only. 50 books. Univ.
Press*

Christ Church Unity
1146 University Ave.
San Jose, CA 95126
(408) 293-7525
*Charlotte T Myers, buyer. Unity books &
tapes. 1100 bks, 20% audio,10% gifts,1%
periodicals. DVrss, Bkpple, New Leaf, Mus.
Design, Unity*

Christian Community Book Store
1407 McLaughlin Ave.
San Jose, CA 95122
(408) 279-3366
Gene Nelson, buyer. Religious.

Christian General Store
2130 4th
San Rafael, CA 94901
(415) 457-9489
*Betty A Kenner, buyer. Christian, bibles.
10,000 bks, 20% audio, 25% gifts.*

Christian General Store
874 Grant
Novato, CA 94947
(415) 897-6644
Joan Kerns, buyer. Religious, general bks.

Christian General Store No 5
571 5th St. West
Sonoma, CA 95476
(707) 996-6888
*Diane McIntyre, buyer. Christian, bibles,
children's. 2,000 bks, 5% audio, 45% gifts,
5% prdicals. Spring-Arbor, Riveride World.*

Christian Life Bookstore
1370 South Novato Blvd.
Novato, CA 94947
(415) 892-6804
Nancy Harris, buyer. Religious only.

ClaireLight
1110 Petaluma Hill Rd., Suite 5
Santa Rosa, CA 95404
(707) 575-8879
*M Grosch, buyer. Women's, children's.
7,000 bks,1% audio, 20% gifts, 3% periodicals. Ing., Bkpple.*

Columbus Books
540 Broadway
San Francisco, CA 94133
(415) 986-3872
*Marilyn Pallister, buyer. College & medi-
cal. 200,000 books. L & S, ARA, Bkpple.*

Comic Collector Shop
73 East San Fernando
San Jose, CA 95113
(408) 287-2254
*Bob Sidebottom, buyer. Comic books, art,
graphic novels, paperbacks, fantasy.*

Comic Relief
2138 University Ave.
Berkeley, CA 94704
(415) 843-5002
Rory Root, buyer. Sci-fi, comics, art. 10,000 books, 2,000 gifts, 60,000 periodicals. Cptl City, Diamond, Fantasy Dist., Wstrn Books.

Comics & Comix
2461 Telegraph Ave.
Berkeley, CA 94704-2397
(415) 845-4091
Carl Davidson, buyer. Comics, pbacks, art, European graphic novels.

Comics & Comix
405 California Ave.
Palo Alto, CA 94306
(415) 328-8100
Mike McCulloch, buyer. Comic books, comic art, illustrations, cartooning. 10,000 books, 20% gifts, 50% periodicals. Diamond, Last Gasp, Cptl City.

Computer Literacy Bookshop
520 Lawrence Expressway, #310
Sunnyvale, CA 94086
(408) 730-9955
Daniel Doernberg, buyer. Computers, technical, business, reference.

Computer Literacy Bookshop
2590 N. 1st St.
San Jose, CA 95131
(408) 435-1118
Daniel Doernberg, buyer. Computers, technical, business, reference.

Cookbook Corner
620 Sutter St.
San Francisco, CA 94102-1018
(415) 673-6281
Taya Monfried, buyer. Cookbooks/ nutrition.

Cotton Patch
1025 Brown Ave.
Lafayette, CA 94549-3901
(415) 284-1177
Carolie Hensley, buyer. Crafts, cross-stitch, quilting & quilting videos, sewing, garments, stencils. 225 books. C & T Publishing

Cover to Cover Booksellers
2254 Clement St.
San Francisco, CA 94121
(415) 668-6004
Nikki Salan, buyer. Children's, cookbooks, travel, folklore.

Coyote Point Museum Store
Coyote Point
San Mateo, CA 94401
(415) 342-7755
Donna Pribble, buyer. Museum, environment, animals, plants. 2,000 books. Price, Stern & Sloan, Nat'l Geo., Landon Hse, L & S.

Crystal Pathway
Suite #14 631 4th
Santa Rosa, CA 95404
(707) 579-4336
Kristina Lentz, buyer. Metaphysical, healing, spirituality. 550 books, 5% audio, 75% gifts. Bkpple, DVrss.

Curios & Candles
289 Divisadero
San Francisco, CA 94117
(415) 863-5669
Mark Sherman, buyer. Occult books & materials.

Dark Carnival Bookstore
2978 Adeline St.
Berkeley, CA 94703
(415) 845-7757
Jack Rems, buyer. Folklore, writers' reference, sci-fi, young adult. 25,000 bks, 1% audio, 1% gifts, 1% periodicals. B & T, L & S, Bkpple, PGW.

Dark Castle Books
1861 Adobe St.
Concord, CA 94520
(415) 687-0407
Paige A Dorais, buyer. Sci-fi, fantasy, horror. 12,000 books.

Davis Publishing Company
219 Highland Dr.
Aptos, CA 95003-4614
Stewart T Davis, buyer. Computers, politics, science.

Dawn Horse Book Depot
750 Adrian Way
San Rafael, CA 94903-3050
(415) 492-9382
*Michael Setter, buyer. Religion, psych.,
spiritual.*

De La Rosa's Latin American Imports
1163 South King Rd.
San Jose, CA 95122
(408) 272-1321
*Gilbert De La Rosa, buyer. Spanish &
English dictionaries, religious, general.*

De Lauer Super Newsstand
1310 Broadway
Oakland, CA 94612
(415) 451-6157
*Bud De Lauer, buyer. In- and out-of-state,
foreign periodicals. 75,000 bks, 1% audio,
10% gifts, 75% periodicals. Cal West, L–S.*

Dearborns Bible Book Store
22481 Foothill Blvd.
Hayward, CA 94541
(415) 881-8411
Tim Duncan, buyer. Religious only.

Deja Vu Metaphysical Book Store
1706 University Ave.
Berkeley, CA 94703
(415) 548-1867
*Rev. Karen Sorrentino, buyer. Metaphysical, healing, physical awareness. 1,900
books, audios, gifts, periodicals. Bkpple.*

Depot Park Museum
270 1st St. West
Sonoma, CA 95476
(707) 938-9765
*Inez Johnson, buyer. Museum, local
history, railroad books, local writers,
children's, California history, Indians.100
titles. Direct from publishers.*

Diane's Health Foods
3233 22nd Street
San Francisco, CA 94110
(415) 285-4454
Diane Rodden, buyer. Health & New Age.

Discount Book Company
24 Woodland Ave.
San Rafael, CA 94901
(415) 454-3122
*Bowman Yager, buyer. Warehouse outlet
for auto-related books; retail & wholesale.
3,000 bks,10% audio, 5% periodicals.
Motorbk Int'l, Price Stern & Sloan,
Crestline, SA Design, Sterling Pub, Auto.
Quarterly.*

Discovery Corner
Lawrence Hall of Science, UC Berkeley
Berkeley, CA 94720
(415) 642-1929
*Judith Timmel, buyer. Children's, science,
math, nature, teachers' guides. 3,000
books, 5% audio, 50% gifts. Ing., Bkpple*

Dragginwood
216 Capitola Ave.
Capitola, CA 95010
(408) 475-0915
Renee Chose, buyer. New Age/metaphysical.

Dragginwood
322 North Santa Cruz Ave.
Los Gatos, CA 95050
(408) 395-8544
Renee Chose, buyer. New Age/metaphysical, beading.

Drama Books
134 9th St.
San Francisco, CA 94103
(415) 255-0604
*Andrew DeShone, buyer. Film, theatre,
dance and related fields. 10,000 books,
some gifts.*

Earle's Christian Books & Gifts
2523 El Portal Dr.
San Pablo, CA 94806
(415) 237-8101
Jessie Kendrick, buyer. Religious.

East West Bookshop
1170 El Camino Real
Menlo Park, CA 94025-4358
(415) 325-5709
*Norman Snitkin, buyer. New Age, psych.,
philosophy. 17,000 books,14% audio,10%
gifts,1% periodicals. Bkpple, Ing., New
Leaf, DVrss.*

Eastwind Books
1435 A Stockton St.
San Francisco, CA 94133
(415) 781-3331
*David Woo, buyer. China, Asian Amer,
Chinese.*

Eastwind Books & Arts
1986 Shattuck Ave.
Berkeley, CA 94704
(415) 548-2350
*Chris Leung, buyer. China, Asian Amer,
Chinese.*

Easy Going
1400 Shattuck Ave.
Berkeley, CA 94709
(415) 843-3533
*Judith Elkins, buyer. Travel, maps,
accessories. 5,000 books, 40% travel
accessories. Bkpple, L & S, Ing.*

Easy Going
1617 Locust
Walnut Creek, CA 94596
(415) 947-6660
*Matt Elkins, buyer. Travel, maps, accesso-
ries. 5,000 books, 40% travel accessories.
Bkpple, L & S, Ing.*

Ecology Center Bookstore
1403 Addison St.
Berkeley, CA 94702-1902
(415) 548-2220
*R Sidney Shaw, buyer. Cookbooks, house/
garden, politics, nature.*

Educational Exchange
600 35th Ave.
San Francisco, CA 94121-2793
(415) 742-3302
*Andre Gustovsky, buyer. Children's,
education, reference, science. 5,500 books,
5% audio, 30% gifts, 1% periodicals.*

Eight-Seventy One Fine Arts
871 Folsom
San Francisco, CA 94107
(415) 543-5812
*Adrienne Fish, buyer. Contemp. and
modern art books, exhibition catalogs.
3,000 books.*

Ethnographic Arts Publications
1040 Erica Rd.
Mill Valley, CA 94941-3798
(415) 383-2998, 332-1646
*Arnold M Rogoff, buyer. Primitive/tribal art
Africa, Oceana, SE Asia, No. Amer. Indian,
Pre-Columbian Latin Amer, ethnology,
anthropology, 12,000 titles, 5% periodicals.*

Exploratorium Store
3601 Lyon St.
San Francisco, CA 94123
(415) 561-0390
*Mary Reid, buyer. Arts, children's, educa-
tion, science. 1500 books, 4% audio, 80%
gifts, 5% periodicals. Bkpple, Inland.*

Family Book Center
725 Mac Arthur Blvd.
San Leandro, CA 94578
(415) 635-5696
*Richard R Blake, buyer. Christian, bibles,
supplies. 5% audio, 5% gifts. Spring Arbor,
Ing.*

**Fantasy Etc Science Fiction & Detec-
tive Bookstore**
808 Larkin St.
San Francisco, CA 94109-7119
(415) 441-7617
*Charles Cockey, buyer. Horror, mystery,
sci-fi, suspense. 5% periodicals. L & S, B &
T, Bkpple, Speclty.*

Field's Book Store
1419 Polk
San Francisco, CA 94109
(415) 673-2027
*Richard Hackney, buyer. Metaphysical,
religious, psych., diet, healing, magic,
occult. 30,000 books, 1% audio, 5% periodicals. Bkpple, Weiser, DVrss.*

Firewind
250 Healdsburg Ave.
Healdsburg, CA 95448
(707) 433-8365
*Soli Alwyn, buyer. Women's, color, astrol-
ogy, crystals. 200 books, 10% audio, 80%
gifts, 10% periodicals. Bkpple, DVorss,
Weiser, Ind. Craftspeople.*

89

Focus Photography Books
1151 Mission
San Francisco, CA 94103
(415) 864-8355
Rob Vaughn, buyer. Photography.

Fong-Plummer Associates
Box 14821
San Francisco, CA 94114
(415) 647-2651
L B Plummer, buyer. Asian books in Western languages, most used; mail or appointment only. 10,000 books, small & specialized periodicals.

Foundation For San Francisco's Architectural Heritage
2007 Franklin
San Francisco CA 94109
(415) 441-3000
Bob Flagg, Buyer, Architecture, Victoriana, historical.

Friedel-Musikalien
1270 Marshall, 420 West Oakwood Blvd.
Redwood City, CA 94061-3937
(415) 369-3868
E Parkinson, buyer. Arts.

Future Fantasy
2033 El Camino Real
Palo Alto, CA 94306-1124
(415) 327-9242
Randall & Juliane Neff, buyer. Mystery, sci-fi.

Gaia Bookstore & Catalog Co.
1400 Shattuck
Berkeley, CA 94709
(415) 548-4172
Donna Ferina, buyer. General, women's spirituality, shamanism, New Age, health.

Gambler's Bookstore
135 North Sierra
Reno, NV 89501
(800) 323-2295
Mark Hicks, buyer. Mail order, gambling, gaming, sports. 2000 books, 2% audio, 25% gifts, 25% periodicals.

Game-A-Lot
110 Cooper St.
Santa Cruz, CA 95060
(408) 429-9009
Frank Kaehler, buyer. Games, sci-fi.

Gardener's Eden
100 North Point
San Francisco, CA 94133
(415) 421-7900
Chuck Williams, buyer. Garden.

Gateways Book & Gift
825 Pacific Ave.
Santa Cruz, CA 95060-4491
(408) 429-9600
B N Dass, buyer. Psych., philosophy, metaphysical. 10,000 books, 15% audio, 40% gifts, 1% periodicals. Bkpple, Ing., DVrss, New Leaf.

Globus Slavic Bookstore
332 Balboa
San Francisco, CA 94118
(415) 668-4723
Veronica Ahrens, buyer. Slavic language books, some in English, some imported.

God's Lighthouse
18 Hillcrest Blvd.
Millbrae, CA 94030
(415) 697-6690
Isabel Boyd, buyer. Religious only.

Golden Gate National Parks Association Bookstores
Fort Mason, Building 201
San Francisco, CA 94123-1322
(415) 556-0693
Rob Schauffler, buyer. Arts, history, nature. 3000 books, 1% audio, 1% gifts, 1% periodicals. Bkpple, L & S, Pblshrs.

Golden Gate University Bookstore
536 Mission St.
San Francisco, CA 94105
(415) 442-7277
Larry Smith, buyer. Business, legal, professional.

Goshado Company Books, Stationary and Records
1748 Buchanan
San Francisco, CA 94115
(415) 921-0200
Japanese. Some audio, some periodicals.

Gospel Christian Books
2550 El Camino Real West
Mountain View, CA 94040
(415) 941-0446
Jim Tholen, buyer. Religious.

Gourmet Guides/Travel Book Center
1767 Stockton St.
San Francisco, CA 94133
(415) 391-5903
Jean Bullock, buyer. Cookbooks, travel. 5,000 books, 1% audio, 1% gifts, 1% periodicals. Bkpple, L & S, B & T, Pac. Pipeline.

Grace Cathedral Gift Shop
1011 Taylor
San Francisco, CA 94108
(415) 776-1272
Josephine Jones, buyer. Religious. 2,500 bks, 1% audio, 45% gifts. Spring Arbor, Bkpple

Graduate Theological Union Bookstore
2465 Le Conte Ave.
Berkeley, CA 94709
(415) 649-2470
Debra Farrington, buyer. Primarily religious.

Grimblefinger Books
242 Commercial St.
Nevada City, CA 95959
(916) 265-5592
Lee Hundley, buyer. Hist., classics. 7,000 books, 1% audio, 1% gifts, 1% periodicals. B & T, Bkpple, Ing.

Guiding Star
469 Miller Ave.
Mill Valley, CA 94941
(415) 389-8432
Wendy Berman, buyer. Metaphysical & New Age. 2,200 books, 10% audio, 50% gifts, 5% periodicals. Bkpple, DVrss, New Leaf.

Guy's Teachers' Supplies
5327 Jacuzzi St.
Richmond, CA 94804
(415) 527-0566
Guy Patterson, buyer. Training manuals, education.

Haas-Lilienthal House
2007 Franklin
San Francisco, CA 94109
(415) 441-3004
Architecture, SF history, Victoriana. 500 books.

Hampton House
Box 67-8000
Placerville, CA 95667
(800) 248-3555
Lisa Herd, buyer. Sales, marketing, business training. B & T.

Hand Goods
3627 Main
Occidental, CA 95465
(707) 874-2161
Nancy Farah, buyer. Metaphysical, self-help, craft. 2000 books, 20% audio. Bkpple, Berkeley

Harvest Christian Bookstore
1239 Noriega
San Francisco, CA 94122
(415) 665-9672
Margaret Lee, buyer. Bibles, books. 1,000 books, 20% audio, 20% gifts, 5% periodicals.

Hastings College Of Law
200 McAllister St.
San Francisco, CA 94102
(415) 565-4610
Peg Meacham, buyer. Business, politics.

Hayward Area Historical Society & Museum
22701 Main
Hayward, CA 94541
(415) 581-0223
Lois Over, buyer. Museum, Cal. hist., victoriana. 10% bks, 90% gifts. Dover.

Hearth Song; A Shop For Families
Magowan Dr. & Farmers Ln., Montgomery
Village Shopping Center
Santa Rosa, CA 95405
(707) 829-1550
Barbara Kane, buyer. Toy store, traditional books for children, parenting.100 books, gifts, also mail order catalogue.

Other location:

156 North Main St.
Sebastopol, CA 95472
(707) 829-1550

Hicklebee's
1345 Lincoln Ave.
San Jose, CA 95125
(408) 292-8880
Valerie Lewis, buyer. Children's, education, family, folklore.

His Dwelling Place
2320 Midway Dr.
Santa Rosa, CA 95405
(707) 544-5555
Religious, deliverance, demonology.15,000 books,15% audio, 30% gifts, 5% periodicals. Spring Arbor, WORD, Zondervan.

If Wishes were Horses
522 Ramona
Palo Alto, CA 94301
(415) 321-9689
Terry Lyon, buyer. Kids', parenting.

Imago
Box 1682
Sausalito, CA 94966-1682
(415) 332-1822
Alfred Cavanaugh, buyer. Arts.

Interfaith Books & Gifts
37 Old Courthouse Sq.
Santa Rosa, CA 95404
(707) 525-8221
Peter Kiep, buyer. Religious, psychology, fiction, spirituality.

Irish Castle Gift Shop
537 Geary
San Francisco, CA 94102-1640
(415) 474-7432
John Whooley, buyer. Irish, lit., geneaology, folk, biography, art, education. 1,000 books, 15% audio, 5% periodicals.

Jack London Bookstore
Box 337
Glen Ellen, CA 95442
(707) 996-2888
Winifred Kingman, buyer. Jack London, Californiana, West. Americana. 12,000 books.

JACP Inc
414 East 3rd Ave.
San Mateo, CA 94401
(415) 343-9408
F M Hongo, buyer. Asian Amer. Only. 21,927 books,10% audio, .1% gifts, .1% periodicals.

Jewish Community Museum
121 Steuart
San Francisco, CA 94105
(415) 543-8880
Marilyn Sugarman, buyer. Museum, Judaica, the arts, Jewish history, children's. Ing., L & S, B & T.

Jewish Museum of the West/Judah L Magnes Museum
2911 Russell
Berkeley, CA 94705
(415) 849-2710
Arlene Sarver, buyer. Museum, Judaica, holocaust, arts, crafts.

John A Brown Kitchen Wares
Book Department, 5940 College Ave.
Oakland, CA 94618-1502
(415) 654-6462
W O Hughes, buyer. Cookbooks.

Kaleidoscope
1820 41st Ave.
Capitola, CA 95010
(408) 475-0210
Gertrude Frye, buyer. Children's, education, Spanish, folklore.

Kaufer's Religious Supplies
1834 Market St.
San Francisco, CA 94102-6295
(415) 431-6827
David Kaufer, buyer. Arts, Catholicism, general. 6,000 books, 5% audio, 40% gifts. Direct from pblshrs.

Kinokuniya Book Stores of America Company Limited
1581 Webster
San Francisco, CA 94115
(415) 567-7625
Y Suguki, buyer. Japanese, some in English.

La Craft Boutique
10073 Saich Way
Cupertino, CA 95014
(408) 257-2303
Phyllis Breller, buyer. Healing, crystals.

La Moderna Poesia
2122 Mission
San Francisco
CA 94110
(415) 861-6775
Maria Sanchez, buyer. Books in Spanish.

Lake Law Books
915 C Linden Ave.
South San Francisco, CA 94080
(415) 873-2900
Larry Lake, buyer. Politics, law.

Lakeshore Toy House
3343 Lake Shore Ave.
Oakland, CA 94610
(415) 451-1156
R Tomasco, buyer. Children's, cookbooks, folklore.

Lane's Books
1900 Park Blvd.
Oakland, CA 94606
(415) 465-9231
Shirley Massengill, buyer. Children's, folklore, adults.17,000 books,1% audio, .5% gifts. B & T, L & S.

Lawrence Hall of Science Gifts & Bookstore
Centennial At Grizzly Peak Blvd.
Oakland, CA 94611
(415) 642-1929
Books for teachers, parents and kids. novels.

Libreria Cristiana- Templo De La Fe
3126 16th
San Francisco, CA 94103
(415) 431-9027
Books in Spanish only.

Libreria La Latina Bookstore
2548 Mission St.
San Francisco, CA 94110-2512
(415) 824-0327
J E Zelaya, buyer. Spanish, ethnic, foreign literature.

Libreria Mexico
2841 Mission
San Francisco, CA 94110
(415) 647-0330
Francisca Mazon, buyer. Books in Spanish only.

Liebers Hebrew-English Book & Gift Store
3240 Geary Blvd.
San Francisco, CA 94118
(415) 387-3077
Laya Myers, buyer. Hebrew, Judaica.

Lifeway Books And Gifts
915 Lootens Pl.
San Rafael, CA 94901
(415) 456-9445
Emory Michael, buyer. Inner devel., children's, psych. 5,000 books, 5% audio, 40% gifts, 3% periodicals. Bkpple, New Leaf, DeVorss, Morning Bks.

Lighthouse New Age
2162 Union
San Francisco, CA 94123
(415) 567-2467
Max Schader, buyer. Children's, philosophy, holistic health, women's.

Limelight Bookstore
1803 Market St.
San Francisco, CA 94103-1107
(415) 864-2265
Roy A Johnson, buyer. Arts, entertainment. 15,000 books, audios, periodicals. L & S, Bkpple, B & T.

Linden Tree Children's Records & Books
170 State St.
Los Altos, CA 94022
(415) 949-3390
Dennis Ronberg, buyer. Kids' records & books.15,000 books, 35% audio,15% gifts. B & T, L & S, Bkpple.

Lioness Books
2224 J St.
Sacramento, CA 95816
(916) 442-4657
*Theresa Corrigan, buyer. Feminist,
women's, politics, recovery, children's.
6,000 bks, 200 audios, 5% gifts, 5%
periodicals. Bkpple, B & T.*

The Listening Post
52 Mission Circle
Santa Rosa, CA 95409
(707) 538-4936
*Audio book store, 2,000 audios, specialize
in business/self-help, Ing.*

Logos Bookstore
2398 Telegraph Ave.
Berkeley, CA 94704
(415) 548-2626
Henry Heerschap, buyer. Religious.

Los Gatos Museum
4 Tait Avenue
Los Gatos, CA 95031
(408) 354-2646
*History, kids art, art history, nature,
science. 500 books.*

Louie Bros Book Store
754 Washington
San Francisco, CA 94108
(415) 391-8866
*Chinese books and magazines.10,000
books, 2% audio, 5% gifts, 20% periodicals.
(Hong Kong/Taiwan).*

Lowie Museum Of Anthropology
UC Berkeley
Berkeley, CA 94720
(415) 643-7648
*Maria Gonzales-Bridges, buyer. History,
women's, sociology, anthropology, folklore.
1,000 books, some audio, 50% gifts.*

Magnes Museum Gift Shop
2911 Russell St.
Berkeley, CA 94705
(415) 849-2710
*A G Sarver, buyer. Arts, history, Judaica,
philosophy, children's, folklore - no phone
calls please/mail only.1% audio,1%
periodicals.*

Mama Bear's
6536 Telegraph Ave.
Oakland , CA 94609
(415) 428-9684
*C Wilson, buyer. Women's, spirituality,
recovery, non-sexist, children's. 7,000
books,1% audio, 2% gifts, 5% periodicals.
Bkpple.*

Mandarin Books
1725 Taraval
San Francisco, CA 94116
(415) 661-3355
Bilingual.

Maps to Anywhere Travel Bookstore
1514 North Hillhurst Ave.
Hollywood, CA 90027
(213) 660-2101
*Robert Crowley, buyer. Travel., language
materials, maps, accesories. 3,500 books,
200 audios.*

Marin Museum of the American Indian
2200 Novato Blvd./Box 864
Novato, CA 94948
(415) 897-4064
*Janet Larson, buyer. Museum, native
Amer. 50 books, 30% gifts, .2% periodicals.
Bkpple, Naturegraph.*

**Marin Teachers' Store & Children's
Books**
901 C St.
San Rafael, CA 94901
(415) 453-9197
*Rosalind Gardner, buyer. Children's,
education.13,000 books, 5% audio, 25%
gifts. Ing.*

Mariuccia Iaconi Book Imports
1110 Mariposa
San Francisco, CA 94107
(415) 285-7393
*Mariuccia Iaconi, buyer. Childen's Spanish
lang. literature, foreign lang. dictionaries,
English as a Second Language, open by
appointment.*

Marxist & Leninist Books & Periodicals
3232 Martin Luther King Way
Berkeley, CA 94703
(415) 653-4840
Marxist, Leninist.

Math Aids/Math Products Plus
Box 64
San Carlos, CA 94070
(415) 593-2839
Theoni Pappas, buyer. Mail order and bookstore, gifts & teaching materials, math, science, computers.

McDonald's Book Shop
48 Turk
San Francisco, CA 94102
(415) 673-2235
Used, out-of-print, hard to find, esoteric. 2 million books, 5% audio, 5% gifts, 50% periodicals.

Meridian Books
319 4th St.
Sausalito, CA 94965
(415) 332-3824
Gail Hurley, buyer. Nautical/aviation.

Michael Olaf
5817 College Ave.
Oakland, CA 94618
(415) 655-7100
Susan & Jim Stephenson, buyers. Children's, mail-order. 3,000 books, 150 audios, gifts, periodicals. Bkpple, Houghton-Mifflin, Ladybird. Suppliers to Montessori schools.

Military Medal Museum & Research Center
448 San Pedro
San Jose, CA 95110
(408) 298-1100
John Yates/ U.S., Victor Sutcliffe/ U.K., buyers. Museum, militaria. 2,100 books.

Milpitas Bible Book Store
220 South Main St.
Milpitas, CA 95035
(408) 946-2200
Jean Scott, buyer. Religious.

Minerva Books
1027 Alma St.
Palo Alto, CA 94301-2406
(415) 326-2006
Robert Clark, buyer. New Age, philosophy, psych., mysticism, religion.10,000 books,5% audio, 5% gifts, 2% periodicals. Bkpple, B & T, Harper & Row.

Modern Times Bookstore
968 Valencia St.
San Francisco, CA 94110-2389
(415) 282-9246
Michael Rosenthal, buyer. Education, gay/ lesbian, history, politics.

Montalvo Association Book Shop
Box 158
Saratoga, CA 95071
(408) 741-3421
Vicki Adams, buyer. "Garden for the arts," children's, cookbooks, Bay Area guide books, Bay Area history.

Mount Shasta Mystic Books
115 South Oregon St.
Yreka, CA 96097
(916) 842-4036
E L Downs, buyer. New Age.

Mr Mopps Children's Bookshop
1405 Martin Luther King Way
Berkeley, CA 94709
(415) 525-9633
Jean Yamashita, buyer. Arts, children's, crafts, folklore, education, tapes, general, special interest.15% audio, 20% gifts.

Museo Italio Americano
Fort Mason
San Francisco, CA 94123
(415) 673-2200
Elaine Romano, buyer. Museum, Italian Amer. books.

Museum Books SFMMA
401 Van Ness Ave.
San Francisco, CA 94102-4582
(415) 863-8800
Debra Lande, buyer. Arts, entertainment, house/garden, travel, children's. 10,000 books, 25% gifts, 15% periodicals. B & T, L & S, Ing.

Museum of Modern Mythology
693 Mission, Suite 900
San Francisco, CA 94105
(415) 546-0202
Robyn Talman, buyer. Museum, popular culture, advertising, Americana, collectibles, mythology.150 books, gifts.

Museum Store - California Palace of the Legion of Honor
Lincoln Park
San Francisco, CA 94121
(415) 750-3642
Valerie Hogan, buyer. Art, architecture. 40% gifts, 1% periodicals.

Museum Store - M H de Young Memorial Museum
Golden Gate Park
San Francisco, CA 94118
(415) 750-3642
Valerie Hogan, buyer. Art, architecture, 1% audio, 40% gifts, 1% periodicals.

Musical Offering
2430 Bancroft Way
Berkeley, CA 94704-1609
(415) 849-0211
Joseph Spencer, buyer. Arts, classical music. 100 books, 98% audio, 1% gifts, 25% periodicals. Polygram, harmonia mundi, Dover.

Mystic Gems
39159 Cedar Blvd.
Newark, CA 94560
(415) 792-0920
Loraine Fujiomoto, buyer. Metaphysical. 50% books, 20% audio, 28% gifts, 2% periodicals. Bkpple, DVrss, New Life.

Nature's Window
2417 Magowan Dr.
Santa Rosa, CA 95405
(707) 528-2201
Michelle Nelligan, buyer. Nature & science, philosophy.

Needle People
2435 South Winchester Blvd.
Campbell, CA 95008-4801
(408) 866-1181
Dalene Coleman, buyer. Needlecraft books and charts.

New Attitudes
5326 Fairfax Ave.
Oakland, CA 94601
(415) 533-7837
Paige Porter, buyer. Tools for recovery. 50 books, 15% audio, 75% gifts. Bkpple.

Nursery Books
4430 School Way
Castro Valley, CA 94546
(415) 538-4249
Sita Likuski, buyer. Children's, cookbooks.

Old Wives Tales Women's Visions & Books
1009 Valencia
San Francisco, CA 94110
(415) 821-4675
Tiana & Sim, buyers. Women's, children's, Third World, recovery. 11,000 books, 5% audio, 15% gifts, 5% periodicals. Bkpple, B & T, L & S.

One Way Book Shop
711 Stony Point Rd.
Santa Rosa, CA 95407
(707) 528-8937
Nick Harrison, buyer. Religious.

OPAMP
1033 North Sycamore Ave.
Los Angeles, CA 90038
(213) 464-4322
Morgan Edwards, buyer. Computer, engineering, film, audio. 150,000 books, 1% gifts, 2% periodicals.

Other Change Of Hobbit
2433 Channing Way
Berkeley, CA 94704-2298
(415) 848-0413
Debbie Notkin, David Nee, Tom Whitmore, buyers. Sci-fi, fantasy. 5,000 books, 100 audios, gifts, periodicals. L & S, Ing.

Pampanito Submarine
Pier 45, Fisherman's Wharf
San Francisco, CA 94133
(415) 929-0202
Tom Richardson, buyer. Museum, World War II memorabilia, including books.

Paper Ships Books & Crystals
630 San Anselmo Ave.
San Anselmo, CA 94960
(415) 457-3799
David Scheeter, buyer. Spiritual, self-healing, awareness.

Pegasus Books
1855 Solano Ave.
Berkeley, CA 94707
(415) 525-6888
Bill Gross, buyer. New Age, used & new, general.

Peninsula Conservation Center Store
2448 Watson Court
Palo Alto, CA 94303
(415) 494-9301
Linda Drey-Nightingale, buyer. Trail guides, travel, field ident. books, children's, education, nature, environment. 500 books, 50% gifts. Bkpple.

Peninsula Scientific Bookstore
2185 Park Blvd.
Palo Alto, CA 94306-1543
(415) 326-4136
Nancy Holmes, buyer. Computers, nature, science.

Phileas Fogg's Books & Maps For The Traveler
87 Stanford Shopping Center
Palo Alto, CA 94304
(415) 327-1754
Dick Butler, buyer. Travel, maps. 8,000 books.

Planetree Health Resource Center
2040 Webster St.
San Francisco, CA 94123
(415) 923-3680
Christine Moen, buyer. Medical, consumer health. 600 books,100 audios. Bkpple, B & T, J A Majors, Ing.

Point Reyes National Seashore Association
Point Reyes National Seashore
Point Reyes, CA 94956
(415) 663-1092
Don Neubacher, buyer. Environment, education. 140 books.

Printers' Shop
4047 Transport St.
Palo Alto, CA 94303-4916
(415) 494-6802
Frederica Postman, buyer. Graphic arts, book arts. 550 books.

Quick Trading Company
Box 477
San Francisco, CA 94101-0477
E Rosenthal, Ed. Marijuana, gardening. 20 books. Direct from publisher only.

Quinby's for the Curious Child
3411 California St.
San Francisco, CA 94118
(415) 751-7727
Mary Swetland, buyer. Children's, foreign lang., parenting, education. 1,500 books,12% audio, 5% gifts. B & T, Ing.

Ram Metaphysical Bookstore
1749 Park Ave.
San Jose, CA 95126-2016
(408) 294-2561
Francoise Beaudoin, buyer. New Age, metaphysical. 4,000 books,10% audio, 20% gifts, 5% periodicals. DVrss, Bkpple, New Leaf, Weiser.

Revolution Books
1541 Grant Ave.
San Francisco, CA 94133-3323
(415) 781-4989
Richard Flemming, buyer. Alternative issues, minority, politics, Marxist.

Revolution Books
2425 Channing Way
Berkeley, CA 94704
(415) 848-1196
Revolutionary Internationalist, progressive books & periodicals, general.

Roaring Camp Mercantile
577 5th St.
Oakland, CA 94607-3591
(415) 451-0863
Peter Bowman, buyer. Language, travel, literature.

Roberts Art Supply & Bookstore
330 South 10th
San Jose, CA 95112
(408) 286-0930
Textbooks, construction, art, study aids.

Rock Shop
468 Santa Clara Ave.
Oakland, CA 94610
(415) 893-5440
Pennie Opal, buyer. New Age/metaphysical. 65 books, 5% audio, 90% gifts, 5% periodicals. Bkpple.

San Francisco African American Historical and Cultural Center
Fort Mason, Building C
San Francisco, CA 94123
(415) 441-0640
Black history, books, magazines.

San Francisco Bay National Wildlife Refuge Bookstore
Box 524
Newark, CA 94560
(415) 792-0222
Steve Handcock, buyer. Animals, nature.

San Francisco Cameraworks Bookstore
70 12th St.
San Francisco, CA 94103-1242
(415) 621-1001
Wendy Oberlander, buyer. Arts, photography. 250 books, 1% audio, 20% periodicals. L & S, Bkpple.

San Francisco Museum of Modern Art
401 Van Ness Ave.
San Francisco, CA 94102
(415) 863-8800 ext 272
Debra Lahoe, buyer. Art. 10,000 books, 15% gifts, 5% periodicals. L & S, Bkpple, B & T.

San Francisco Mystery Bookstore
746 Diamond St.
San Francisco, CA 94127
(415) 282-7444
Bruce Taylor, buyer. Mystery, detective fiction, 10,000 books, 5% gifts. B & T.

San Francisco Opera Shop
199 Grove St.
San Francisco, CA 94102-4505
(415) 565-6414
Gabrielle Harmer, buyer. Classical performing arts. 1,000 books, 80% gifts.

San Jose Bookshop
1231 East Kentwood Ave.
San Jose, CA 95129-3602
(408) 446-0590
Shirley Bartlett, buyer. Health, New Age, philosophy, women's, sci-fi.

San Jose Historical Museum & Gift Shop
635 Phelan Ave.
San Jose, CA 95112
(408) 287-2290
Carol Carlson, buyer. Calif history, 800 books, 1% audio, 50% gifts, 1% periodicals.

San Jose Korean Christian Book Center
2454 El Camino Real
Santa Clara, CA 95051
(408) 246-2300
Mr. Chun, buyer. Religious.

San Jose Museum of Art
Museum Store, 110 South Market St.
San Jose, CA 95113
(408) 294-2787
Christina Miller, buyer. Arts, biographies, children's, cookbooks, crafts.

Sanchez Spanish Book & Music Store
2122 Mission
San Francisco, CA 94110
(415) 861-6775
Maria M Sanchez, buyer. Spanish lang. only.

Sand Dollar Books
Box 7400 Landscape Station
Berkeley, CA 94707-0400
(415) 527-1931
Poetry.

Schoenhof's Foreign Language Books
76 A Mount Auburn St.
Cambridge, MA 02167
(617) 547-8855
David Leyenson, buyer. North America's only comprehensive European bookstore. 30,000 books.

Science of Mind Bookstore
1195 Clark St.
San Jose, CA 95125-5702
(408) 294-1828
Wilma Riley, buyer. Metaphysics.

Second Timothy 2-15 Christian Bookstore
6016 Mac Arthur Blvd.
Oakland, CA 94609
(415) 632-3259
Religious.

Shambhala Booksellers
2482 Telegraph Ave.
Berkeley, CA 94704
(415) 848-8443
Philip Barry, buyer. East. & West. religions, Jung, acupuncture, environmental ethics, mail orders.

Sierra Club Bookstore
730 Polk
San Francisco, CA 94109
(415) 923-5600
Ginger Reding, buyer. Nature, trail guides. 3,500 books,1500 gifts. Whleslrs.

Sierra Club San Francisco Bay Chapter
6014 College Ave.
Oakland, CA 94618
(415) 658-7470
Nature, trail guides.

Sierra Club Store
530 Bush St.
San Francisco, CA 94108-3623
(415) 981-8634
Rebecca Evans, buyer. Nature.

Sisterspirit Women's Bookstore - Coffeehouse
1040 Park Ave.
San Jose, CA 95126
(408) 293-9372
Rose Sebastian, buyer. Women's, feminist, lesbian fiction, 3,000 books,10% audio, 5% periodicals. Bkpple, Ing., Inland.

Sisterwrite
190 Upper St.
London, England
NI United Kingdom
Women's.

Skool Daze Teacher's Supplies
806 Piner Rd.
Santa Rosa, CA 95403
(707) 544-6775

Small Press Traffic
3599 24th St.
San Francisco, CA 94110
(415) 285-8394
M B Condon, buyer. Specializes in small press and poetry, periodicals, nonfiction, records.

Smith & Hawken
25 Corte Madera
Mill Valley, CA 94941-1829
(415) 383-4415
Betsy Blew, buyer. Gardening, horticulture, nature, children's.1000 books, few magazines. Ing., Pblshrs.

Society of Pioneers
456 Mc Allister
San Francisco, CA 94102
(415) 861-5278
Museum.

Sonoma Bookends Bookstore
201 West Napa St., #18
Sonoma, CA 95476
(707) 938-5926
Jeff Simmons, buyer. Trade, computers, wine, special order. 25,000 books, 2% audio, 2% gifts, 5% periodicals. Ing., B & T, Bkpple.

Southern Sisters
411 Morris St.
Durham, NC 27701
Melody Ivins, buyer. Women's, feminist. 2,500 books, 2% audio, 20% gifts,3% periodicals. Ing., B & T, Inland, New Leaf, Bkpple.

Spice House
2343 Birch
Palo Alto, CA 94306
(415) 326-8811
Charlotte Lamb, buyer. Cookbooks. 2,000 books, 200 gifts.

Spring Valley Bible Church
220 South Main
Milpitas, CA 95035
(408) 262-2013
Jean Scott, buyer. Religious only.

Start-Up Books Etc
105 Serra Way
Milpitas, CA 95035
(408) 946-0115
G Hammer, buyer. Business. 350 books.

Store of Knowledge
1524 North Main
Walnut Creek, CA 94596
(415) 945-7562
Frede S Hammes, buyer. Children's, cookbooks, lang., sci-fi.

Store of Knowledge
1989-D Santa Rita Rd.
Pleasanton, CA 94566
(415) 462-TOYS
Frede Hammes, buyer. Kids' and teachers' books & art supplies. 200 books, 2% audio, 10% gifts. B & T, PSS, Bksllrs.

William K. Stout, Architectural Books
804 Montgomery
San Francisco, CA 94111
(415) 391-6757
Alan Silver, buyer, Architecture, design, graphics.

Sunnyvale Christian Bookstore
161 El Camino Real
Sunnyvale, CA 94087
(408) 738-3155
Religious.

Sunrise Bookshop
3054 Telegraph Ave.
Berkeley, CA 94705-2037
(415) 841-6372
Richard C Cook, buyer. Health, New Age, East. philosophy & religion. 10,000 books, 2% audio, 5% periodicals. Bkpple, DVrss, Samuel Weiser, Moving Bks, Ing.

Sweet Dreams
2901 A College Ave.
Berkeley, CA 94705
(415) 549-1211
Coral Mocklod, buyer. Children's, sci-fi.

Szwede Slavic Books
Box 1214
Palo Alto, CA 94302-1214
(415) 327-5590
Slavic. 250,000 books, 10% periodicals. European.

T'Olodumare Bookstore
2440 Durant Ave.
Berkeley, CA 94704
(415) 843-3088
Ade. Y Aro, buyer. African studies, metaphysical, religion. 500,000 books, 2% audio, 5% gifts. T'Olodumare Dist., Bkpple, Pblshrs.

Tammy's Bible & Book Store
3515 38th Ave.
Oakland, CA 94609
(415) 530-2788
Religious.

Tattoo Art Museum
#30 7th St.
San Francisco, CA 94103
(415) 775-4991
Judith Tuttle, buyer. Museum, historical/contemp. tattooing. 1,200 books, 10% gifts, 20% periodicals.

Teacher's Supply House Learning Rainbow Inc
2839 Meridian Rd.
San Jose, CA 95124
(408) 265-7744
Marion Elkerton, buyer. Children's, parenting, recovery, cooking, travel, reference, health, inspirational, home and garden. Ing., Beyda.

Teaching With Love
10 Enterprise Dr.
Santa Rosa, CA 95404
(707) 586-1866
Allison Keith, buyer. Education, children's. 5,000 b ks, 2% audio, 50% gifts. Troll, Milliken, Frank Schaffer, David S Lane.

Terrie Brill Gift Shoppe
770 El Camino Real
Belmont, CA 94002
(415) 593-3068
Michael Brill, buyer. New Age. 200 books, 25% audio, 70% gifts, 5% periodicals. Bkpple, Summit Univ. Press.

Tex's Toys Book Department
655 South San Antonio Rd.
Mountain View, CA 94040
(415) 941-1018
Cindy Harris, buyer. Children's, folklore, science. 4,000 books, 7% audio.

The Academy Store
California Academy of Science, Golden
Gate Park
San Francisco, CA 94118
(415) 750-7290
*Linda Chalmers, buyer. Natural history,
planetarium, aquarium. 15,000 books, 1%
audio, 70% gifts. L & S.*

The Antiquarian Archive
160 South Murphy Ave.
Sunnyvale, CA 94086
(408) 739-5633
*David B Ogle, buyer. Used hardcovers
only, militaria, aviation, maritime, Western
Americana. 30,000 books, periodicals.*

The Bearded Giraffe
6927 Stockton Ave.
El Cerrito, CA 94530
(415) 524-9325
*Rush Greenly, buyer. Metaphysical,
astrology, psychology.*

The Book Center
518 Valencia St.
San Francisco, CA 94110
(415) 626-2924
*Roberta Goodman, buyer. Marxist-Leninist,
some general, poetry, periodicals,
children's, some Spanish.*

The Book Nest
376 Greenwood Beach Rd.
Tiburon, CA 94920
(415) 388-2524
*Brian Hubbard, buyer. Animals, nature,
field guides, natural history, texts, environmental education. 1,000 books, 5%
audio, 10% gifts. Cmmn Grnd Dist.*

The Children's Bookshelf
1965 5th Ave.
Sacramento, CA 95818
(916) 456-6787
Children's, education.

The Crystal Cluster
510 Kelly Ave.
Half Moon Bay, CA 94019
(415) 726-7644
*Judy Johnson, buyer. New Age. 50 books,
2% audio, 20% gifts. Bkpple, New Leaf.*

The Hollow Reed
1149 First St.
Napa, CA 94559
(707) 226-9230
*Janis, Doreen, buyers. New Age/meta-
physical. 800 books, 150 audio, 50% gifts.
Bkpple, DVrss.*

The Little Land of Counterpane
139 Kearny
San Francisco, CA 94109
(415) 986-7745
*Stephanie Hardgrave, buyer.   Children's.
10,000 books, 30% gifts. L & S, B & T.*

The Map Center
2440 Bancroft Way
Berkeley, CA 94704
(415) 841-6277
*Barbara Jackson, buyer. Reference,
recreation, travel, atlases, land navigation,
cartography, natural hist. 1,000 books.
Bkpple, Rndm Hse, Falcon Press, Chronicle Bks.*

The Maritime Store
Historic Hyde Street Pier
San Francisco, CA 94109
(415) 775-2665
*Beverly Pikutis, buyer, Maritime, San
Francisco/California history, children's.*

The Mexican Museum
Fort Mason
San Francisco, CA 94123
(415) 441-0404
*Ann Barios, buyer, Museum, Mexican
history, Mexican artists.*

The Nature Company
*Catherine Kouts, Book buyer at corporate
offices for all Nature Company stores.
(415) 644-1337. Retail chain - books re
nature, science, field guides, natural sci.*

Store locations:

750 Hearst Ave.
Berkeley, CA 94710
(415) 644-1337
*2,000 books, 50% audio, 10,000 gifts.
Bkpple, Sunbelt, PGW, Book Whleslrs,
Koen Book Dist., Pac. Pipeline.*

The Nature Company (con't)
1530 Redwood Highway
Corte Madera, CA 94925
(415) 924-9470

2855 Stevens Creek Blvd.
San Jose, CA 95128
(408) 249-3535

4 Embarcadero Center
San Francisco, CA 94111
(415) 956-4911

6 Stanford Shopping Center
Palo Alto, CA 94306
(415) 321-9833

Ghirardelli Sq.
San Francisco, CA 94133
(415) 776-0724

Hillsdale Mall
San Mateo, CA 94403
(415) 345-5786

1236 Broadway Plaza
Walnut Creek, CA 94596
(415) 935-9556

The Oakland Museum Store
1000 Oak St.
Oakland, CA 94607
(415) 834-2129
*Joyce Ambrosini, buyer. Museum, Calif art,
natural science, history, children's. 40%
gifts,1% periodicals. Bkpple, Ing.*

The Scroll
4436 Pearl Ave.
San Jose, CA 95136
(408) 266-8317
*John Johnson, buyer. Religious, bibles.
4,000 books, 25% audio,15% gifts,1%
periodicals. Spring Arbor.*

The Sonoma County Museum
425 7th
Santa Rosa, CA 95404
(707) 579-1500
*Barbara Noel, buyer. Museum, history of
Sonoma Co., children's, Sierra Nevada,
Mexico.*

The Sorceress
900 North Point
San Francisco, CA 94109
(415) 928-1592
*Sharron Autiere, buyer. Metaphysical,
crystals.*

The Storyteller
2 Lafayette Cir.
Lafayette, CA 94549
(415) 284-3480
*Linda Higham, buyer. Children's litera-
ture, parenting.*

The Travel Shop
56 1/2 North Santa Cruz Ave.
Los Gatos, CA 95030
(408) 354-9909
*Ditty Smith, buyer. Travel. 5,000 books,
50% gifts. L & S, Bkpple, Ing.*

The Unicorn
1304 Scott St.
Petaluma, CA 94952
(707) 762-3362
*Lars Malmberg, buyer. Craftsmen. 10,000
books.*

Thinker Toys
196 Stanford Center
Palo Alto, CA 94304
(415) 326-2555
Mark Phillips, buyer. Children's.

Thomas Brothers Maps
550 Jackson
San Francisco, CA 94133
(415) 981-7520
Travel books, maps.

Tom Davis Books
Box 1107
Aptos, CA 95001-1107
(408) 476-6655
*Tom Davis, buyer. Biographies, history,
politics, current events. 740 books, 1%
periodicals. B & T, Ingram, Bkpple.*

Toronto Women's Store
73 Harbord St.
Toronto, Ontario M5SIG4
Women's.

Tower Books
1280 East Willow Pass Rd.
Concord, CA 94520
(415) 827-2920
Karen Lyberger, buyer. Tarot, I-Ching, art, drama, children's, music. 100,000 books, 1% audio, 10% gifts, 12% periodicals. Bkpple, Ing.

Toy World
Book Department, 319 Corte Madera
Town Center
Corte Madera, CA 94925-1308
(415) 276-9233
Harry Clayton, buyer. Children's, education.

Toyhouse Schoolhouse
Book Department, 322 Woodside Plaza
Redwood City, CA 94061
(415) 366-9374
Tom Farley, buyer. Animals, children's, crafts, education, science.

Travel & Things
5919 College Ave.
Oakland, CA 94618
(415) 547-6560
Travel.

Travel Quest
20103 La Roda Ct.
Cupertino, CA 95014-4410
(408) 446-0600
Cooking, travel, foreign lit., folklore.

Travelmarket
Golden Gate Commonway, 130 Pacific
Ave. Mall
San Francisco, CA 94111-1905
(415) 421-4080
Anne Brunswell, buyer. Cookbooks, language, reference, travel, literature.

Treasure Island Museum
1939-40 World's Fair-China Clipper Bldg
1 Treasure Island
San Francisco, CA 94111
(415) 765-6182
Phyllis Chaix, buyer. Museum, history of Navy, Marines, Coast Guard, Treasure Island.

UBC Book Company Inc
494 44th
Oakland, CA 94609
(415) 653-2022
G B Rumsey, buyer. College textbooks. 50,000 books.

UCSF Millberry Union Book & Supply Store
500 Parnassus Ave.
San Francisco, CA 94143-0230
(415) 476-1666
Christian Brust, buyer. Health science. 24,000 books, 1% audio. Matthews, Majors, Ing., L & S, PGW.

Unity Metaphysical Bookstore
1871 Geary Rd.
Walnut Creek, CA 94596
(415) 827-4708
Sandra Ortner, buyer. New Age/metaphysical.

University Art Museum Bookstore
2625 Durant Ave.
Berkeley, CA 94720
(415) 642-1475
John Douglas McCallister, buyer. Arts, history, architecture, photography, aesthetics. 4,000 books, 5% gifts, 15% periodicals. Bkpple, Eastern News, DeBoer Dist, L & S.

University Bookshops
34 Princess St.
Auckland 1
New Zealand
Women's.

University Press Books
2430 Bancroft Way
Berkeley, CA 94704
(415) 548-0585
Chloe Redon, buyer. 100 univ. publishers; history, lit.erature, sociology, science.10,000 books,10% periodicals. Univ. Presses, Metheun, Feminist Press.

Valley Bible & Book Shop
3295 Claremont Way
Napa, CA 94558
(707) 255-5985
Mark Peterson, buyer. Religious.

Vedanta Society Bookshop
2323 Vallejo
San Francisco, CA 94123
(415) 922-2323
Marilyn Pearce, buyer. Indian philosophical literature, religion, children's. 15,000 books, 10% gifts. Bkpple, direct from Pblshrs.

Victorian Books
2510 Hill Ct.
Berkeley, CA 94708-1910
(415) 644-4466
R L Ciochon, buyer. Animals, nature.

Videobook Store
2515 South El Camino Real
San Mateo, CA 94403
(415) 578-8303
Jacob Sleto, buyer. Instructional, educational. 3,000 books, 1% audio.

Videobook Store
3512 Geary Blvd.
San Francisco, CA 94118
(415) 578-8303
James Wong, buyer. Books on video tape, education, travel, children's, arts. 4,000 books, 1% audio, 5% gifts.

Waldenkids
3320 Northgate Mall
San Rafael, CA
94901
(415) 472-4533
Kids.

Walt Whitman Bookshop
2319 Market St.
San Francisco, CA
94114-1679
(415) 861-3078
Bernard Sinkler, buyer. General, gay/lesbian. 6,000 bks, 60% periodicals. Ing.

West Coast Church Supplies
369 Grand Ave.
South San Francisco, CA 94108
(415) 583-5153
Maxine Kotwituz, buyer. Religious.

Western Aerospace Museum
Oakland Int'l Airport
Oakland, CA 94621
(415) 638-7100
Ron Ruther, buyer. Museum, aviation, nature, history, pilot bio's.

Whales and Friends
Box 2660
Alameda, CA 94501
(415) 769-8500
Christine Gonsalves, buyer. Whales, nature, art, science. 2,000 books, .5% audio, 80% gifts. Bkpple, B & T, Harper & Rowe, Price, Stern & Sloan.

Williams-Sonoma
100 North Point
San Francisco, CA 94133
(415) 421-7900
Anne Mitchell Kupper, buyer. Cookbooks.

Windows Bookstore
400 West Franklin St.
Monterey, CA 93940-2303
(408) 372-7200
Alice Hofer, buyer. Biographies, children's, computers, cookbooks, entertainment.

Znanie Bookstore
5237 Geary Blvd.
San Francisco, CA 94118
(415) 752-7555
Mrs. Sapelkin, buyer. Russian lang. only, some children's.

5 Radio/TV Stations and Programs

Radio/TV Stations and Programs
Bay Area and Elsewhere

ABC Business World
47 West 66th St.
New York, NY 10023-6201
(212) 887-4993
Eleanor Prescott, Producer. Business news & interviews.

American Public Radio
444 Cedar St., Suite 700
St. Paul, MN 55101
(612) 290-1466
Dan Jensen. Largest distrib of public radio programs. "Marketplace," host, Michael Creedman, produced by Jim Russell. "Good Evening," producer, Tom Voegli, variety, music, literature, interviews.

AMEX Business Talk
86 Trinity Place
New York, NY 10006
(212) 306-1637
Tom Mariam. Radio program re business news, some author interviews.

"As It Happens"
Box 500, Station A
Toronto, Ontario
Canada M5W 1ER
(416) 975-6262
Syndicated radio program, general cultural interests.

BBC (British Broadcasting Corporation)
639 Fifth Ave.
New York, NY 10020
(212) 581-7100
"World of Books" program.

"Bookmark"
666 Broadway
New York, NY 10012
(212) 473-2230
Cynthia McFadden. Weekly public TV program on current books, Lewis Lapham, editor of Harpers magazine is host, panel of authors, critics.

Cable News Network (TV)
5 Penn Plaza
New York, NY 10001-1878
(212) 714-7800
Eric Scholl, Assign.desk. Several business-related shows weekly. Call for producer's name appropriate to your book subject.

"Cafe Society"
De Anza College TV Center
Cupertino, CA 95014
(408) 996-4426
Eliot Margolis. Cable TV show featuring poetry and other readings by authors, jazz music.

"Car Talk"
WBUR FM
630 Commonwealth Ave.
Boston, MA 02215
(800) 332-9287

CATV
340 Inverness
Pacifica, CA 94044
(415) 355-8000
Doug Edwards, Gen Mgr. Pacfica Community TV. "Seniors in Action," "Living Free," "Veteran's Viewpoint," "Discovery."

CBS News
524 W 57th St.
New York, NY 10019
(212) 975-7135
Eric Marcus, CBS Morning News features on books/authors.

Children's Journal
Box 682
Athens, OH 45701
593-1759
Programs re children, families.

Cultural Media Services
11750 Lake Blvd.
Felton, CA 95018
(408) 335-2878
Jay Wagner, Program "Food for the Thoughtful," syndicated to public radio, interviews & mentions authors frequently, nutrition, environment, agriculture, etc.

FNN
6701 Center Dr, West
Los Angeles, CA 90045
(213) 670-1100
Catherine Abraham, segment producer. "Business Tonight," cable program distributed to No. Calif stations, hosted by Bill Griffith, Diana Koricke and Gary Salen, finance & business, includes author/book. Business books, advertising, marketing, interna, global, social, economic, media, entertainment, new authors in literature.

Hour Magazine (TV)
5824 Sunset Blvd.
Los Angeles, CA 90028
(213) 960-2412

K101 FM Radio
700 Montgomery St.
San Francisco, CA 94111
(415) 956-5101
Bobby Cole, Program Director, John Evans, News Director. Primarily adult contemp hit music. Some pub affairs shows: community, major public issues, women, youth, minorities. "This Week:" Doug Sovern. "Funny books" send to Terry McGovern, morning DJ show, does brief interviews.

KABL AM, FM Radio
1025 Battery St.
San Francisco, CA 94111
(415) 788-5225
Dave McKinsey, Prog Director. Primarily easy listening music. "Public Voice," local issues, Olivia Goodson. "Speaking Freely," Tom Winston, pub opinion call-in, community concerns, women, minorities, discussion, interviews, religious.

KALW FM Radio
2905 21st St.
San Francisco, CA 94110
(415) 648-1177
Julia Randall, Prog Dir & Producer of "Interview" program."Information radio," SF Unified School District, interna news & information programs. Program guide & newsletter identifies show hosts. "People, Places & Ideas:" locally produced general interest program, interviews, authors & others. 1900 watts.

KALX FM Radio
2311 Bowditch St.
Berkeley, CA 94704
(415) 642-1111
Staff varies, Univ of Calif students. Progressive: pub affairs, community, women, minorities, interview, call-in programs, music, magazine format.

KARA FM Radio
Box 995
San Jose, CA 95108
(408) 293-8030
John McLeod, Prog Dir. Primarily oldies, adult contemp music. Some interviews, community news.

KATD FM Radio
227 N Santa Cruz
Los Gatos, CA 95030
(408) 354-6622
Bob Harlowe, Prog Dir. Primarily contemp music. Talk show.

KAZA FM Radio
Box 1290
San Jose, CA 95108
(408) 984-1290
Victor Barrios Mata, Prog Dir. Primarily Spanish music. Some Hispanic community discussion.

KBAY FM Radio
Box 6616
San Jose, CA 95150
(408) 370-7377
Bob Kohtz, Prog Dir. Primarily easy listening. Some interviews & news of commmunity issues; minority issues, health, education, social issues, environment. Carla Perez (Mental Health).

KBHK TV, CH 44
420 Taylor
San Francisco, CA 94102
(415) 885-3750
Tom Spitz, Prog Dir. Programs: "Black Renaissance," "El Amanecer" (Hispanic). Interview & talk shows. "Weekday:" misc. interviews re community.

KBLX Radio, AM, FM
601 Ashby
Berkeley, CA 94710
(415) 848-7713
Tony Kilbert, Prog Dir. Primarily adult contemporary music. "Bay Point," social issues. Health, Harvey Smith. Politics, Keith Carson. "Bay View," arts. 6600 wts.

KBRG FM Radio
39111 Paseo Padre Pkwy.
Fremont, CA 94538
(415) 791-1049
Salvador Campos, Prog Dir. Spanish language, Top 40 music. 3000 watts. Interviews re community.

KCAF AM 1510
1623 Fifth Ave.
San Rafael, CA 94901
(415) 456-1510
Susan Bice, General Manager. Primarily classic country music, some current issues.

KCBS AM Radio
1 Embarcadero Center
San Francisco, CA 94111
(415) 765-4000
Ed Cavagnaro, Prog Dir. Barbara Kaufman: consumer issues, "Call for Action." Ron Lyons: Health and Real Estate. Harvey Steiman, Narsai David: Food. Jane Riley: Bay Area women. Jerry McKay: science. 50,000 watt, CBS affiliate. Robert McCormack, "Night Beat," misc. talk show and interviews. "Jan Black's Journal:" gen'l interest and consumer interviews. John Holmgren, travel. Bert Bertolero, gardening. Larry Green, fishing, outdoors. Don Mosley, automotive.

KCDS FM Radio
Broadcast Center
Angwin, CA 94508
(707) 965-7141
Religious music and programing. "On the Line," Jennifer Lyons, interviews.

KCSM FM Radio
1700 W Hillsdale Blvd.
San Mateo, CA 94402-3784
(415) 574-6427
Clifford Brown Jr, Prog Director. Cultural programs, news, big band, art, public radio. 14,000 watts. "People," hosted by Claire Mack, interviews, community affairs, produced by Sandy Firpo.

KCSM TV 60
1700 W Hillsdale Blvd.
San Mateo, CA 94402
(415) 574-6586
Wendell Jones, Program Director. Cultural programs.

KDFC AM, FM Radio
2822 Van Ness
San Francisco, CA 94109
(415) 441-5332
Cal Haves, Prog Dir. Primarily classical music. Interviews re arts, community, consumer. 5000 watts. Cultural, consumer affairs, educational.

KDIA AM Radio
100 Swan Way
Oakland, CA 94621
(415) 633-2548
Jeff Harrison, Prog Dir. Primarily adult contemp music, black urban audience. Sunday general interview show & Sunday religious interview show.

KDTV TV, Ch 14
2200 Palou Ave.
San Francisco, CA 94124
(415) 641-1400
Emilio Nicolas, Gen Mgr. 100% Spanish lang. "En La Bahia," talk show. Jorge Belon, Program Director.

KEAR FM Radio
1234 Mariposa St.
San Francisco, CA 94107
(415) 626-3010
Thad McKinney, Station Manager. Interviews & talk shows re religion, community. 80,000 watts.

KEEN AM Radio
Box 6616
San Jose, CA 95150
(408) 370-7377
Christopher Snell, Prog. Dir. Primarily country music. Some discussion of community & social issues, health, education, environment.

KEST AM Radio
1231 Market St.
San Francisco, CA 94103
(415) 626-5585
Tom Johnson, Prog Dir. Primarily gospel music. Some discussion, interviews re health, community. "Bay Area Perspective" talk show. 1000 watts.

KEZR FM Radio
Box 2337
San Jose, CA 95109
(408) 287-5775
Lisa Dominique, Prog. Dir. Primarily adult music. Sunday interview show, community.

KFAX AM Radio
3106 Diablo Ave.
Hayward, CA 94545
(415) 782-1100
Janine Lundberg, Pub. Affairs Dir. Primarily religious music. Talk shows, community, social. "Saturday Morning Live," hosted by Dr Joseph Busey, produced by Janine Lundberg.

KFJC FM Radio
12345 El Monte Rd.
Los Altos Hills, CA 94022
(415) 960-4260
"P 2," hosted by Don Subath. "Brainwaves," hosted by John Porter.

KFOG FM Radio
55 Green St.
San Francisco, CA 94111
(415) 986-1045
Tony Salvador, Gen Mgr. Primarily rock, soft music. Street Beat & Foghorn: gen'l int & interview programs. 7900 watts.

KFRC AM Radio
500 Washington St.
San Francisco, CA 94111
(415) 986-6100
Harry Valentine, Prog Dir. Primarily news & oldies music, 5000 watts. "On the Positive Side," Robin Fahr, misc interview/ discussion. "Bayview," Don Sainte Johnn, misc including minority, interview/ discussion. "In the Medicine Cabinet," Linda Bernstein. "Delancey St.," Lew Lillian, city politics & government. "Dupont Guy," Janice Hom, Asian Amer issues. "Daily Dose," Joanne Greene, health & fitness. "Talk with Joanne Greene," interview/talk show, misc..

KFTY TV, Ch 50
Box 1150
Santa Rosa, CA 95402
(707) 526-5050
Chuck Snyder, Prog Dir. Magazine format show: "California North," regional general interest, people and places, Afton Ault, host.

KGO AM Radio
900 Front St.
San Francisco, CA 94111-1450
(415) 954-8100
News & Talk shows. Assign Ed: Ken Berry. Misc interview/talk shows, authors & others: Michael Krasny. Ronn Owens (call Mikel Cleland), Owen Spann, Dean Edell (health). Jim Eason (call Cindy Slay), Lee Rodgers, Ray Taliaferro, Dave Scott, Jay Snyder (recreation). Jim Jorgenson (money), Barbara Simpson, Carla Perez (mental health), Terry Lowry (The Home Show, home, garden, lifestyle). Michael Bernstein (religion). Carolyn Craven, Russ Riera (restaurants). Bill Bresnan (money). Quentin Kopp (politics), John Hamilton (California weekend, travel).

KGO TV, Ch 7
900 Front St.
San Francisco, CA 94111
(415) 954-7777
Assignment Desk 954-7321
John Moczulski, Prog Dir. Dr. Edell's Medical Journal," Dean Edell, host. "Good Morning Bay Area": Susan Sikora, Don Sanchez hosts, celeb talk show, audience interviews, features, Randy Barone, producer. Sylvia Ramirez: "AM weekend," community topics. Sunday on Seven; pub affairs, interviews.

KHQT FM Radio
2860 Zankar Rd, Suite 201
San Jose, CA 95134
(408) 948-0977
Steve Smith, Prog Dir. Primarily top 40. Some interviews, talk shows re religion.

KHTT AM Radio
1420 Koll Circle
San Jose, CA 95112
(415) 288-5400
Steve Moore, Prog Dir. Primarily oldies, 60's and 70's. Local interviews: Dick Cownie. Pub affairs, community.

KICU TV, Ch 36
Box 36
San Jose, CA 95109
(408) 298-3636
Mike Knoczal, Assign Ed. Michelle Ball, Prog Dir. "Left, Right & Center," politics. Pub Affairs, Roy Avila. "Liveline," live gen'l interest interviews, Michelle Blaine.

KIQI AM Radio
2601 Mission St.
San Francisco, CA 94110
(415) 648-8800, (415) 965-1024
Pilar Garcia, Prog Dir. Spanish lang music & news, some public service. Interviews, talk shows re Hispanics. Sally Jessy Raphael, interviews, lifestyle, psych. "Nuestra Invitados y Ud," hosted by Pilar Garcia & Raul Colindres, produced by Pilar Garcia. (695-1024)

KITS FM Radio
1355 Market St., #152
San Francisco, CA 94103
(415) 626-1053
Primarily rock music. 15,000 watts. Interviews: Alex Bennett.

KJAZ FM Radio
1131 Harbor Bay Parkway
Alameda, CA 94501
(415) 769-4800
Tim Hodges, Prog Dir. Primarily jazz music. Interviews w/musicians, some community, social.

KKHI AM, FM Radio
Hotel St. Francis, 335 Powell St.
San Francisco, CA 94102
(415) 986-2151
Victor Ledin, Prog Dir. Primarily classical music. Some interviews, community, social. Jeff Hirsch, fine arts, theatre.

KKIQ FM Radio
1603 Barcelona St.
Livermore, CA 94550-6401
(415) 455-4500
Jim Hampton, Prog Dir. Primarily adult contemp music. Some interviews and discussion of community, general issues.

KKIS AM Radio
1975 Diamond Blvd.
Concord, CA 94520
(415) 682-2832
Pat Finn, Prog Dir. Contemp music. Some discussion of pub affairs, community.

KKSF FM 103.7
77 Maiden Lane
San Francisco, CA 94108
(415) 788-2022
Dave Kendrick, Gen Manager. Primarily adult contemporary music, some discussion of community issues.

KKUP FM Radio
10221A Imperial Ave.
Cupertino, CA 95015
(408) 253-0303
Joe Sodja, Prog Dir. Music, interviews, talk shows re community.

KLIV AM Radio
Box 995
San Jose, CA 95108
(408) 293-8030
John McLeod, Prog Dir. Big Band music, discussion of community, social issues.

KLOK AM 1170
Box 21248
San Jose, CA 95151
(408) 274-1170
Bill Weaver, Gen Manager. Primarily contemporary music, some community issue reports.

KMEL FM Radio
2300 Stockton St.
San Francisco, CA 94133
(415) 391-9400
Keith Naftaly, Prog Dir. Primarily contemp music, some interviews, pub affairs. Community concerns, environment, new technologies, interviews. 69,000 watts. "Dialogue," "Health Beat."

KMGG FM Radio
Box 6673
Santa Rosa, CA 95406-0673
(707) 578-0977
Interviews: Bob Garrison. General interest.

KNBR AM Radio
1700 Montgomery St.
San Francisco, CA 94111-1071
(415) 951-7093
Rick Sadle, Jennifer Johnson, Prog. Dir.'s. News, adult contemp music & talk shows. Call-in sports show. Morning talk show, Frank Dill and Mike Cleary, phone interviews. "Leo LaPorte & Co," music, talk, phone interviews. "Hollywood Calling," Jan Wahl, talk show, call-in. "Betty Kamen's Nutrition Watch," call-in. "C J Bronson's Bay Today," music & area events. Sportsphone 68," Dave Newhouse.

KNEW AM Radio
66 Jack London Sq
Oakland, CA 94607
(415) 836-0910
Assignment Ed., Ron Baker. Primarily C & W music. "The Forum," pub affairs program, some interviews. "Bay Area Update," hosted by Marcey Levinson.

KNTA Radio
Box 631
Santa Clara, CA 95052-0631
(415) 244-1430
Armida Cabello, Prog Dir. Spanish music. Interviews, Armida Cabella, general interest. Spanish lang, 2500 watts.

KNTV TV
645 Park Ave.
San Jose, CA 95110
(408) 297-8780
Stewart Park, Prog Dir. Interviews, pub affairs. "Date Book," Yolanda Perez.

KOFY AM, FM Radio
642 Harrison, #404
San Francisco, CA 94107
(415) 442-1800
Randy Bailey, Gen Mgr. Adult contemporary, jazz, blues, folk music, some interviews re consumer tips, community interest.

KOFY TV, Ch 20
2500 Marin St.
San Francisco, CA 94124
(415) 821-2020
Rita Hughes, Prog Dir.

KOHL FM 89.3
Ohlone College
Box 3909
Fremont, CA 94539
Tom Briseno, Prog Dir. Adult contemp. music, community, education.

KOIT AM & FM Radio
77 Maiden Lane
San Francisco, CA 94108
(415) 434-0965
Suzy Mayzel, Prog Dir. Primarily light rock music. Interviews, Mike Phillips, state & local. 35,000 watts. "Today's World," community, social issues, minorities, women, senior citizens.

KOME FM Radio
3031 Tisch Way, Suite #3, Plaza West
San Jose, CA 95128
(408) 985-9800
*Ron Nenni, Prog Dir. Primarily rock music.
"Expressway," phone-in talk show re
general interest, women, minorities,
environment, society.*

KOVR TV, Ch 13
1216 Arden Way
Sacramento, CA 95815
(916) 927-1313
*Carl Dewing, Prog Dir.News, features.
"Midday," hosted by Dewey Hopper,
produced by Janice Torres.*

KPFA FM RADIO
2207 Shattuck
Berkeley, CA 94701
(415) 848-6767
*Jeanie Berson, Prog Dir. Progressive,
listener sponsored station, news, music,
world news, social issues, misc. 59,000
watts. "Booktalk," hosted by Peter Caroll,
SF Review of Books editor. Iris Frost,
People Section Editor (some book-related
stories & author interviews). Wings
Omnibus: re women worldwide, syndi-
cated prog., Katherine Davenport. Kris
Welsh, Bill Sokol, Denny Smithson: morn-
ing talk shows & interviews. "The Other
Americas Radio Journal," Eduardo Cohen:
public affairs program re Latin America &
Caribbean. "Heritage," Robin Gianattassio-
Mall producer: re older women. Morning
Reading and Evening Reading: Book
excerpts. "Here's to Your Health," Deborah
Lee, producer/host.*

KPIX TV, Ch 5
855 Battery St.
San Francisco, CA 94111
(415) 765-8600
*Ann Miller, Prog. Dir. "People Are Talking"
(call DeAnne Hamilton), general interest
interviews, features, Anne Fraser, Ross
McGowan, hosts. Evening Magazine" (call
Melanie Chilek), 1/2 hour magazine format
& interviews. "Afternoon Show," Barbara
Lane, variety/talk. CBS "Mac & Mutley,,"
animal related stories. Jim Lutton, Prog Dir.*

KPOO FM Radio
1329 Divisadero
San Francisco, CA 94115
(415) 346-5373
*Jerome Parson, Prog Dir. Primarily jazz,
reggae, R & B, some talk shows, interviews: educa, alternative issues, women,
world, arts, health.*

KQED FM Radio
500 8th St.
San Francisco, CA 94103
(415) 553-2129
*Carol Pierson, Prog Dir. Listener-supported,
news, pub affairs, genl interest, arts,
culture. NPR. Highly-educated audience.
110,000 watts. "Forum": pub affairs,
Kevin Purseglove. Dr. David Watts, medical. Kevin Boden, money. "West Coast
Weekend," hosted by Sedge Thomson.*

KQED TV, Ch 9
500 8th St.
San Francisco, CA 94103
(415) 864-2000
*Michael Scwarz, Sen. Story Ed. (PBS)
"Express," weekly news mag. on No. Calif.
pub affairs, Ginger Casey, host. "Science
Notes" (Bob Hone),"Art Notes" (John Rosak).*

KRON TV, Ch 4
1001 Van Ness Ave.
San Francisco, CA 94109
(415) 561-8905, assign desk.
*Dave Wilson, Prog Mgr. "Weekend Extra":
pub affair, Bob Roush (561-8648). "Bay
Area Backroads": magazine show &
interviews, Jerry Graham, host, Jessica
Abbe, producer (561-8084). "Home Turf,"
Saturday morning interviews, misc. (NBC
affiliate).*

KRPQ FM Radio
6640 Redwood Dr, #202
Rohnert Park, CA 94928
(707) 584-1058
*Ron Castro, Prog Dir.
Interviews: Dr. Carl Hendel, Health.*

KRQR FM Radio
1 Embarcadero Center
San Francisco, CA 94111
(415) 765-4097
Chris Miller, Prog Dir. Primarily rock music, some interviews & discussion of community, social issues. 82,000 watts. John Evans, pub affairs program.

KSAN FM Radio
Box 95
Oakland, CA 94604
(415) 836-0910
Betsy O'Connor, Assignment Editor. Primarily country music, some discussion of community issues, events. "Bay Area Focus," hosted PJ Ballard.

KSFO AM Radio
300 Broadway
San Francisco, CA 94133
(415) 398-5600
Bob Hamilton, Prog Dir. Noah Griffin, interviews,pub affairs. Primarily news, oldies & pop music, some discussion of community, social issues.

KSJO FM Radio
1420 Koll Circle
San Jose, CA 95112
(408) 288-5400
Ken Anthony, Prog Dir. Primarily rock music, some discussion of community, women, youth, interviews. Pub affairs program: "This is Santa Clara County."

KSOL FM Radio
1730 S Amphlett Blvd., #327
San Mateo, CA 94402
(415) 341-8777
Dave Padilla, Prog Dir. Primarily contemp. music. Some interviews, documentaries, community, social issues. Kids & parents: Brian Gardner. Lifestyle: Ray Jones. Money: Eleanor Curry.

KSRO AM Radio
Box 1598
Santa Rosa, CA 95402
(707) 545-3313
John Burgess, Prog Dir. Newstalk, interviews, discussion of community, general interest. "Diana Walter Show," hosted by Diana Walter, produced by Sandi Hansen. "Ed Lafrance Show," hosted by Ed Lafrance, produced by Sandi Hansen.

KSTS TV, CH 48
2349 Bering Dr
San Jose, CA 95131
(408) 435-8848
Dante Betteo. Interviews, game shows, soap opera, cooking show, talk show, movies, magazine show, news, music video, sports magazine show, sports, documentaries, variety. "Noticentro 48," hosted by Celina Rodriguez and Dante Betteo. "Ask the Expert," finance & investment, Gary Salem.

KTID FM Radio
1623 Fifth Ave.
San Rafael, CA 94901
(415) 456-1510
Dennis Coppola, Prog Dir. Primarily contemp music. Some interviews, talk shows, community, general interest. "Close-Up"; hosted by Jamye Lee.

KTOB AM Radio
12 E Washington
Petaluma, CA 94952
(707) 763-1505
Robert Taylor, Prog Dir. Primarily pop, rock music. Some interviews, discussions of na & local news, general interest. "Ed & Alan Show" hosted by Ed Weber/Alan Goldstock.

KTSF TV, Ch 26
100 Valley Drive
Brisbane, CA 94005
(415) 468-2626
Minda Logan, Prog Dir. Noah Griffin, "In Focus," interviews. "Chinese Journal," Asian Journal," discussion & interviews in several languages. "The Journal," hosted by Rose Shirinian.

KTVU TV, CH 2
2 Jack London Square
Oakland, CA 94607
(415) 834-1212, Assign desk: 874-0242.
Carol Chang, Prog Dir. "Studio A," general interest, Rosy Chu, Prod., Ian Zellick, host. (874-0180)

KUSF FM Radio
2130 Fulton St.
San Francisco, CA 94117-1080
(415) 386-5873
Melissa Metz, Prog Dir. Univ of SF, ethnic & pub affairs, student run, progressive music.

KVON AM Radio
1124 Foster Rd
Napa, CA 94558
(707) 252-1440
Barry Martin, Prog Dir. Local & na newstalk, interviews, community, hispanic. "Doubletalk," hosted and produced by Barry Martin. "Saturday Morning," hosted and produced by Rick Rafner.

KWSS FM Radio
1589 Schallenberger
San Jose, CA 95131
(408) 297-5977
Mike Preston, Prog Dir. Primarily contemp. music. Some interviews, discussion of community, minority interests, environment.

KWUN AM 1480
300 Holly Drive
Concord, CA 94521
(415) 685-1480
Joe Buerry, Gen Man. Primarily adult contemp. music, some discussion of community concerns, major public issues.

KYA FM Radio
300 Broadway
San Francisco, CA 94133
(415) 391-1260
Bob Hamilton, Prog Dir. Primarily R & R music, some interviews, discussion of community concerns. "Noah Griffin Show."

KYUU FM Radio
530 Bush St.
San Francisco, CA 94108
(415) 951-7200
Joe Alfenito, Prog Dir. Primarily contemp music, some interviews, discussion of community, consumer, general interest, psych. Julie Anderson, kids, families. Aldy Swanson, talk show, pub affairs. (NBC).

KZSU FM Radio
Box B
Stanford, CA 94309
(415) 725-4868
Ben Betenber, Prog Dir. Primarily jazz music, some discussion of community, other interests.

Marketplace, c/o Pacific Public Radio
1945 Palos Verdes, #204
Long Beach, CA 90815
(213) 430-6920
Syndicated program for APR re business news and behind the scenes views of business news.

Monitoradio
Dept C30, 1 Norway St.
Boston, MA 02115
(617) 450-2000
Program "Monitoradio," general interest, syndicated to public radio stations.

Musical Starstreams
Box 44
Mill Valley, CA 94942
(415) 383-STAR
New Age, syndicated music program, over 50 stations, ads available.

National Public Radio
2025 M St.,NW
Washington, D.C. 20036
(202) 822-2323
Alice Winkler. "All Things Considered," hosted by Robert Siegel, produced by Neal Conan, general interest, (Marilyn Robinson, Editor). "Latin File" - Hispanic American issues and arts. "Morning Edition," host Bob Edwards, produced by Ellen McDonnel. "Weekend Edition," host Scott Simon, prod. by Cindy Carpien, Saturdays. "Weekend Edition," host Susan Stamberg, prod. by Robert Malesky, Sundays.

New American Gazette
271 Huntington Ave., #240
Boston, MA 02115
(617) 437-5800
*Host: Barbara Jordan, Producer:
Deborah J Stavro, (617) 437-5800
"Some of the country's most provocative
thinkers from politics, educa, journalism,
medicine, science, the arts." Live audience.
Program syndicated to public radio
stations.*

New Dimensions
Box 410510
San Francisco, CA 94141
(707) 468-5215
Justine Toms, Prod., Michael Toms, host.

New Letters on the Air
5216 Rockhill
Kansas City, MO 64110
(816) 276-1168

*Carla Fisch.
Weekly 1/2 hr program of contemporary
authors reading from and talking about
their writing. Produced by New Letters
magazine and broadcast over NPR stations. "New letters on the Air," hosted and
produced by Rebekah Presson.*

Parenting Network
5432 West 102nd St.
Los Angeles, CA 90045
(213) 337-3382
*Bob Males.
Syndicated TV news features on kids,
parents, education, health, safety, behav-
ior, news, appears on local TV newscasts
nationally.*

Radio Smithsonian
Box 0609
Washington, DC 20073-0609
(202) 357-1935

Read More About It
51 West 52nd St.
New York, NY 10019
Jeannine Cattie. Program on books

SANE Education Fund
5808 Greene Street
Philadelphia, PA 19144
(215) 848-4100
Beth Parke, Producer.
"Consider the Alternatives," nationally syndicated, 30 min., weekly radio mag. on nuclear weaponry issues, foreign and military policy, labor and the economy, civil rights and liberties.

Soundings
Box 12256
Research Triangle Park, NC 27709-2256
(919) 549-0661
Na. Humanities Center, weekly, 30-minute public affairs program featuring fellows and visitors at the Na. Humanities Center, hosted by Dr Wayne J Pond.

The Today Show, NBC TV
30 Rockerfeller Plaza, #304
New York, NY 10112
Emily Boxer, Gene Shalit,
"Christmas Gift Book Round Up."

The Travel Show
150 Broad Hollow Rd, Penthouse 7
Melville, NY 11747
(516) 549-1202
David Kruter, Exec Prod.
2-hr weekly show, interviews with travel writers, authors or destination orientation guests. Frank Gelman, Coordinating Prod.

KIXE TV
Box 1719
Redding, CA 96099
(916) 549-4752
Theresa L. Bach, Producer.
Syndicated radio program, PBS, including book reviews. "Bach on Books".

USA Today, The TV Show
150 E 52nd St.
New York, NY 10022
(212) 593-7450

WAMC FM Radio
PO Box 1300
Albany, NY 12212
(518) 465-5233
"The Book Show," Tom Smith, interviews w/authors. "NPR Book Show," interviews: fiction writers, journalists, critics & poets.

WCOL AM Radio
c/o Jeanne Bonham
101 E Wilson Bridge Rd
Columbus, OH 43085-2303
(614) 885-1031
Daily program re books/authors by editor of Columba Review.

WFMT
303 East Wacker Dr
Chicago, IL 60601
(312) 565-5020
Sydney Lewis.
"Studs Terkel Almanac".

20/20 - ABC News
157 Columbus Ave.
New York, NY 10023
(212) 580-6000
Meredith White.
Author interviews, weekly TV shows.

 **Distributors and Wholesalers**

Distributors and Wholesalers

Advanced Marketing Services
4747 Morena Blvd. #200
San Diego, CA 92117-3469
(619) 581-2232
*Allen Orso, Mass market, cookbooks,
juvenile, calendars, video. Distrib in U.S.,
Canada Bookstores, Mass Market.*

AIMS International Books
3216 Montana Ave., Box 11496
Cinncinati, OH 45211
(513) 661-9200
*Georgia Crowell, Imports & distributes
Spanish-language books.*

Alpha Book Distributors
303 West 10th St
New York, NY 10014
(800) 221-8112
*Richard Epstein, National distributor,
specializes in small publishers, all subjects.*

AM Vakharwala
22 Union Ave.
Passaic, NJ 07055
*Distrib in India, specializes in business
books.*

Anne McGilvray & Co.
2505 Dallas Trade Mart,
2100 Stemmons Fwy
Dallas, TX 75207-3006
(800) 442-1495
Wholesaler to gift retailers.

Annex Book Distributors Inc
1889 Wantagh Ave.
Wantagh, NY 11793
(516) 781-3343
*Sandy Fellman, Primarily stationery store
racks, mass market books and maps,
specialty and reference books for schools.
Distrib to East Coast, Long Island.*

ARA Services
2340 South Fairfax Ave.
Los Angeles, CA 90016
(213) 933-7581
Wholesale magazines, all types, LA area.

Associated New, Inc.
3710 Main
Houston, TX 77002
(713) 528-3351
*Distrib mass market paperbacks to
bookstores, book fairs, SE Texas.*

Associations Book Distributors, Interna
503 Thomson Park Dr
Mars, PA 16046
(412) 772-0070, FAX (412) 772-5281
*Maureen Schwab, Distrib for engineering,
technical, scientific societies and publishers.*

Astran Inc
Rene Navarro
7965 North West 64th St.
Miami, FL 33166
(305) 591-8766
*Wholesaler of Spanish lang books in U.S.,
Puerto Rico, Dominican Republic.*

Auto-Bound
Andrew DeFrancesco
2313 Santa Clara Ave.
Alameda, CA 94501-4521
(415) 521-8630
*Auto parts stores, auto dealerships,
bookstores, libraries, repair manuals,
history, motorcycles. U.S. bookstores,
libraries.*

Baker & Taylor
652 East Main St., Box 6920
Bridgewater, NJ 08807-0920
(201) 218-0400
*Sue Pizza, Small Press Buyer
One of the largest and most important
wholesalers. Na, interna. Bookstores,
schools, libraries, colleges.*

Baker & Taylor Western Division
380 Edison Way
Reno, NV 89564-0099
(702) 786-6700
Ms. Vita Balsino, (201) 218-3968. One of the largest and most important wholesalers. 110,000 titles. Na, interna Bookstores, schools, specialty stores, libraries, colleges, government. Send for info packet.

Ballen Booksellers
66 Austin Blvd.
Commack, NY 11725-5765
(800) 645-5237
Barry Bernstein, Wholesaler specializing in academic, research, med. libraries. Na, interna. Colleges, special and corporate libraries.

Benton Ross Publishers
46 Parkway Drive
Glenfield, Auckland 10, New Zealand
479-5230, FAX 47802644
R.M. Ross, Distributes U.S. publishers in New Zealand.

Berkeley Educational Paperbacks
2480 Bancroft Way
Berkeley, CA 94704-1609
(415) 848-7907
Ed Hunolt, Schools, libraries.

Bevan & Michelle Davies
680 BRd.way
New York, NY 10012
(212) 254-1360
Distrib of contemp art books and art gallery catalogs, primarily European, small and large publishers.

Blackwell North America Company
Matt Nauman
6024 SW Jean Rd., Bldg G
Lake Oswego, OR 97034
(503) 684-1140
Wholesale/jobber to academic and research libraries. Interna.

Book Brokers of Australia
108 Rundle St.
Kent Town, South Australia 5067
08-42-7052
John V Gallehawk, (61-8-3627052) General non-fiction, distributors in Australia (AKA Axion Distrib, Aussie Proud Pub). Bookstores, schools, newstands, mass market, remainders.

Book Dynamics
330 Dalziel
Linden, NJ 07036
(800) 441-4510
Christopher J Fountas, Wholesaler, full line distrib. U.S. Bookstores, schools, newsstands, mass market, airports.

Book Inventory Systems
5451 South State Rd.
Ann Arbor, MI 48108-9789
(313) 995-7262
Kathleen Richardson, Small press books. Wholesaler of books & tapes. Midwest U.S. bookstores.

Book Promo Services, Ltd.
108, Federal Bldg
369 Lockhart Rd
Hong Kong, China
5-8339092, FAX 5-729531
Distrib in China.

Book Sales Inc
110 Enterprise Ave.
Secaucus, NJ 07094
(800) 526-7257
Promotional wholesalers of paperbacks.

Book Service California
2620 Del Monte St.
West Sacramento, CA 95691-3810
(916) 371-0359
Woodie Woodard., Wholesalers/distributors, West Coast & Midwest, paperbacks, trade, juvenile, remainders to chain stores, some independents.

Book Service Unlimited Inc
15030 Highway 99 South
Lynnwood, WA 98037
(800) 521-0714 ext #673
Woodie Woodard, Same as Book Service California, West Coast chainstores.

Bookazine Company
303 West 10th St.
New York, NY 10014
(800) 221-8112
*Richard Epstein, Wholesaler, paperback
and hardback, to bookstores, East Coast
libraries, mostly New York, some U.S.*

Booklink Distributors
Box 840
Arroyo Grande, CA 93420-0840
(805) 473-1947
*Lachland P. MacDonald, Distrib to book-
stores, schools, spec stores, libraries,
catalogs. In Calif, Nevada. Specialize in
nature, travel.*

Bookpeople
2929 4th St.
Berkeley, CA 94710-2776
(800) 624-4466
*Randall Beek, David Russ (549-3030)
Wholesaler, 4000 Na & interna accounts,1500 small publishers, all major
trade & mass market publishers. All
subjects, specializes in New Age, women's
travel, gay, health. Bookstores, specialty
stores,libraries, mass market, catalogs.*

Bookslinger
502 North Prior Ave.
Saint Paul, MN 55104
(612) 649-0271
*Rod and Hanje Richards (call collect)
Small press, literary, prose/poetry, essay,
the arts, children's literature, gay/lesbian,
theatre, mystery. All U.S. Bookstores,
specialty stores, libraries, colleges.*

Brodart Co
500 Arch St.
Williamsport, PA 17705
(800) 233-8467
*John Moore, Na wholesaler for libraries,
hardcovers, pbacks, juvenile, audio/video,
full service. Schools, libraries, colleges,
mass market.*

Cal-West Periodicals
2400 Filbert St., Box 2049
Oakland, CA 94604
(415) 444-3570
*Bookstores, schools, newstands, libraries,
mass market, catalogs.*

Charles E Tuttle Company
28 South Main St., Box 410
Rutland, VT 05701-0410
(802) 773-8930, FAX (802) 773-6993
*Stephen R Marro, English language books
& tapes on Asia distributed in Japan,
books on Asia distrib in North and South
America. Bookstores, schools, specialty
stores, libraries, colleges.*

China Books & Periodicals, Inc.
2929 24th St
San Francisco, CA 94110
(415) 282-2994
*Joe Katz, Mail order and retail books; all
subjects related to China, in English. No.
America distrib. Bookstores, libraries,
colleges.*

Conference Book Service
80 South Early St.
Alexandria, VA 22304
(703) 823-6966
*Mark Trocchi, Specialized exhibit and
promo. service for publishers of professional literature. Distrib in U.S., Canada.*

Consortium Book Sales & Dist., Inc
213 East 4th St.
St Paul, MN 55101
(612) 221-9035
*Stephen Williamson, Bobbie Rix. Distrib for
limited no. of independent publishers,
literary and/or art, U.S. primarily, bookstores, library wholesalers, trade wholesalers,*

Consulting Psychologists Press
577 College Ave.
Palo Alto, CA 94306
(415) 857-1444
*Psych. testing, self-awareness, assertive-
ness training, self-development, industrial
psych, career devel, marriage/family/
child. Na distrib, Bookstores, schools,
colleges.*

Contemporary Arts Press
Box 3123, Rincon Annex
San Francisco, CA 94119-3123
(415) 431-7524
*Anna Couey, Susan Weiner , Distrib of
books on new art activities, performance
art, video, film, computers, contemporary
theory. Na, interna. Bookstores, schools,
specialty stores, libraries, colleges. Send
sample copies w/documentation.*

Critique Book Service
Box 11368
Santa Rosa, CA 95406
(707) 525-9401
*Bob Banner, "Paradigm" type books,
metaphysical, healing.*

Cromland
4417 18th Ave. #312
Brooklyn, NY 11204-1202
(718) 797-0100, FAX (718) 935-9042
*Miriam Rotenstein., Wholesaler & exporter
of computer books, na and interna markets, largest assortment of computer
books, magazines & software in the world.*

David McKay Company Inc
2 Park Ave.
New York, NY 10016
*Bookstores, specialty stores, libraries,
direct mail workshops, newsletter.*

DeVorss & Company
Box 550
Marina Del Rey, CA 90294
(800) 331-4719
*New Age, self-help, health, audio, meta-
physical. Na, interna. Bookstores, specialty stores.*

Distribuidora del Libro
6521 North West 87th Ave.
Miami, FL 33166
(305) 592-5929, (800) 635-4276
*Felipe Calderon, Dist. & importer of Span-
ish-language books in U.S. Bookstores,
schools, specialty stores, libraries, colleges, mass market.*

Double M Press
16455 Tuba St
Sepulveda, CA 91343
(818) 360-3166
*Charlotte Markman Stein, Parenting, early
ed books & materials, Greek mythology
books, imagery, young adults. Distrib in
U.S. Schools, specialty stores, libraries,
colleges, mass market.*

DreamHaven Books & Art
300 Fourth St. South East
Minneapolis, MN
55414-2029
(612) 379-8924
*Greg Ketter, Comics, graphic art novels,
science fiction, fantasy, horror novels,
small presses. Bookstores, specialty
stores, libraries, colleges, catalogs.*

Eastwind Books & Arts
1435-A Stockton St.
San Francisco, CA 94133-3816
(415) 781-3331
*Mr. Doroteo Ng, Distrib of Asian language
books and English lang books on Asian
subjects, bookstores and libraries in U.S.,
college and univ text and reference books,
specializes in So East Asia.*

Educational Book Distributors
Box 551
San Mateo, CA 94401-0551
(415) 344-8458
*Robert Toms, Children, education, pre-
school, elementary, distrib in U.S. Bookstores, schools, catalogs, school supply
companies.*

European Book Company
925 Larkin
San Francisco, CA 94109
(415) 474-0626
*Distrib of books and magazines in French,
German, Spanish. Bookstores, schools,
libraries, newstands.*

Faherty & Associates
1670 South Amphlett #203
San Mateo, CA 94402-2511
(800) 824-2888
*Thomas Faherty, Distrib trade books.13
Western States. Bookstores.*

Far West Book Service
3515 North East Hassalo
Portland, OR 97232
(503) 234-7664
Katherine McCanna, Regional.

Firefly Books
3520 Pharmacy Ave.
Unit 1-C Scarborough M1W 2T8
Ontario, Canada
(416) 499-8412
*Lionel Koffler, Distrib books in Canada for
Amer. and Canadian publishers, small
presses.*

**First Editions/Crystal Coyote
Company**
North Payne Place
Sedona, AZ 86336
(602) 282-9574
*Distrib for New Age, metaphysical, in U.S..
Bookstores, specialty stores, libraries,
direct mail, workshops, newsletter.*

Forest Sales & Distributing Company
2616 Spain St.
New Orleans, LA 70117
(504) 947-2106
*Titles re New Orleans, Louisiana,
Mississippi subjects, distrib in Louisiana,
Mississippi, Alabama, Arkansas, East
Texas. Bookstores, specialty stores,
libraries, colleges.*

Forsyth Travel Library
9154 West 57th St., Box 2975
Shawnee Mission, KS 66201
Mail-order dist.

Forum Publishing Company
383 East Main St.
Centerport, NY 11721
(516) 754-5000
*Martin Stevens, Business books via retail,
mail order, import & export, catalogs. U.S.
market.*

Gazelle Books Services Limited
Falcon House, Queen Square
Lancaster, LAI IRN, England
(524) 68765
*Chris Tinns, Dist. of English lang. in U.K.
and Europe, all trade, academic & STN
subjects except mass market pbacks,
educa., fict. and children's. Distib in
U.K.,Ireland, Western Europe, South
Africa. Bookstores, specialty stores.*

Golden-Lee Book Distributors
16030 Carmenita Road
Cerritos, CA 90701
(800) 544-1490
*Debbie LeBoy, W Coast Sales Mgr. Cloth,
trade, mass market, computer science.
Distrib in West Coast, Southwest, Pacific
NW Bookstores, specialty stores, colleges.*

Gordon's Books Inc
2323 Delgany
Denver, CO
80216-5129
(800) 525-6979
*Sandy Revielle, New releases, backlist
titles, calendars, audio.Rocky Mountain
States. William Brown, hardcover; Tim
Cooper and Ken Eveleigh, buyers of small
press/regional titles; Jeanne Stevenson,
juveniles; John Cunningham, trade
paperback buyer; Tami Newlin, mass-
market paperbacks.*

Great Tradition
750 Adrian Way #111
San Rafael, CA 94903-3050
(415) 492-9382
*David Rosen, New Age, religions, Jungian
psych., holistic health, bookstores, libraries, colleges. Distrib in U.S., Canada, Australia, New Zealand. Bookstores, libraries,
colleges.*

Greatway Books
Box 590641
San Francisco, CA 94159
(800) 548-9990
*Jim Pinter, Distrib of books, tapes, in-
cense, Eastern religion, philosophy,
martial arts, healing in U.S., Canada.
Bookstores.*

Hippocrene Books
171 Madison Ave.
New York, NY 10016
(415) 898-8825
Peter McMillan (415) 898-8825
Frederick Schmalz-Riedt (415) 939-9756
Publishers & distrib of travel books,
general trade nonfic., Jewish interest,
Polish interest. Distrib in U.S., Canada.
Bookstores, schools, book fairs, libraries,
colleges, catalogs, museums.

Homestead Book Company
6101 22nd Ave. North West
Seattle, WA 98107-2496
(206) 782-4532
Marlin Ayotte, Distrib small presses,
counter-culture.

Horizon Publishers & Distributors
Box 490
Bountiful, UT 84010-0490
(801) 295-9451
Duane Crowther, Distrib in U.S., religious,
stitchery, family life, books and tapes to
bookstores, schools & specialty stores.

Hunter House Inc
Box 847
Claremont, CA 91711-0847
(714) 624-2277
J Trzyna, Publisher, distributor, rights
agent, book production service. Book-
stores, schools, libraries, catalogs, trade.
Specialize in family, health & psych.

Illinois Literary Publishers Association
Box 816
Oak Park, IL 60303
(312) 383-7535
Disrib for small literary publishers.

Independent Publishers Group
814 North Franklin St.
Chicago, IL 60610
(312) 337-0247
Mark Suchomel, Distrib in U.S. Bookstores,
schools, specialty stores, libraries, col-
leges, catalogs.

Ingram Book Company
347 Reedwood Dr
Nashville, TN 37217
(800) 937-8000
Bella Stringer (615) 793-5000, Wholesaler,
New & backlist titles, video, software,
periodicals, audio cassettes, CD's. 20,000
titles. Calif warehouses, buys from re-
gional wholesalers. Na, interna.

Inland Book Company
Box 261
East Haven, CT 06512
(800) 243-0138
Wholesalers, 6000 new & backlist titles,
small press, audio, video.

International Book Marketing
210 Fifth Ave.
New York, NY 10010-2102
(212) 683-3411
Judith Davenport, Subsidiary rights,
English book packaging. Distrib in U.S.,
Canada. Mass market.

Jelm Mountain Publications
209 Park St.
Laramie, WY 82070
(307) 721-5058
Jean R Jones, Regional interest. Distrib
from Sierra to Rockies. Bookstores,
schools, libraries.

Johnson Books
1880 South 57th St.
Boulder, CO 80301
(303) 443-1576, *Richard Croog*
Nature, travel, history, recreation.Distrib in
U.S., Canada. Bookstores, specialty stores,
libraries.

Kampmann & Co
9 East 40th St
New York, NY 10016-0402
(212) 685-2928

Ken Barden
11 High Mesa
Richardson, TX 75080-1519
(214) 231-0216
Western, cowboy, Texas, Texas
history.Distrib in Texas, Oklahoma, New
Mexico western-wear stores.

Klassen International
5781 Sherwood Blvd
Tswwassen
BC V4L 2K5, Canada
Distributor for books & tapes in Canada.

Koen Book Distributors
514 North Reed Ave.
Cinnaminson, NJ 08077
(800) 257-8481
New & backlist trade titles, small press.

Kyobe Book Centre
Box 1658
Kwangwhamun, Seoul, Korea
English lang. distrib in Korea.

L-S Distributors
480 Ninth St.
San Francisco, CA 94103-4411
(415) 861-6300
*Richard Seifert, All subjects, 20,000 titles,
every m;ajor Amer pubisher & selected
small presses, univ presses. Distrib from
Montery to Oregon border.*

Lectorum Publications Inc
137 West 14th St.
New York, NY 10011
(800) 345-5946
*Nerissa Moran, Cloth & paper bestsellers,
classics, regional, reference. Distrib in U.S.
Bookstores, schools, libraries, colleges.*

Magickal Childe
35 West 19th St.
New York, NY 10011
(212) 242-7182
*Herman Slater, Dist. of New Age, meta-
physical books. National, interna distrib.
Bookstores, specialty stores, libraries,
catalogs.*

Mariuccia Iaconi Book Imports
1110 Mariposa
San Francisco, CA 94107
(415) 255-8193
*Languages, literature, ethnic, childrens.
Distrib in U.S. Schools, libraries.*

Merle Distributing
27222 Plymouth Rd.
Detroit, MI 48239
(800) 233-9380
*Kevin Lentz (313) 937-8400. Cloth, mass
market, trade pback. Na distrib. Bookstores, schools, specialty stores, libraries,
colleges, mass market, drug stores, dept
stores. Specialize in golf books.*

Michael Olaf
5817 College Ave.
Oakland, CA 94618
(415) 655-7100
*Susan & Jim Stephenson, Children's, mail-
order.*

Milligan News Company
150 N Autumn St.
San Jose, CA 95110-2388
(408) 298-3322
(408) 286-7604, educational div.
*Billie Jo Winger, Fred Silva , General,
education. Distrib in U.S., Hong Kong.
Bookstores, schools, spec stores, libraries,
colleges, mass market.*

Moon Publications
722 Wall St.
Chico, CA 95298
(916) 345-5413
*Deke Castleman, Donna Galassi, Publish-
ers, travel, exclusive distribution rights
only. Interna. Bookstores, specialty stores,
libraries, mass market, catalogs, outdoor
retail product stores.*

Motorbooks International
729 Prospect Ave.
Osceola, WI 54020
(800) 458-0454
*Kaye Broom, Publisher and wholesaler of
books on autos & aviation, trains, modeling, tractors, hobby shops. Na, interna
readership. All markets except mass
market.*

Mountain N'Air Books
Box 12540
La Crescenta, CA 91214
(818) 957-5338
FAX 957-5376
Gilberto d'Urso, Outdoor, sports, travel,
automotive, aviation, motorcycles, trains,
boats, modeling, tractors. Distrib in U.S.,
Canada. Specialty stores, catalogs.

Moving Books, Inc
Box 20037
Seattle, WA 98102
(800) 777-6683
(206) 325-9077
Michael Brasky, New Age, metaphysical,
self-help, alcoholism, addiction. Na,
interna. Bookstores, schools, specialty
stores, libraries, colleges, mass market.

NACSCORP Inc
528 East Lorain St.
Oberlin, OH 44074-1298
(800) 321-3883
Pam Schuck, Front & backlist, academic,
course adoptions, calendars. U.S., Can-
ada. Colleges & Univ. bookstores only.
Non-profit book wholesaling subsidiary of
Na Assoc of College Stores, distrib only to
members of NACS.

National Book Network
4720 Boston Way #A
Lanham, MD 20706-4310
(301) 459-8696
Emphasis on politics, government.

National Book Store, Inc.
Socorro C. Ramos, General Mgr.
Box 1934
Manila, Philippines 49-43-06
Importer, wholesaler & retailer.

Naturegraph Publishers
3543 Indian Creek Rd., Box 1075
Happy Camp, CA 96039-1075
(916) 493-5353
Barbara Brown, Nature, American Indian,
health. Na, interna distrib. Bookstores,
schools, specialty stores, libraries, col-
leges, catalogs, museums, gift shops.

New & Unique Video
2236 Sumac
San Diego, CA 92105
(619) 282-6126
FAX (619) 283-8264
Mark Schulze, Distrib of how-to, sports,
instructional videos. Interna. Foreign
rights.
All markets except newsstands.

New Concepts
9722 Pine Lake, Box 55068
Houston, TX 77055
(713) 465-7736
Jacqueline Ellis, New age, self-help, alter-
native health, psych., children's. Book-
stores, schools, newsstand, spec stores,
libraries, catalogs. South Texas.

New Leaf Distributing Company
5425 Tulane Drive South West
Atlanta, GA 30336
(404) 691-6996
Judith Hawkins, New Age, holistic health
(Aisha Lamumba), metaphysical (Judith
Hawkins), calendars, New Age, music
(Mary Grider), childrens (Tracy Coppedge).
Na, interna distrib. Bookstores, specialty
stores, health food stores. Books, audio,
video.

Nolo Press Distribution
Box 544
Occidental, CA 95465
(707) 874-2818
Cathy Stevenson, Self help legal and
business.

NorCal News
2040 Petaluma Blvd., Box 2508
Petaluma, CA 94953-2508
(707) 763-2606
Robert Erwin, Mass markets, newsstands.
No. Calif. distrib.

Omnibooks
456 Vista Del Mar
Aptos, CA 95003-4832
(408) 688-4098
Distrib to libraries, mostly No Calif,
scientific.

Pacific Northwest Books Company
Box 314
Medford, OR 97501
(503) 664-4442
Bert Webber, Libraries, historical societies,
schools. specialize in pioneer trail, Indians.
Small presses. Distrib in Pac North West.
Bookstores, schools, libraries, colleges.

Pacific Pipeline, Inc
19215 66th Ave., South
Kent, WA 98032-1171
(206) 872-5523
Jane Suddarth, Distrib in Pacific NW,
Southwest, Rocky Mountains, Washington,
Oregon,Montana, Idaho, Calif., Alaska,
West. Canada. Northwest regional interest
books, history, guidebooks, fiction. News-
letter. Bookstores, schools, specialty
stores, libraries.

Pacific Search Press
Box 18000
Florence, OR 97439
(503) 997-6668
Northwest travel & adventure, cooking,
crafts.

Pacific Trade Group
Box 668
Pearl City, Oahu, HA 96782
(808) 671-6735
Publisher & distributor for books related to
Hawaiian Islands.

Partners Book Distributing
154 Frost
Williamston, MI 48895
(800) 336-3137
Sam Speigel, Hardcover frontlist, trade,
mass mkt paperbacks, test guides, kids.
Distrib in U.S. Bookstores, colleges.

Portland News Company
Box 1728
South Portland, Maine 04104
(207) 774-2633
Leslie Carver, Wholesale distrib of books,
maps, calendars, hardcover, trade, New
Age. Distrib in New England, New York,
bookstores, schools, newstands, spec
stores, libraries, mass market.

Professional Book Service
415 Sargon Way, Babylon Bus. Campus
Horsham, PA 19044
(800) 648-8040 FAX 441-803
Wholesale distrib. Computer, business &
electronics. U.S. Bookstores, schools,
specialty stores, libraries, colleges.

Publishers Group West
4065 Hollis St
Emeryville, CA 94608
(415) 658-3453
Distrib for independent publishers, general
non-fic, hardcover, trade paperback, mass
market, U.S., bookstores, jobbers, shcools,
colleges, libraries.

Publishers Interna Management
The Old Church
Ley, Liskeard, U.K. PL14 6PE
0579-21280, FAX 0579-21293
Maria Holt, Sales & marketing for U.S.
publishers in US & Australia, handles
foreign rights.

Publishers Marketing Services
11661 San Vincente Blvd. #206
Los Angeles, CA 90049
(213) 820-8672
Claudia Forman, Distrib of nonfic. some
self-help. U.S, Canada. Bookstores,
schools, libraries, colleges.

Publishers Overstock
149 Madison Ave
New York, NY 10016
(212) 481-0055, FAX 212-213-6074

Publishers Services
Box 2510
Novato, CA 94948
(415) 883-3530
Warehousing and fullfillment only.

Quality Books, Inc.
918 Sherwood Drive
Lake Bluff, IL 60044
(312) 295-2010
Tom Drewes, All subjects, adult nonfict,
how-to, travel, health, business, career.
Distrib in U.S., Canada. Direct sale
marketer to libraries. "Always hungry for
new, quality, small press non-fiction.
America's only natioal library distributor
specializing in small presses."

Rainforest Publishing
Box 101251
Anchorage, AK 99510
(907) 373-7277
Distrib in Pacific Northwest, Alaska.
Bookstores, schools, libraries, colleges.

Robert Silver Associates
Randall Book Co., 307 East 37th St.
New York, NY 10016-3233
(212) 686-5630
Robert M Silver, Art.

Ron Belanger & Assoc
170W Beaver Creek Rd.
Richmond Hill, ON, Canada L4B 1B4
(416) 764-8858
Canadian distrib.

Royal Publications, Inc
Publications Department
Box 5793
Denver, CO 80217
(303) 778-8383
Wholesale distrib of books, magazines,
audio, video, deals only in non-entertain-
ment, how-to materials. Distrib in U.S.
Specialty stores, libraries, health food
stores, maternity shops, sporting goods,
pharmacies, craft shops.

Samuel French Trade
7623 Sunset Blvd.
Hollywood, CA 90046
(213) 876-0570
Gwen Feldman, Performing arts books,
film, theater, U.S., Canada

Samuel Weiser Inc
Box 612
York Beach, Maine 03910
(207) 363-4393
Pat Stanton, Eastern philosophy, astrol-
ogy, tarot, metaphysical, New Age. Distrib
in U.S., Europe. Bookstores, specialty
stores, libraries, catalogs.

Sandhill Book Marketing
Box 197, Station A
Kelowna, BC, Canada V1Y 7N5
(604) 763-1406
Nancy Wise, Distrib specializing in small
press & self-published trade books in
British Columbia, Alberta. Outdoor recrea-
tion, railway books, cookbooks. Book-
stores, specialty stores.

Serendipity Couriers
470 Du Bois St.
San Rafael, CA 94901
(415) 459-400
Distributors of magazines to newstands.

Seven Hills Book Distributors
49 Central Ave. #300
Cincinnati, OH 45202-3438
(513) 381-3881
Ion Itescu, Publisher and distributors,
photography, travel, art, antiques, cooking,
military, history, self-help. Na, interna.
Bookstores, schools, newstands, spec
stores, libraries, mass market, catalogs.

Shamus Publications
689 Florida St.
San Francisco, CA 94110-2023
(415) 821-2912
Tony Uruburu, Sports, games, mystery,
interna. Bookstores, schools, specialty
stores, mass market, catalogs.

Shelter Publications
Box 279
Bolinas, CA 94924-0279
(415) 868-0280
Fitness, health, architecture, business,
humor. U.S., Foreign Translations. Book-
stores, schools, specialty stores, libraries,
colleges.

Slawson Communications
165 Vallecitos de Oro
San Marcos, CA 92069
(619) 744-2299
Leslie S. Smith, Exclusive distrib rights
only. Distrib in U.S., England, Australia,
New Zealand. Bookstores, specialty stores,
libraries, colleges.

Small Changes
3443 12th Ave. West
Seattle, WA 98119
(206) 282-3665
*Shari Bascom, Northwest distrib of maga-
zines and calendars, no wholesale. Distrib
in Northwest U.S., Canada. Bookstores,
newstands, specialty stores.*

Small Press Distribution
1814 San Pablo Ave.
Berkeley, CA 94702-1624
(415) 549-3336
*Steve Dickison, Fict, poetry, essays, criti-
cism, literary books from small presses,
does not handle self-published. National
distrib.*

Small Press Traffic
3599 24th St
San Francisco, CA 94110
(415) 285-8394
*Katharine Harer, Nonprofit, small press
distribution outlet & literary center. Na,
interna distrib. Schools, colleges, mass
market.*

Southern Booksellers
3710 Main
Houston, TX 77002
(713) 528-3351
*Chris Swanzy, buyer. Distrib mass mkt
paperbacks to bookstores in Texas. Sells
paperbacks at fund raising bookfairs, So.
Texas schools.*

Southern Book Service
Palmetto Lakes Industrial Park
Hialeah, FL 33014
(800) 843-6568
*Cloth, quality paper, mass market,
regional.*

Spring Arbor Distributors
10885 Textile Rd
Belleville, MI 48111
(800) 521-3690
*Mike Kehoe (313) 481-0900, #410
Religious/inspirational, music,audio/
video. U.S. & interna. Bookstores, specialty stores, colleges, catalogs. Warehouse in Calif.*

St Martin Press, Inc
175 Fifth Ave.
New York, NY 10010
(212) 674-5151
Publisher, distrib.

Stanislaus Imports
75 Arkansas St.
San Francisco, CA 94107-2494
(415) 431-7122
*Crafts, hobbies, fiber arts. Distrib in U.S.,
Europe, Canada. Specialty stores.*

Sun and Moon Press
6148 Wilshire Blvd
Los Angeles, CA 90048-9377
(213) 653-6711
*Douglas Messerli, Ann Kletstad Distrib to
bookstores, libraries, catalogs, U.S.,
Canada, specialize in fiction.*

Sun/Day Distributors Corporation
8175 D Signal Court
Sacramento, CA 95824-2327
(916) 381-7617
*Stitchery, Don Patterson, U.S., Canada, to
shops.*

Sunbelt Publications
8622 Argent St, #A
Santee, CA 92071
(619) 448-0884
*Diana Lindsay, Wholesaler of Baja and
Mexico books, bicycles, regional, travel,
outdoor, field guides, nature guides.
Regional distrib for B. Dalton Bookseller &
Waldenbooks. Bookstores, specialty
stores, museums, associations, parks,
bicycle stores, travel & map stores.*

Talman Company
150 Fifth Ave.
New York, NY 10011-4311
(212) 620-3182
*Marilee Talman, Distributor for small press
who have published several books; black
studies, women's, travel, Judaica, outdoor,
Latino, juvenile. Distrib in U.S., Canada.
Bookstores, schools, specialty stores,
libraries, colleges, catalogs, map stores.*

Ten Speed Press/Celestial Arts
Box 7123
Berkeley, CA 94707
(415) 845-8414
Mariah Bear, How-to books, cookbooks, New Age, national, interna distribtution. Bookstores, schools, newstands, specialty stores, libraries, mass market, catalogs.

Texas Monthly Press
Box 1569
Austin, TX 78767
(512) 476-7085
Scott Lubeck, Publisher & distrib. of general trade books about Texas, or by Southwest area publishers. Bookstores, schools, specialty stores, libraries, colleges. Distrib in U.S.

The Booklegger
12693 Oak Drive
Grass Valley, CA 95945-9019
(916) 272-1556
Gutherie Kraut., Distrib of golf books & videos, other sports, U.S., foreign, golf shops, sporting goods shops.

The Bookmen
525 North Third St.
Minneapolis, MN
55401
(800) 328-8411
Norton Stillman, Regional wholesaler for major titles and children's books.

The Children's Small Press Collection
719 North Fourth Ave.
Ann Arbor, MI 48104
(313) 668-8056
Kathleen Baxter, Distrib of children's books, games, tapes, records.

The Creative Source
20702 El Toro Rd.
El Toro, CA 92630
(714) 458-7971
Distrib of spiritual growth & personal devel. materials, books.

The distributors
702 South Michigan
South Bend, IN 46618
(219) 232-8500
Paul Ray (small press) Distrib for trade paperbacks, all subjects, U.S., Canada, Europe.

The Sewall Company
74 Davidson Drive, Box 529
Lincoln, MA 01773
(617) 259-0090
Susan M Sewall, Nature & history titles.

Thomas Brothers Maps
550 Jackson St.
San Francisco, CA 94133-5188
(415) 981-7520
Travel/geography.

TV Tempo Publishing Company
822A Rittwater Rd.
Dee Why, NSW, Australia 2099
02-971-2107
Book importer, distributor, publisher.

Unique Books
4200 Grove Ave.
Gurnee, IL 60031
(312) 623-9171
Jud Krick, Distrib of small press titles to libraries.

Vivekananda Foundation
Box 1351
Alameda, CA 94501
(415) 521-4745
New Age. Bookstores, schools, libraries, colleges, catalogs.

Washington Toy Company
220 9th St.
San Francisco, CA 94103-3891
(415) 863-5965
Children's, languages, crafts. Distrib in Bay Area, No. Calif., Nevada. Schools, specialty stores, mass market, toy stores, gift shops.

Western Book Distributors
2970 San Pablo Ave.
Berkeley, CA 94702-2498
(415) 849-2929
*Matt Wyse, Tamara Austin Trade,
children's. Distrib in U.S., U.K. Bookstores,
specialty stores, colleges.*

Western States Books Services
Box 855
Clackamas, OR 97015
(503) 657-9838
Pacific Northwest & Rocky Mountains.

Wilderness Press
2440 Bancroft Way
Berkeley, CA 94704
(415) 843-8080
*Thomas Winnett, Nature, recreation, pub-
lisher, distributor of some books from other
publishers. Specialize in Western U.S.
subjects, wilderness hiking, outdoor
recreation. Bookstores, schools, specialty
stores, libraries, colleges, catalogs.*

Willow Tree
Box 1439
San Rafael, CA
(415) 456-9335
*Linda Brunner, Order fulfillment only,
assistance w/distribution.*

Wine Appreciation Guild
155 Connecticut St.
San Francisco, CA 94107-2414
(415) 566-3532
Cookbooks, wine.

Wishing Well Distributing
Box 529
Graton, CA 95444
(707) 823-9355
*Debra Giusti, Metaphysical, New Age,
health, educa. videos. Na, interna distrib.
Bookstores, specialty stores, libraries,
catalogs.*

Womontyme Distribution Company
Box 50145
Long Beach, CA 90815-6145
(213) 429-4802
*Gwen Tucker, Books, videos, cassettes for
women and children, feminist, New Age,
metaphysical, lesbian. U.S. Bookstores,
schools, catalogs.*

7 Directory of Mailing Lists

Making Extra Money
Through Mailing List Rental

By Elaine O'Gara

Author and publisher of Travel Writers' Markets, a Writer's Digest Book Club selection, and author of Smokefree Travel Guide. Winterbourne Press, Box 7548, Berkeley, CA 94707.

I entered the world of mailing rental quite by chance. Another publisher called and asked if I rented my list, and as it was already on my computer, I said, "Sure".

I knew mailing lists could be lucrative and I heard the siren call of Easy Money.

My book, *Travel Writers' Markets*, lists newspaper travel editors and periodicals, and my first customer wanted the editors' addresses for his news releases.

Since the list was so specialized, I set a price of ten cents per label, with a five dollar setup charge.

In order to print on small labels as requested by the client, we delved into label formats and compressed print. We managed to get out that order, but figured the pay rate to be about fifty cents per hour.

Next, we put together a flyer with all our lists and formats, and offered labels in one, two, three and four-across format.

Our first orders from the Great American Public came after a small notice in Dan Poynter's newsletter, *Publishing Poynters*.

We offered several kinds of databases: newspaper travel editors, magazines that take travel articles (broken down according to category), travel writers, specialty travel companies and convention and visitors' bureau. Some customers wanted a combination of these lists, but as we had not originally planned to merge the lists, the structures were all different. Some lists had a title field, some did not, and they were different lengths.

While processing the orders, we created a new temporary database called WORKFILE, to merge and meld information from various databases. A useful field we eventually added to all databases was called SOURCE, telling us where and when we got the name. We started with dBASE III, but now use a clone of that program called dBXL.

Once the structure was mastered, our printer presented problems. Sometimes it printed three characters in place of one, and one day, when we blithely left the printer alone, we found it would also do this triple play with carriage returns and print half an address on one label and half on another.

We came to hate city names like Rolling Hills Estates, because another quirk of the printer was that each label could only be 26 characters in length, and some names would be wrapped around onto the next line.

Eventually, we bought a new state-of-the-art printer, but found the mailing labels caught on the plastic paper guide. We'd take out the plastic piece, scrape off the label, reinsert the plastic, start all over and hold our breath. Nervewracking.

One policy is for one time use, but we also give customers the option of paying more and getting the list on disk. In California, there is no sales tax on list rental, but tax does apply to disk sales. (Check your state laws).

To monitor list rental, I chane names slightly. For instance, if the real jame is John Jones, I modify it to Jon Albert Jones for one list rental, Jon Bernard Jones for the next, and so on, then ask Mr. Jones to let me know if they get more mail for that name.

I haven't had any problems with this, since my lists are often updated and customers rent again and again.

Another area to consider is where to find customers for your lists. Most of my book sales are direct mail and I just stick a flyer about the lists in with flyers about the book. If you publish cookbooks and have developed a list of newspaper food editors, other cookbook publishers might be interested in renting that list.

I've also had a number of offers to trade lists with other publishers. For instance, if two publishers have New Age books, they might want to trade customer lists.

Our policy on payment is not to ask for any money in advance. We send an invoice with the labels and add a variable shipping fee. Most people have paid promptly but some require a second or third reminder. These eventually pay, often with a notation that the bill was lost or their landlord kicked them out of their old office.

Since starting this sideline, I've been keeping a folder of brochures from other companies offering mailing lists. Some want payment in advance with a constant shipping fee such as three dollars. Prices range from four cents a name on up.

If you decide to rent your lists, it's important to remember you're really a publisher and not a mailing list maven. For a one-book publisher such as myself, this is sometimes difficult. My book sells for $12.95, and my average list order is about $40, with some as high as $200.

I try to look on the list business as my straight job, the thing that keeps me from having to work as a secretary to pay for my publishing habits.

Directory of Mailing Lists

ABC Children's Booksellers list
175 Ash St.
St. Paul, MN 55110
(612) 490-1805

Ad Lib Publications
51 N Fifth St., Box 1102
Fairfield, IA 52556
(800) 624-5893
*John Kremer. Specialty booksellers, maga-
zine editors, distributors, newspapers, 450
radio interview shows, TV shows, syndicates. Databases for small press & self-
publisher, many lists for book marketers/
publishers/writers. Produced by well-
known publisher of books & directories for
small press & self- publisher.*

Blue Bird Publishing
1713 E Broadway, #306
Tempe, AZ 85282
(602) 968-4088
Cheryl Gorder. 7,000 antique dealers.

Blue Heron Publishing, Inc.
Route 3, Box 376
Hillsboro, OR 97123
*1,800 NW libraries and NW English
teachers (OR,WA,ID,AK,MT) 2,600 publishers, 550 publishers' resources.*

Command Productions Radio/TV List
Box 26348
San Francisco, CA 94126-6348
(415) 332-3161
Warren Weagant.

Communications Unlimited
Box 6405
Santa Maria, CA 93456
(805) 937-8711
*Freelance writers, attendees and book
buyers from Burgett seminars (see calendar), primarily in California. Seminars are
re general & travel writing, book publishing, self-publishing. 16,500 seminar
participants, 1,100 professional publishers, 3,000 speaking seminar participants,
4,050 professional speakers.*

COSMEP, Int'l Assoc. of Independent
Publishers, Box 703
San Francisco, CA 94101
(415) 922-9290
*Richard Morris, Exec Dir. 5,000 small
press & and self-publishers, 1,300 membership. $45/thousand, 1,479 self-
publishers, all over U.S., few foreign,
3,600 U.S. small book publishers.*

Directors Guild Publishers
Box 369
Renaissance, CA 95962
(916) 692-1355
*Art-related lists: 8,500 visual artists, art
publications, publishers, consultants,
schools, U.S. & Canadian galleries, univ.
galleries, foreign, organizations, museums.*

Dustbooks
Box 100
Paradise, CA 95969
(916) 877-6110
*2,000 bookstores, 660 organizations,
5,000 U.S. & foreign small press operations, 170 book distributors, 4,000 U.S. &
foreign small press book publishers,
13,000 publishing-related and/or interested in publishing or writing, 600 public
libraries, 1,800 univ. & other libraries,
2,400 U.S. and foreign small magazine
publishers, 1,600 self-publishers, 660
printing manufacturers, 400 reviewers.
(Publishers of Int'l Directory of Little
Magazines & Small Presses).*

Fair Oaks Publishing Co.
941 Populus Place
Sunnyvale, CA 94086
(408) 732-1078
*Carol O'Hare. 3,400 interested in books on
home business.*

FBN
Box 882554
San Francisco, CA 94188
(415) 626-1556
*350 feminist, gay, alternative & indepen-
dent bookstores.*

First Editions
Box 1158A
Sedona, AZ 86336
(602) 282-9574
New Age marketing resources, 2,100 meta-physical bookstores, 300 New Age periodi-cals, 2,000 crystal related, plus many more New Age. Rental & trade.

Foreign Markets Database
Three Kings Communications Co.
Box 574
Collegedale, TV 37315
300 overseas buyers of English language material for periodicals, inflight, company, business and travel.

Gallopade Publishing Group
Main St.
Historic Bath, NC 27808
(808) 923-4291
Carole C. Marsh. Repeat buyers of books related to publishing/writing.

Gebbie Press
Box 1000
New Paltz, NY 12561-9990
Na mailing lists on disk. Daily, weekly newspapers, radio, TV, magazines, syndicates.

IBIS Information Services
152 Madison Ave.
New York, NY 10016
(800) 433-6226
One of the largest distributors of interna mailing lists, also co-op mailings.

Jeffrey Lant Associates
50 Follen St., #507
Cambridge, MA 02138
Business and marketing-related publica-tions.

Market Data Retrieval
147 Lomita Ave., #D
Mill Valley, CA 94941-1451
(800) 624-5669, (800) 332-6777
Business, children's, education, comput-ers, religion.

Museum Store Association
501 South Cherry St., #460
Denver, CO 80222
Mailing list of members.

Name-Finders Lists
2121 Bryant St.
San Francisco, CA 94110-2135
(800) 221-5009
Wide variety of lists.

Names in the News
530 Bush St.
San Francisco, CA 94108-3691
(415) 989-3350
Politics, political donors.

National Women's Mailing List
Box 68
Jenner, CA 95450-0068
(415) 824-6800

New Age Mailing Lists
Box 778
Berkeley, CA 94701
(415) 644-3229, FAX (415) 486-8032
Long established owner & broker of extensive variety of New Age-related lists: Catalogs, periodicals, book buyers, retail-ers, conference participants, natural food-stores, health & bodyworkers, therapy centers and more.

New Age Retailer
Box 489
Greenbank, WA 98252-0489
(206) 678-7772
3,000 New Age/metaphysical bookstores nationwide. Monthly Report to Booksellers is sent to this list.

New Age Yellow Pages
Box 5978
Fullerton, CA 92635
(714) 871-2489
Lists of consciousness-raising services, products, organizations, publishers, everything New Age-related.

New Pages
Box 438
Grand Blanc, MI 48439
(313) 743-8055
Bookstores, public libraries, colleges.

Pacific Lists
131 Camino Alto, #D
Mill Valley, CA 94941-2295
(415) 381-0826
*Paula Huntley, Gen'l. Mgr. 40 managed
lists: Psych, all types of New Age,
mothering, Oakland museum, Vegetarian
Times, Whole Earth Review, Yoga Journal,
Tom Peters Group, education, publishers,
Esalen Institute, bookbuyers, more.
Experienced, reliable broker. Can get any
list that exists.*

Panorama Publishing Co.
14640 Victory Blvd., #210
Van Nuys, CA 91411-1623
(818) 988-4690
*Extensive mailing lists for rent or ex-
change: self-help books & tapes on
hypnosis, psych, behavioral, etc.*

Paradise Publications
8110 SW Wareham
Portland, OR 97223
(503) 246-1555
Christie Stilson. 150 travel bookstores.

Para Publishing
Box 4232
Santa Barbara, CA 93140
(805) 968-7277, FAX (805) 968-1379
Dan Poynter. *Long established and
reliable. Book promotion mailing lists of
various kinds. Book reviewers, book
review magazines, radio/TV Talk shows,
writers, publishers, printers, book clubs,
business magazines, newspapers with
book review columns, legal, military, police
magazines, more.*

Perspectives Press
Box 90318
Indianapolis, IN 46290-0318
(317) 872-3055
1,400 infertility, foster care and adoption.

Poets and Writers Magazine
201 W 54th St.
New York, NY 10019
*30,000 writers, readers & literary organi-
zations.*

Publishers Databank
Box 3190
Vista, CA 92083
(619) 941-2235
*Mailing lists on disk for publishers,
thousands of periodicals by category.*

Strawberry Media
2460 Lexington Dr.
Owosso, MI 4867
(517) 725-9027
650 Armed Forces libraries & Dept of
Defense school libraries.

**The Canadian Book
Information Centre**
260 King St., E
Toronto, Ontario M5A 1K3
(416) 362-6555, FAX (416) 361-0643
*Comprehensive print and broadcast media
in Canada, including specific programming
& personnel.*

The Denali Press
Box 021535
Juneau, AK 99802-1535
(907) 586-6014
*Libraries: large budgets, academic,
Alaska, Canada; also U.S. bookstores.
Hispanic: Canada, Northwest, Southwest,
business, theatre, publishers, periodicals,
organizations.*

Thrust Publications
8217 Langport Terrace
Gaithersburg, MD 2877
Science fiction and fantasy lists, rental.

Twin Peaks Press
Box 129
Vancouver, WA 98666
(206) 694-2462
*Libraries: U.S., Canada, medical, hospi-
tals, schools, colleges. Publications for
disability/health market. Travel agencies
for disabled persons. Daily newspapers.
Wire services.*

Westar Media
2317 Broadway, #330
Redwood City, CA 94063
(415) 368-8800
*50,000 subscribers to No. California Home
& Garden.*

Williams-Sonoma Mailing Lists
100 North Point
San Francisco, CA 94133
(415) 421-7900
Bonnie Allen-Carpender. Cookbooks,
house/garden, 720,000 catalog buyers.

Willowood Press
Box 1846
Minot, ND 58702
(701) 838-0579
Established, reliable lists of public, college
and high school libraries, English depart-
ments.

W.I.M. Publications
Box 137
2215R Market St.
San Francisco, CA 94114
3,000 readers interested in women's
subjects, Afro-American, gay. 1,000 misc.
media, booksellers, publishers, writers.
100 women in mail order. Mail order
publications offering classified ads.

Winterbourne Press
Box 7548
Berkeley, CA 94707
(415) 527-9885
Elaine O'Gara. 250 U.S. newspaper travel
editors. 20 Canadian newpaper travel
editors.1,600 travel writers. 178 foreign
government tourist offices in U.S. 2,400
local and regional convention and visitors
bureaus, chambers of commerce, misc.
magazine and travel-related lists, one time
use or disk.

Writer's Connection
1601 Saratoga-Sunnyvale Rd., #180
Cupertino, CA
(408) 973-0227
Steve Lester. 4,500 membership
list.18,000 writing, publishing, business
seminar participants. 10,000 business &
corporate publications, technical writing.
Established, reliable lists from association
for writers/publishers.

Book Publicists and Book Packagers

Marketing Your Book

By Carol C. Butterfield, President, Butterfield & Associates, 5925 Doyle St, Emeryville, CA 94608 and President, Northern California Book Publicists.

A marketing campaign for your book should include everything that needs to be done to let your potential customers know your book exists and to make it easy for them to buy.

If you neglect marketing, yu may end up like a self-published author who recently called me from San Diego. She had so many books left she made a wall divider out of them and put plants on top of it.

Distributors and Wholesalers: To make it easy for people to buy your book, you need a distributor. For selling nationally or regionally through bookstores, you'll want to contact distributors like Publishers Group West, Slawson Communications, Kampmann & Company or The Talman Company. You will also need to work with your local wholesalers — Bookpeople, for example — who supply books to bookstores and often buy from distributors.

It's the distributor's and the wholesaler's job to get your books into the bookstores, but it's your job to create the demand through publicity.

Publicity helps get the customer into the bookstore to buy the book and motivates the bookstore buyer to reorder the book. And if you're interested in fame and fortune, publicity creates the fame, if not necessarily the fortune.

I want to emphasize the importance of publicity, because small presses, start-ups and self-published individuals frequently think once they have a distributor or wholesaler, their marketing cares are over. This simply isn't so. Distributors and wholesalers are a vital, but just a part, of your total marketing plan.

Publicists: Publicists vary widely in the services they offer small presses and entrepreneurial publishers. Here's a list of the services a publicist might offer you and an idea of when you should contact one:

Pre-publication services: Ideally, you should begin marketing your book or contact a publicist as long as six months before your book is published, because of the long lead time on first serial rights, book club sales and for major book industry reviewers. The publicist may also have valuable input on the cover art and copy, resulting in more media attention and better sales.

Here is a laundry list of the pre-publication services a publicist could offer you. Almost all publicists offer the asterisked services:

- *Writing up a marketing plan and schedule for your book.
- *Preparing press materials including at least a press release and a full press kit if you plan to do TV and radio publicity.
- Sending out bound galleys or pages for first serial rights and following up on those queries.

- Book club rights.
- Setting up your distribution and wholesale network.
- *Sending out galleys or pages to major publishing industry reviewers that need to see your materials four months ahead of publication.

Post publication services: After your book is published, there is a whole second wave of publicity available through your publicist:

- *A national, regional or local author tour where the author is booked to appear on the media - usually a combination of TV, radio and print.
- *A local Bay Area author tour including TV, radio, print and newspapers.
- *National or regional phone interviews by phone so you can get live publicity in cities you don't plan to visit.
- *Querying print media on a national or local basis for reviews or feature stories.
- Querying print media for sale of second serial rights.
- Querying catalog wholesalers who might want to include your book in their mail order catalog.
- Special or premium sales.
- Direct mail campaigns.

Why hire a publicist? You should consider hiring a publicist, rather than doing the work yourself, hiring an in-house person or skipping publicity altogether.

First, the fourteen projects listed above must be accomplished within a brief period of time, to maximize the sales of your books. All are labor intensive and most involve having contacts in the industry (book clubs, industry reviewers, serial rights) or the media (print reviews, TV, radio or newspaper bookings). A few, such as direct mail, require previous experience if you want to succeed.

Second, if you're a small press, it's difficult to spend time on publicity and marketing while you're developing your next product. A publisher of children's books asked me to do their publicity because they had been too successful with their Christmas list. They were so busy with pre-Christmas marketing and publicity, they neglected to put out any Spring list at all.

During the heat of a media campaign for a book, we may be juggling 20-40 phone calls a day plus resending books and press materials to media who mislaid them the first time around. We're on the phone to the East Coast at 7 a.m. and not off the phone locally until 6 p.m. or later.

Third, you could hire an in-house staff who will cost less per hour than an experienced publicist. The drawbacks are that you pay salary and employment taxes all year long and an inexperienced person may not have the media contacts and expertise you need.

Fourth, if you're self-published, you probably have a career or another job. I would advise you against taking on the publicity yourself unless you can easily fit 20-40 extra phone calls and call-backs into your daily work, and you have facilities for packing and mailing.

Fifth, if you're self-published or the major author for a small press, you'll find many media people do not like to deal directly with the author. They feel the author is too close to the book and they are embarrassed to ask the questions they ask the publicist, such as, "Is she a knock-out or just so so?" "Is he going to show up in a suit or that weird thing he's wearing on the cover?" "Can she down-play that Southern accent?" "Who's going to coach him on media presence?"

Fees: Don't shy away from contacting a publicist because you've made assumptions about fees. Most West Coast fees are reasonable and negotiable.

It helps to know that most publicists work in one of three ways. First, they may prefer to give you an estimate for each project, such as national print and magazine reviews. Second, a publicist may ask for a retainer for the number of months it takes to accomplish the tasks you need.

Third, a publicist may work on an hourly fee. Most prefer not to work this way, because it's so time consuming to keep track of minutes and hours. And, I think you have more control if you work on a project by project or retainer basis. If you pay on an hourly basis, you'll need to know if your publicist works quickly or takes dozens of coffee breaks.

Traditionally, publicists' fees do not include out-of-pocket expenses such as Xeroxing, postage, telephone, etc. Ask your publicist, and if those expenses are not included, ask for a ballpark estimate.

Finally, although there are many reasons to use a publicist, one of the most important is the professional presentation of your book or your press to the media.

Book Publicists and Book Packagers

About Books, Inc
Marilyn Ross
Box 1500
Buena Vista, CO 81211
(719) 395-2459
All phases of publishing, marketing, consulting, editing, ghost writing, design, typesetting, printing, specialists in regional & national book marketing & PR, book packager, work with small presses & self-publishers, publishers of several books re entrepreneurial publishing/marketing.

Alice Acheson
2962 Fillmore St, 3rd Floor
San Francisco, CA 94123
(415) 563-5122
Publicity, subsidiary rights, consulting, works with small presses.

American Graphic System
Ruth DeJauregui
111 Pine St., Suite 1410
San Francisco, CA 94111
(415) 989-2450
Book packager, all phases of production.

Gail Anderson
25 San Andreas
San Francisco, CA 94127
Publicist, marketing & communications consultant, media tours, program review.

Authentic Marketing
Dan Kassell
545 Wisconsin
San Francisco, CA 94107-2731
(800) 771-INFO
New Age specialty, consultant in advertising, sales promotion and publicity, business management, marketing, book packager, production, design, editing, works with small presses and self-publishers, no foreign rights.

Avant Books
Leslie S Smith
165 Vallecitos de Oro
San Marcos, CA 92069
(619) 744-2299
Book packagers, distributors, publishers, assoc w/Slawson Communications, Inc. Book packager, production, design, editing, works with small presses and self-publishers, foreign rights & marketing.

Sue Avila, Publicist
Sue Avila
1301 Teneighth Way
Sacramento, CA 95818
(916) 444-5130
Book publicity, radio interviews, media tours anywhere in U.S., escort service in Sacramento area, serial rights, copy markets, mostly Sacramento area clients, works with small presses and self-publishers, no foreign rights.

BMR/Business Media Resources
Jack Jennings
150 Shoreline Hwy, Bldg B-27
Mill Valley, CA 94941
(415) 331-6021
Book packagers, all phases from acquisition to production and marketing, also video and software.

Book Publicists Northwest
Anne Damron
Box 19786
Seattle, WA 98109
Information on book publicists in NW.

Bookline Advertising
Nancy M Ringler
216 McAllister Ave.Kentfield, CA 94904
(415) 456-0516
Literary agent, also ad manager for "San Francisco Review of Books."

Robert Briggs Associates
3030 Bridgeway
Sausalito, CA 94965
(415) 331-5967
Literary agency, publishing consultants.
No PR.

Britt & Associates
Trisha Britt
1980 Washington St. #106
San Francisco, CA 94109
(415) 474-0326
Speciality in medical practitioners, clinics, and health care products, mostly Bay Area clients, works w/small presses.

Butterfield And Associates
Carol C Butterfield
5925 Doyle St., Suite U
Emeryville, CA 94608
(415) 428-1991
Full marketing set-ups, distribution networks, publicity, author tours, direct mail, repackaging, consulting. Fiction, non-fic, New Age, business, professional books, kids, audiocassettes, textbooks. 50% Bay Area clients, works with small presses and self-publishers, handles foreign rights, President of No Calif Book Publicists Assoc.

Michael Bass & Associates President:
Michael Bass
220 Redwood Highway, #288
Mill Valley, CA 94941
(415) 383-8312
Book packager, all phases of production, distribution, works with small presses,and self-publishers, no foreign rights.

Henry Berry
Box 176
Southport, CT 06490
Consulting for independent publishers, critiques, subsidiaries advice, video, audio, acquisitions advice. Publisher of Small Press Book Review.

Kathlene Carney & Associates
Kathlene Carney
108 Orange St.
San Rafael, CA 94901
(415) 459-4596
Public relations, local and na media exposure for small business and professionals. Mostly Bay Area clients, works with small presses and self-publishers, no foreign rights. Local & na media tours, newspaper, magazines, radio, TV interviews.

Joyce K Cole & Associates
Joyce K Cole
797 San Diego Rd.
Berkeley, CA 94707
(415) 526-5165
Media escort, coordinator of Cody's Books author appearances.

The Compage Company
Ken Burke
55 New Montgomery, Suite 706
San Francisco, CA 94110
(415) 957-9855
Book packager, all phases of production. Develop and produce publishing products from concept through printed and bound books, manuals, newsletters, magazines, marketing pieces. Works with small presses rarely works with self-publishers, no foreign rights.

Creative Communications & Research
Gini Graham Scott
308 Spruce St.
San Francisco, CA 94118
(415) 567-2247
Book packager, all phases of production, writing & promotion. Business, group dynamics, sales & creativity, specializes in self-help, education, training books. Works with small presses and self-publishers, no foreign rights.

Emerald Marketing
116 Sandpaper Circle
Corte Madera, CA 94925-1081
(415) 927-3240
Marketing & product development consultant and VAR, to specialty stores, catalogs, producers, directors, production companies, photographers, No. Calif primarily, specialize in books on photography, electronics, computers, marketing, theatre arts.

Empire Publishing Service
Joseph W Witt
7645 Le Berthon St.
Tujunga, CA 91042
(818) 784-8918
Book packager, all phases of production, editing, design. Distribution, advertising, trade, library, exhibit services. Specialize in film, TV, theater, entertainment industry, entertainment personalities, plays, musicals. Works with small presses &self-publishers, foreign rights.

First Editions
Sophia Tarila
Box 1158
Sedona, AZ 86336
(602) 282-9574
New Age marketing, publisher of New Age Marketing Opportunities. (see Section 13).

Candice Fuhrman Literary Agency
Candice Jacobson Fuhrman
30 Ramona
Forest Knolls, CA 94933
(415) 488-0161
Literary agency and book packager (Wink Books) specializing in nonfiction, self-help and how-to. Consulting service available. Production, design, editing, works with small presses, handles foreign rights.

Future Source
Debra Giusti
Box 529
Graton, CA 95444
(707) 823-9355
Marketing assistance for New Age products, distributor, broker, audio, video, na and interna. To bookstores, libraries and other markets. Video packager, handles foreign rights.

Kathi Goldmark Media Escorts
Kathi Goldmark
2259 14th Ave
San Francisco, CA 94116
(415) 386-0759
Escorts, logistics for book/author tours in Bay Area.

Kathryn Hall, Publicist
Box 2402
Mill Valley, CA 94942
(415) 381-2911
Since 1979, full service publishing, electronic and print media promotion, professional TV coaching/media escorts, local, regional & na campaigns, client list & info available. Works with small presses and self-publishers, no foreign rights. "Books that carry a message of empowerment, either for the business community or the human potential movement."

Hi-De-Ho Enterprises
H. Holman
Box 1168-224
Studio City, CA 91604
(818) 761-0945
Promo services, tours in So. Cal.

Christine Hopf-Lovette
1345 Edgewood Rd.
Redwood City, CA 94062
(415) 369-6286
Sales, marketing & publicity, production, press releases, reporting systems. Mostly Bay Area clients, works with small presses & self-publishers, handles foreign rights, specializes in childrens' fiction & non-fic, books with appeal to gift markets, calendars. 15 years experience in publishing, print production.

Linda Jones PR
Linda Jones
16689 Rock Creek Rd.
Nevada City, CA 95959
(916) 265-8095
New Age, media tours for books & tapes re health, metaphysics, personal & spiritual growth, global issues.

The Kelly Company
Paul Kelly
14618 Tyler Foote Blvd.
Nevada City, CA 95959
(916) 292-3487
*Book marketing services, design, press
materials, reviews, publicity, tours,
signings. Mostly West Coast, works with
small presses and self-publishers, no
foreign rights, specializes in self-help, non-
fiction titles.*

Lawrence Communications
Bonnie Lawrence
1515 Beverly Pl.
Albany, CA 94706
(415) 525-0544
*Design, production of promotional materi-
als for small publishers, specializes in non-
profit organizations.*

The Live Oak Press
David M Hamilton
2620 Emerson St.
Palo Alto, CA 94306
(415) 853-0197
*Publishing consulting services, manage-
ment, production(specialize in electronic
publishing), editing, design, marketing.
Mostly West Coast and Rockies, works
with small pressesand self-publishers, no
foreign rights,specializes in corporate/
association books, monographs, magazines & periodicals.*

Lowell Moss/Omni Publishing Inc.
Robert Walter
870 Market St., #1260
San Francisco, CA 94107
(800) 222-6657
*Complete book packaging, from editing,
design, printing to promotional materials,
media tours, direct mail campaigns, all
phases of promotion. Specializes in small
publishers.*

Marketing by Mail
Sally A. Leete
2331 Fifth St.
Berkeley, CA 94710
(415) 548-2201
*Complete direct mail campaigns, design,
lists, marketing strategies, promotion
consulting, all phases production, printing,
graphics, tutoring/consulting. Book packager, mostly Bay Area clients, works w/
small presses & self-publishers. No foreign
rights.*

John McHugh
5747 N Ames
Glendale, WI 53209
(414) 351-3056
*Publishing consultant, all aspects market-
ing. Author of The McHugh Publishing
Report Series, contracts, financial analysis, planning, product development.
Management consultant to publishing
organizations, works with small presses
and self-publishers,foreign marketing.*

Mark Nolan & Associates
Mark Nolan
Box 2069
Citrus Heights, CA 95611
(916) 723-3070
*Advertising, marketing, publicity, cover
design & copywriting, news releases,
sales letters, display ads for mail order.
Specialize in placing books w/mail order
catalogs. Book packager, designer. Works
with small presses & self-publishers, no
foreign rights, specializes in non-fiction.*

Caroline O'Connell Public Relations
Caroline O'Connell
9046 Sunset Blvd. #208
Los Angeles, CA 90069-1819
(213) 276-2121
*Na publicity campaigns for publishers/
authors, media kits, coaching. Many Bay
Area clients, work w/small presses & self-
publishers. Specialize in how-to, psych,
business, entertaining. No fiction. Works
with small presses &self-publishers, no
foreign rights, but, handles foreign PR.
Brochure and references avail.*

Penmarin Books/Bookman Productions
President: Hal Lockwood
16 Mary St., Suite 8
San Rafael, CA 94901
(415) 457-7746
Book packager, all phases of production. Originates or develops book ideas for general, nonfiction market. Sells finished books to publishers with na distribution. Works w/small presses and self-publishers. Specializes in trade non-fiction.

Players Press Inc
Box 1132
Studio City, CA 91604
(818) 789-4980
Distribution, advertising, production service, theatrical publishers. Works with small presses and self-publishers, handles foreign rights, specializes in books on plays, musicals, cinema, TV, theatre, entertainment industry.

Professional Media Services
Ron Montana
1201 Melville South #408
Richmond, CA 94804
(415) 232-9983
Wordsmith, lit. & editorial consultants, workshops.

Publishing Consultants
Mimi Luebbermann
6452 Hillegass Ave.
Oakland, CA 94618
(415) 654-8419
All aspects of book publicity, consulting, marketing. Specializes in cookbooks, Bay Area regional guides. Mostly Bay Area clients, works with small presses, and self-publishers, handles foreign marketing.

Sue Rayner Warburg Public Relations
Sue Rayner Warburg
2390 Powell St., #407
San Francisco, CA 94133
(415) 921-0461
Authors' P R and special events, media ours, advertising, works with small presses, non-profit and fund raising.

S J Shepard Public Relations
Sally-Jean Shepard
100 Avenida Mira Flores
Tiburon, CA 94920
(415) 435-3571
Publicist specializing in food, art, book and travel related accounts and events, publicity programs, media tours, consultations. Mostly Bay Area clients, works with small presses, rarely works with self-publishers, no foreign rights.

Solem & Associates
Anne Solem
545 Mission St., 5th Floor
San Francisco, CA 94105
(415) 957-0957
Public relations, marketing, advertising.

Suzy Strauss & Associates
Suzy Strauss
1570 Chestnut St.
San Francisco, CA 94123
(415) 673-4773
Media tours, promo and advertising for authors/books.

Toni Werbell Public Relations
Toni Werbell
730 Columbus Ave., 6J
New York, NY 10025
(212) 662-5450
Public relations & publicity for books, magazines, cultural events and public policy issues, writes press material, authors' tours, placement of stories nationally and locally. Works with small presses, rarely works with self-publishers, serious nonfiction, self-help, biographies, news-connected fiction.

Willow Tree
Ginny Brunner, Linda Mackay
Box 1439
San Rafael, CA 94915
(415) 456-9335
Order fulfillment house for self-publishers, warehousing, mailing services, mailing list support, bookkeeping, etc.

Syndicates, Wire Services and News Gathering Agencies

Syndicates, Wire Services, and News Gathering Agencies

Associated Press
Box 7247
San Francisco, CA 94120
(415) 621-7432
Peggy Walsh, Bureau Chief. Na & interna news syndicate.

Audio/TV Features
149 Madison Ave, #804
New York, NY 10016
(212) 889-1327
Syndicates news, features & spots to radio & TV stations; fee.

Baltimore Sun
120 Grandview, #3
San Francisco, CA 94114
(415) 641-9090
Ellen Uzelac. Western states bureau.

Bay City News Service
1232 Market St
San Francisco, CA 94102
(415) 552-8900
Dick Fogel, Editor. Regional wire service, greater Bay Area.*also, 70 W. Hedding St., San Jose, CA 95110 (408) 299-3832

Book Beat/Here-Abouts
401 East 65th St, #14J
New York, NY 10021
(212) 734-9497
Joan Orth. Syndicated column, book reviews.

BusinessWire
44 Montgomery St
San Francisco, CA 94104
(415) 986-4422
Joe Harikian. For a reasonable fee, your news release is disseminated to major news syndicates, newspapers, magazines, TV, radio, databases, US & interna. Assistance with formatting.

Center for Investigative Reporting
54 Mint St
San Francisco, CA 94103
(415) 543-1200
David Weir. Non profit, produces in-depth reports for media: human rights, crime, environmental, women's issues, health care, etc.

Center for Science Reporting
314 V Street
Sacramento, CA 94818
(916) 441-4096
Bruce Bashin. Group of journalists producing pieces on science, environment and public affairs.

Copley Radio Network/News Service
Box 190
San Diego, CA 92112
(619) 293-1818
Disseminates features & spots to radio stations, columns, articles, cartoons to print media. Also sells excerpts and materials from/for books and audiotapes.

Creators Syndicate, Inc.
1443 S. Sepulveda Blvd
Los Angeles, CA 90025
(213) 4767-2776
Syndicates columns, articles, book excerpts & other.

Fairchild Publications
760 Market St, #857
San Francisco, CA 94102
(415) 781-8921
SF bureau for several dozen trade periodicals.

Feature News Service
Book Review Editors
2330 S Brentwood Blvd
St Louis, MO 63144-2096
(314) 961-9825

Feminist Press Association
c/o Womannews, Box 980
Village Station, NY 10014.
Assoc of women's newspapers, news service.

Jericho News Service
152 11th St, S.E.
Washington, D.C. 20003
(202) 547-1707
Disseminates features & spots to radio stations, including many author/book.

Maturity News Service
National Press Bldg, #968
Washington, DC 20045
(202) 662-8895
Syndicated wire service, nationwide. Features & news for 55-plus age group, of national interest.

Newspaper Feature Report
c/o Bradley Communications
101 W Baltimore Ave, #333
Landsdowne, PA 19050
(215) 259-1070
For a fee: newspaper feature stories in camera ready column form on consumer subjects; assistance provided for editing to AP style, typesetting, etc. 9200 daily & weekly newspapers & shoppers.

News/Radio Network
9431 W Beloit Rd
Milwaukee, WI 53227
(414) 321-6210
Syndicates news, features & spots to radio stations; fee.

Newsweek
505 Sansome St, #1501
San Francisco, CA 94111
(415) 788-2651
Bureau Chief: Tony Clifton.

Pacific News Service
604 Mission St, #800
San Francisco, CA 94105
(415) 986-5690
Non-prof research org & daily news service for hundreds of newspapers, magazines, electronic outlets. In-depth stories of long term interest only.

Singer Media Corporation
3164 Tyler Ave
Anaheim, CA 92801
(714) 527-5650
Natalie Carlton, Editor. Interna syndication; subjects & news must be of interna interest and "timeless." Material is resold in many interna markets for long periods of time. Interested in new, reprint & out of print books, especially those for which you hold foreign rights, fic & non-fic.

The Los Angeles Times
1390 Market St, #210
San Francisco, CA 94102
(415) 431-1600
Bay Area Bureau: Philip Hager.

The Los Angeles Times Syndicate
Times Mirror Square
Los Angeles, CA 90053
(213) 972-5000, (800) 252-0664
Syndicates features, book excerpts, misc., to US & interna periodicals, newspapers.

The New York Times
1 Embarcadero Center, #1310
San Francisco, CA 94111
(415) 362-3912
Bureau Chief: Robert Lindsey.

**The New York Times
Syndication Sales Corp.**
130 Fifth Ave
New York, NY 10011
(212) 645-3000, FAX (212) 645-3949
Syndicates columns, previously published articles, book excerpts.

Time
2 Embarcadero Center, #1900
San Francisco, CA 94111
(415) 982-5000
Bureau Chief, Paul A. Witteman.

Tribune Media Services
Box 119
Orlando, FL 32802-0119
(305) 422-8181
News spots & features, cable TV programs.

UPI
1212 Fox Plaza
San Francisco, CA 94102
(415) 552-5900
*Mark Lowe, Bureau Mgr. Na & interna
news syndicate.*

Whitegate Features Syndicate
71 Faunce Dr
Providence, RI 02906
(401) 274-2149

Wings (Women's International News
Gathering Service)
Box 6758
San Francisco, CA 94101
(415) 861-5434

10 Co-Op Marketing/Catalog Opportunities
Associations, Organizations and Clubs

Saving Money With Co-Op Marketing

By Dan Poynter

Author/publisher of The Self-publishing Manual, Publishing Short-run Books, Book Fairs and co-author of the Writers' Digest selection, Is There a Book Inside You? Para Publishing, Box 4232-M, Santa Barbara, CA 93140-4232.

Book promotion is expensive. Books are a low-ticket item — they don't cost much so you have to sell a bunch to pay for promotion. They're usually targeted to a small interest group and there is no recurring consumption (customers don't often buy a new copy of the same book).

Some savvy publishers are finding the answer to these problems by joining together in mailings, exhibits and buying advertising space.

Co-operative marketing allows us to lower promotional costs and save valuable time through the sharing of work. By sharing the expenses with other publishers, we all get our messages to the customer affordably.

It's easy to participate in co-op programs, because most of the work is done for us for a fraction of the cost of doing the promotion ourselves. One person (who has done it before) does it all. You just pay the money and go on to other projects. Or, you may take in other publishers to share costs in your program.

Fortunately, very few books compete with each other. Since it's a rare publisher who feels threatened by another publisher's product, it is easy to band together with compatible, non-competing products, to lower costs, save time and gain more attention in the marketplace.

Some publishers join in mailings to special lists. For example, Para Publishing promoted *The Self-Publishing Manual* while sharing the envelope with seven other publishers of books on various aspects of publishing. They used a list of 21,000 publishers. Since eight sheets of paper could be sent at the basic Bulk Rate, there was a tremendous postage savings. A mailing by a single publisher would have cost much more, but when split eight ways, it dropped to less than eight cents each and most of this cost was for printing.

If you find a good list and want to spread your costs, offer the service to other publishers of like books. Look for titles that complement but do not compete with yours. Keep the focus narrow.

Make sure your mailing house can stuff eight or more folded flyers and ask if they want Z or letter fold. Equipment varies.

Place a good teaser on the envelope.

The Postal Service will provide a certificate of mailing when the mailing house makes the drop. It is good practice to send copies of the certificate to your mailing praticipants to prove the quantity you mailed.

Four times a year, the Publishers Marketing Association mails individual book flyers to 2600 public libraries across the U.S. which have a purchasing budget of $25,000 or more. They can afford to buy.

Or, you might want school, medical or law libraries, or maybe you have a regional book and just want New England libraries.

"Sales Call in an Envelope" is a creative mailing to 4400 independent bookstores, designed by Peggy Glenn of Aames-Allen Publishing. Six times a year, she mails a booklet containing individual tear-out sales sheets, each with a worksheet on the back to help the buyer locate customers for the book. This format allows the buyer to peruse the offers at his/her leisure, a non-intrusive sales call.

Twice a year, PMA mails a slick flyer offering 37 different titles to 4400 independent bookstores, with each book pictured and described.

PMA also targets periodic mailings to cookbook, health and fitness, metaphysical, children's self-help and travel book reviewers.

Many publishers stuff brochures from other publishers and associations into their packages. Here at Para Publishing, we stuff brochures from the U.S. Parachute Association and *Skydiving Magazine* in with each parachute book we ship. Every publishing book shipped is accompanied by a brochure from *Small Press* magazine and an "Invitation to Join" brochure from the Publishers Marketing Association.

Para Publishing wants to be known as a publishing information center and we find that new publishers are grateful for all the free information. This brochure stuffing builds good will, spreads the word and makes new and small publishing stronger.

Some magazines will give you a free subscription for stuffing their brochure into your packages. And, there is an added bonus – an implied endorsement of your book.

Some publishers have joined together to share the costs for an 800 telephone number used by customers to order books. Others have used order-taking services. (Many services charge about $1.50 per order.)

For co-op exhibiting at book fairs, ABA, ALA, Frankfurt and others, PMA and COSMEP rents blocks of space. Association reps staff the booths and represent your book for you. Participants are represented in a catalog and orders may be taken at the show for forwarding to you.

PMA also purchases space in *Publishers Weekly*, *Library Journal* and other trade publications by the page. Members purchase individual blocks of space as small as 1/12 of a page at the full page rate, a considerable savings. This is a good example of how small publishers can compete with the big publishers, as all pay the same rate for advertising.

By cooperating with other publishers, you add interest and breadth to an offer, save time and money, take advantage of the expertise of the project coordinator and increase the impact of your promotion. The quality of the job can elevate measurably when expenses are shared and the print run can be increased, enabling you to reach a wider audience.

Co-op promotion makes good sense.

Co-Op Marketing and Catalog Opportunities

Ad-Lib Publications
Box 1102
Fairfield, IA 52556-1102
((515) 472-6617
*John Kremer. Catalog of publishing/
writing/marketing related books in "Book
Marketing Update" newsletter.*

American Bookdealers Exchange
Box 2525
La Mesa, CA 92041
(619) 462-3297
*Al Galasso. Mail order bookdealers; co-op
at gift and trade shows, interna membership.*

Arrow Connection
Box 899
Pollock Pines, CA 95726
(916) 644-2341
*Al Beechick. Co-op mailings to computer
owners.*

Aslan Publishing
310 Blue Ridge Dr.
Boulder Creek, CA 95006-9657
(408) 338-7504
*Brenda Plowman, Dawson Church. Co-op
mailings to chiropractors.*

Authors on Air
Box 1179
Eastsound, WA 98245
(206) 376-5660
*Linda Jones. Co-op mailings to 1,000 key
program directors, hosts & producers
responsible for booking the top talk shows
nationwide, New Age oriented.*

Backroads Distributors
47 Tamal Plaza
Corte Madera, CA 94925
(800) 845-4848
Catalog of audio listings, New Age.

Book Marketing Group
1106 Main St.
Huntington Beach, CA 92648
(714) 536-4926
*Peggy Glenn. Ad brochure distributed to
bookstores & retail stores.*

Books & Tapes
561 Tyler
Monterey, CA 93940
(408) 372-1658
*Ruby Grace. Mail order catalog tapes,
music, puzzles, incense, books.*

Books & Tapes Catalog
Box 2250
Santa Cruz, CA 95063
*Free catalog of Sanskrit chanting &
meditation music, books.*

Borderland Sciences Research
Box 429
Garberville, CA 95440
*Books & videos catalog distributed to
consumers, retail, mail order & wholesale,
New Age, spiritual, alternative therapy,
healing.*

Bradley Communications
Box 299
Haverford, PA 19041
(215) 896-6146
*Bill Harrison. Radio-TV interview report to
3000 TV and radio producers.*

Buddhist Bookstore
1710 Octavia
San Francisco, CA 94109
(415) 776-7877, FAX (415) 771-6293
*Sarah Grayson. Buddhist books - catalog,
co-op mailings, newsletter.*

Carousel Press
Box 6061
Albany, CA 94706
(415) 527-5849
*Catalog: books on family travel, family
recreation, travel games.*

China Books & Periodicals, Inc.
2929 24th St.
San Francisco, CA 94110
(415) 282-2994
Mail order catalog of books & periodicals from and about China.

Conference Book Service, Inc.
80 South Early St.
Alexandria, VA 22304
(703) 823-6968, FAX 370-3371
Established, reliable exhibition service or many trade shows, conferences, meetings nationwide, all subjects.

Continuity Publishing
Box 489
Greenbank, WA 98253
(206) 678-7772
Emily Sweeney. New Age, co-op mailings.

COSMEP
Box 703
San Francisco, CA 94101
(415) 922-9490
Richard Morris, Exec Dir
Association of independent publishers . Co-op exhibits and representation of small publishers at ALA and ABA, newsletter.

Critique:
A Journal Exposing Consensus Reality
Box 11368
Santa Rosa, CA 95406
(707) 525-9401
Bob Banner. Co-op mailings, "paradigm" type books.

Discount Book Company
24 Woodland Ave.
San Rafael, CA 94901
(415) 454-3122
Bowman Yager. Warehouse outlet for auto-related books; retail & wholesale.

Empire Publishing
7645 Le Berthon St
Tijunga, CA 91042
(818) 784-8918
Co-op mailings to libraries, high schools & universities.

Esquire Books
1127 S Mannheim Rd., #111
Westchester, IL 60153
(312) 865-0888
S. Jim Rahman. Co-op mailings re consumer health.

First Editions
Box 2578
Sedona, AZ 86336
(602) 282-9574
Sophia Tarila. New Age marketing, mailings to metaphysical bookstores, crystal retailers, workshops, co-op hotline, newsletter, directory.

Flatland
2250 Shattuck Avenue, #56
Oakland, CA 94606
(415) 532-3865
Mail order catalogue, distrib to consumers, misc. small press books.

Focus on Books
7744 31st Ave NE
Seattle, WA 98115
(206) 527-2693
Kristen Nelson. Newsletter of book reviews re women, children, family issues, distrib to 3500 librarians, 500 reviewers.

Forum Publishing Co
383 East Main St.
Centerport, NY 11721
(516) 754-5000, FAX 754-0630
Martin Stevens, President. Catalog for consumers, books, tapes & magazines on business, self-improvement.

Gaia Bookstore & Catalog Company
1400 Shattuck @ Rose
Berkeley, CA 94709
(415) 548-4172
Catalog of objects, jewelry, books, tapes, tarot, sacred arts & ritual instruments.

Good Living Catalog
Box 13257, Northgate Station
San Rafael, CA 94913
(800) 632-2122
Catalog of books, cassettes, New Age music,direct mail to consumers.

Hampton House Publishing Co
Box 67-8000
Placerville, CA 95667
(916) 622-777
E. Hamilton Hensley. Catalog for books re business, sales, mktg.

Harsand Financial Press
Box 515
Holman, WI 54636
(800) 451-0643
Jeff Sweet. Personal finance and parenting books, co-op mailings.

Health Research
Box 70
Mokelumne Hill, CA 95245
Catalog of health and metaphysical material.

Institute of Noetic Sciences
475 Gate Five Road, #300
Sausalito, CA 94965
Barbara McNeill. Catalog of books, audio and video tapes re mind/body connection, healing, consciousness, transpersonal psychology, spiritual quest, etc.

International Titles
931 East 56th St.
Austin, TX 78751
(512) 451-8874
Loris Essary. Interna exhibiting co.: ALA, ABA, London Book Fair, etc.

Jaffe Publishing Management Service
Kunnuparampil Bldg. Kuridty
Kerala State, India
686549
Catalog of small press books for foreign export & subsidiary rights.

Jeffrey Lant Associations
50 Follen St, #507
Cambridge, MA 02138
(617) 547-6372
Dr. Jeffrey Lant. Books, tapes for Sure-Fire Business Success Catalog, mail order.

Lagoon Publications
9 Channel Lndg.
Tiburon, CA 94920
(415) 381-4601
Karen Misuraca. Direct mail co-op to No. California publishers, writers, re self-publishing, book marketing.

Leading Edge Review
Box 5010
St Cloud, MN 56302
(612) 259-6364
Consumer newsletter available through bookstores, many New Age books.

Markets Abroad
2460 Lexington Dr
Owosso, MI 48867
Michael Sedge. Sells books, directories re writing, photography, in quarterly newsletter re world-wide periodicals markets for writers.

Math Aids/Math Products Plus
Box 64
San Carlos, CA 94070
(415) 593-2839
Elvira Monroe, Theoni Pappas. Catalog of math, science, computer, game, puzzle books.

Mehitabel
Box 60357
Palo Alto, CA 94306
(415) 326-6530
Catalog of books & materials on publishing, writing, editing, design.

Network Marketing
545 Wisconsin St.
San Francisco, CA 94107
(415) 821-3652
Dan Kassell. Cooperative mailings directed to health product users.

New Pages
Box 438
Grand Blanc, MI 48439
Co-op mailings, bookstores & libraries.

New & Unique Videos
2336 Sumac Drive
San Diego, CA 92105
Catalog of videotapes.

Olivia Records
4400 Market St.
Oakland, CA 94608
(415) 655-0364
Free catalog of women's music, tapes, posters, books, distributed to consumers.

Panorama Publishing Co
18607 Ventura Blvd.1
Tarzana, CA 91356
John Kappas. Catalogue of self-help books, tapes on hypnosis, psych, behavioral, etc.

PARA PUBLISHING
Publishers Book Club
Box 4232-867
Santa Barbara, CA 94140-4232
(805) 968-7277, FAX (805) 968-1379
Dan Poynter. Catalogs of books for publishers on all aspects of book publishing, marketing, promotion and distribution. Large co-op mailings to magazine reviewers, catalog buyers, radio/TV talk shows.

Parenting Press
Box 15163
Seattle, WA 98115
(206) 527-2900
Elizabeth Crary. Co-op mailings to parents, kids, educa & library lists.

Phileas Fogg's Books & Maps For The Traveler
87 Stanford Shopping Center
Palo Alto, CA 94304
(415) 327-1754
Dick Butler. Catalogue of travel books, maps.

Publisher's Clearing House
382 Channel Dr.
Port Washington, NY 11050
(516) 883-5432
Jeannie Clarke. Direct mail, nonfiction books, hi volume.

Publishers Marketing Association
2401 Pacific Coast Hwy, #206
Hermosa Beach, CA 90254
(213) 372-2732
Jan Nathan. Wide variety of co-op mailings: libraries, kids, travel, how-to and more. Co-op exhibits and representation at ABA, ALA, other conventions & trade shows.

Pussywillow Publishing House
Box 1806
Gilbert, AZ 85234
(602) 892-1316
Terry Latterman. Co-op mailings to libraries.

Rada Press Mailings
2297 Folwell Ave.
St Paul, MN 55108
(612) 645-3304
Daisy Campbell. Co-op mailings to school libraries.

Radio-TV Interview Report & Newspaper Feature Report
101 West Baltimore Ave.
Lansdowne, PA 19050
(215) 259-1070
Bill Harrison. Co-op newsletter to radio/TV & newspapers.

Rainforest Publishing
Box 101251
Anchorage, AK 99510
(907) 274-8687
Co-op book catalog for retail & library markets, Alaska/Pacific NW titles.

Rights from USA Review
Hunter House Inc. Publishers
Box 847
Claremont, CA 91711
(714) 624-2277
Foreign rights marketing newsletter & direct mail co-op opportunities.

Robert Anderson Publishing
Box 276297
Sacramento, CA 95827-6297
(916) 369-0223
Healthcare catalog: nursing.

Scholar's Bookshelf
51 Everett Dr.
Princeton Junction, NJ 08550
(609) 799-7233
Books on fine arts, music, history, literary, philosophy, co-op mailings.

Small Press Center
20 West 44th St.
New York, NY 10036
(212) 764-7021
Non-profit facility for exhibiting books by independent publishers, library of books and catalogs, window display space, meeting space, annual book fair.

SPL Group
Box 31
Fountaintown, IN 46130
(317) 835-7683
Stephen Laykauf. Personal financial investing books, co-op mailings.

Spotlight
Box 51103
Seattle, WA 98113
(206) 527-2693
Co-op newsletter to TV, radio stations, interview programs, to parents, domestic violence groups, kids librarians, school counselors, shelters, day care directors, more child-related, newsletter: reviews of small press books on women, children and family issues, for librarians.

Sunbelt Publications
8622 Argent St., #A
Santee, CA 92071
(619) 448-0884
Diana Lindsay. Co-op mailings on books re Baja, Mexico and cycling.

The Unicorn, Books for Craftsmen, Inc
1304 Scott St.
Petaluma, CA 94952
(800) 289-9276
Catalog for books on weaving, crafts, textiles, knitting, etc.

The Wine Appreciation Guild Catalog
155 Connecticut St.
San Francisco, CA 94107
(415) 864-1202
E. Marchez. Catalog of over 600 titles, plus video tapes, gifts, posters, prints, re wine.

Towers Club
Box 2038
Vancouver, WA 98668-2038
(206) 574-3084
Catalog of how-to & reference books for publishers.

Trans Pubs Bookstore
1259 El Camino Real #209
Menlo Park, CA 94025
(415) 325-6487
Catalog: Education, health, family, psych, transactional analysis, Gestalt & family therapy, child devel, substance abuse.

Troll Associates
100 Corporate Dr.
Mahway, NJ 07430
(800) 247-6106
Marian Schecter. Catalog for families, including books.

Tudor Publishers
3712 Old Battleground Rd.
Greensboro, NC 27408
(919) 282-5907
Co-op mailings, family, marriage , seniors.

Twin Peaks Press
Box 129
Vancouver, WA 98666
(206) 694-2462
Helen Hecker. Exhibits travel titles at trade shows , U.S. & Canada.

VHW Publishing
930 Via Fruteria
Santa Barbara, CA 93110
(805) 687-4087
Co-op mailings to libraries, US & Canada, schools; interna book exhibits.

Vocational Marketing Services
18510 Carpenter St.
Homewood, IL 60430-3534
(312) 799-6560
Michael Walsh. Extensive calendar of co-op mailings & exhibition service to the vocational, technical, adult, indust. training market, many conference & trade shows. Also offers fulfillment, distribution, media consulting.

W.I.M.
Box 137
2215R Market St.
San Francisco, CA 94114
S Diane Bogus. Co-op mailings - poetry.

Whale Publishing Co
Box 21696
St. Louis, MO 63109
Gus Theodore. Co-op mailings, books re humour, games.

Whole Earth Catalog
27 Gate 5 Rd.
Sausalito, CA 94965
(415) 332-1716
Catalog to consumers, books, tools, ideas, outdoor clothing, environ. related items.

Winterbourne Press
1407 Gilman St.
Berkeley, CA 94706
(415) 527-9885
Elaine O'Gara. Co-op mailings re travel, co-op exhibits at travel trade shows.

Writer's Connection
1601 South Saratoga-Sunnyvale Rd.
Cupertino, CA 95014
(408) 973-0227
Steve Lester. Mail-order catalogs of a wide variety of books and tapes relating to the business, production & promotion of books and writings.

Marin Small Publishers Association

A non-profit organization for the benefit of small, independent book publishers, our membership consists of self-publishers, small presses, writers, printers, editors, design and production professionals, publicists, related associations and businesses.

Meetings, free to the public, are held on the second Sunday of each month at two in the afternoon. Meeting programs include sharing of information and resources by members and guests, and presentations from industry experts on the subjects of book selling, promotion, printing, editing and all phases of production and the business of publishing.

MSPA sponsors an annual seminar day in May, including workshops of benefit to new and established small publishers, a book fair and vendors' exhibits.

Membership includes a subscription to the bimonthly newsletter, SPEX (Small Publishers Exchange), a publication dedicated to members' news, marketing tips, book reviews, press releases, informational articles and a calendar of events, classes and trade shows of interest to the publishing community.

Information: MSPA, Box 1346, Ross, CA 94957
Karen Misuraca, (415) 381-4601
Jayne Murdock, (415) 454-1771

Organizations and Associations

African American Publishers & Booksellers Association
Haki Madhubuti, 3rd World Press
7524 South Cottage Grove
Chicago, IL 60619
(312) 651-0700

American Bookdealers Exchange
Box 2525
La Mesa, CA 92041
(619) 462-3297
Mailorder booksellers, newsletter, co-op mailing.

American Library Assoc
50 E Huron St.
Chicago, IL 60611
(312) 944-6780
45,000 members, benefits include job listings, discounts, magazine, trade shows, conferences, more.

American Society of Composers, Authors, and Publishers
One Lincoln Plaza
New York, NY 10023
(212) 688-5111

American Society of Indexers
265 Arlington Ave.
Kensington, CA 94707
(415) 524-4195
Nancy Mulvany. Trade organization of indexers.

American Society of Journalists & Authors, Inc.
1501 Broadway, #1907
New York, NY 10036
(212) 997-0947
Na org of 750 independent nonfiction writers of articles, books & other nonfiction. Annual conference, local chapters, publishing-related events, benefits.

Association for Authors
4189 Bellaire Blvd., #222
Houston, TX 77025
(713) 666-9711
Na, non-profit.

Association of American Publishers
220 East 23rd St.
New York, NY 10010
(212) 689-8920
Na trade organization.

Association of American University Presses
1 Park Ave.
New York, NY 10010
(212) 889-6040

Association of Business Communicators
870 Market St., #910
San Francisco, CA 94109
(415) 433-3400
Lin A. Lacombe. Na & local chapters, monthly meetings.

Association of Magazine Editors in the Bay Area
568 Alvarado St.
San Francisco, CA 94114
(415) 282-3570
Michael Castleman. Irregular meetings, informal org.

Bay Area Book Reviewers
1117 Geary
San Francisco, CA 94109
(415) 771-1252
Peter Carroll. Literary emphasis, mostly editors, freelance reviewers, annual awards.

Bay Area Lawyers for the Arts (BALA)
Bldg C, Fort Mason Center
San Francisco, CA 94123
(415) 775-7200
Legal advice for writers and artists, workshops.

Bay Area Publishers Network
New Harbinger Publications
5674 Shattuck Ave.
Oakland, CA 94609
(415) 652-0215
Bi-monthly, networking, small presses.

Bay Area Travel Writers
2634 43rd Ave.
San Francisco, CA 94116
(415) 564-7941
Pat Lee. Monthly networking meetings for
professional travel writers.

Bay Area Video Coalition
1111 17th St.
San Francisco, CA 94107
(415) 861-3280
Low cost editing to members, networking.

BMUG
1442A Walnut St.
Berkeley, CA 94709
(415) 849-HELP
*Berkeley Macintosh-users group, one of
largest & best in U.S.*

Book Industry Study Group, Inc.
160 5th Ave.
New York, NY 10010
(212) 929-1393, FAX 989-7542
*Wm. Raggio. Extensive research programs,
trends, reports, statistics, publishes
information of all kinds for publishers &
booksellers.*

Book Publicists Northwest
Anne Damron
Box 19786
Seattle, WA 98109
(206) 285-2665

Book Publicists of Southern California
6430 Sunset, #503
Hollywood, CA 90028
(213) 461-3921

Book Publishers of Texas Association
3208 Amberway Dr.
Arlington, TX 76014
*Lee Anne Hammond. Only statewide
publishing assoc.*

Bookbuilders West
Box 883666
San Francisco, CA 94188-3666
(415) 995-4208
*Pat Brewer, newsletter. Paul Butzler,
Pres.; professional organization of book
producers, publishers, printers, typogra-
phers, manufacturers, color separators,
photograhers, etc. Conferences, meetings,
awards.*

Bookbuilders West/South
c/o Unisource, 2600 Commerce Way
Commerce, CA 90040
(213) 725-3700
*Helen Hawekotte. So. Cal. division of
Bookbuilders West.*

California Writers Club
2611 Brooks
El Cerrito, CA 94530
East Bay Chapter.

California Writers Club
333 Ramonda Ave.
Berkeley, CA 94530
(415) 526-8356
Ray Nelson. Berkeley chapter.

California Writers Club
2435 Coronet Blvd.
Belmont, CA 94002
(415) 593-6161
Blanche Watson. Peninsula chapter.

California Writers Club
4720 Bellue St.
Carmichael, CA 95608
Sacramento chapter.

California Writers Club
3757 Macbeth Dr.
San Jose, CA 95127
(408) 258-7125
Madge Saksena. So. Bay chapter.

Children's Book Council
Box 706
New York, NY 10276-0706
(212) 254-2666

Computer Alliance
Building D, Fort Mason Center
San Francisco, CA 94123
(415) 771-1671
Lee Haskell, Director. Members receive discounts on classes, Macintosh lab, other benefits. Extensive slate of classes.

Computer Press Assoc
1260 25th Ave.
San Francisco, CA 94122
(415) 681-5364
Saul Feldman. Interna professional organization of computer journalists and industry associates, editors, writers, broadcasters, PR, including many authors.

COSMEP
Box 703
San Francisco, CA 94101
(415) 922-9490
Richard Morris, Exec Dir. Trade association for independent publishers, newsletter and many services, co-op exhibiting and representation at trade shows, conferences.

Creative States Quarterly, Inc.
Box 22438
Carmel, CA 93922
(408) 647-8086
Non-profit, literacy programs & support for writers, learning center, classes.

editcetera
2490 Channing Way, Suite 507
Berkeley, CA 94704
(415) 849-1110
Hazel White. Nonprofit corp. to help freelancers improve skills, clearing-house for freelancers.

Feminist Writers Guild
Box 9396
Berkeley, CA 94709
(415) 524-3692

Interna Women's Writing Guild
Box 810
Gracie Station
New York, NY 10028
Networking, writing for publication, newsletter, annual conference in NY.

International Association of Business Communicators
870 Market St., #940
San Francisco, CA 94102
(415) 433-3400
SF chapter, newsletter, research service, job hotline, annual conference, monthly meetings.

Marin Small Press Association
9 Channel Landing
Tiburon, CA 94920
Karen Misuraca, (415) 381-4601
Jayne Murdock, (415) 454-1771
Networking and support group for small publishers in the Bay Area, monthly presentations by industry experts, annual seminars, newsletter, book fair .

Media Alliance
Bldg D, Ft Mason
San Francisco, CA 94123
(415) 441-2557
Media: writers, publishers, radio & TV, support group, classes, jobs service, special events, monthly newspaper.

Mid-America Publishers Assoc
Box 1102
Fairfield, IA 52556
(800) 624-5893
John Kremer. Midwest publishers, authors & related businesses. Seminars, co-op promotions, awards, annual conference.

Mystery Readers International
Box 8116
Berkeley, CA 94707-8116
Janet Rudolph. Organization for mystery readers, critics, editors, publishers, writers, reviewers.

Mystery Writers of America, No Calif
48 Valley Rd.
San Anselmo, CA 94960
(415) 457-5179

Na Assoc of Desktop Publishers
Box 508
Kenmore Station
Boston, MA 02215-9919
(617) 437-6472

National Writers Union, SF Chapter
236 W Portal Ave., #232
San Francisco, CA 94127
(415) 654-6369
Networking meetings, newsletter, events, benefits. Works to improve working conditions & pay through collective action, negotiation w/publishers, grievances, contracts.

New Age Publishing and Retailing Alliance
Box 9
Eastsound, WA 98245
(206) 376-2702
Marilyn McGuire. Metaphysical publishers & marketing association.

Northern California Booksellers Assoc
c/o Cody's Books
2454 Telegraph Ave.
Berkeley, CA 94704
(415) 845-9033
Annual trade show.

Northern California Book Publicists
5925 Doyle St.
Emeryville, CA 94608
(415) 428-1991
Carol C Butterfield. Monthly meetings & lecturers, workshops, small & large presses, marketing, self-publishers, periodical editors, etc.

Pacific Northwest Book Publishers Association
Box 1931
Mt. Vernon, WA 98273

Poets and Writers Assoc.
201 West 54th St.
New York, NY 10019
(212) 757-1766

Publishers Marketing Assoc. (PMA)
2401 Pacific Coast Hwy
Hermosa Beach, CA 90254
(213) 372-2732
Jan Nathan. Trade assoc of independent book, audio and video publishers. Extensive co-op marketing, exhibition service, newsletter, conferences, other benefits.

Redwood Writers Club
Marion McMurtry
3382 Glen Echo Dr.
Santa Rosa, CA 95404
(707) 545-1244
Redwood Empire branch of California Writers Club, meetings, conference.

Romance Writers of America, SF Chapter
2808 Morgan Dr.
San Ramon, CA 94583
JoAnne Dreyfus (209) 658-7282
Bonnie Hearn (209) 432-7881

Society for Scholarly Publications
2000 Florida Ave., NW
Washington, D.C. 20009
(202) 328-3555

Society of Children's Book Writers
Box 20233, Park West Finance St.
New York, NY 10001
(212) 243-4370
Conferences.

Society of Children's Book Writers
Box 505
St Helena, CA 94574
(707) 963-0704
Gay N Finkelman. Writers, illustrators, editors, publishers, agents, monthly meetings in SF, full slate of speakers.

Society of Technical Communications
Paul LiBeu, IMCO
3883 Airway Drive
Santa Rosa, CA 95401
Professional organization of techical writers, documentation specialists, publishers. Meets monthly.

Society of the Black Marble
820 Hooshang Ct.
Cupertino, CA 95014
Carole Girvan. Fiction writers' group.

Textbook Authors Assoc
Mike Keedy
Box 535
Orange Springs, FL 32682
(904) 546-1000

Women's National Book Association
379 Burning Tree Ct.
Half Moon Bay, CA 94109
SF chapter, bi-monthly meetings, events.

Writers Connection
1601 Saratoga-Sunnyvale Rd., Suite 180
Cupertino, CA 95014
(408) 973-0227
*Steve Lester. Trade & networking assoc
for writers/publishers/related businesses,
extensive series of classes & seminars all
year re fiction, nonfiction, screenplay,
technical writing, mktg, etc. Publishers of
California Publishing Marketplace, a
directory for writers, newsletter, other
benefits. Free catalog.*

Calendar of Special Events, Trade Fairs, Shows, Conventions, Classes, Seminars, Workshops

Calendar of Special Events, Trade Fairs, Shows, Conventions, Classes, Seminars, Workshops

(Most of these events are annual, occurring every year during the same month)

JANUARY

January 7-12
American Library Assoc Midwinter Conference, Washington, D.C.
ALA, 50 E Huron St, Chicago, IL 60611
(312) 955-6780

January 12-14
National Assoc of Hispanic Publications annual convention, Las Vegas, NV
Eddie Escobedo (702) 384-1514

January 14
Publishers' Marketing Association Annual Seminar/Suppliers' Fair, LA
Speakers re book business, book public-ity, media, marketing, vendors, exhibits.
2401 Pacific Coast Highway, #206
Hermosa Beach, CA 90254
PMA, Jan Nathan (213) 372-2732

January 20-22
The Days of Wine & Proses, Writers Conference, No Calif. Chapter of Amer Soc of Journalists & Authors
310 MacAlvey Dr, Martinez, CA 94553
Linda-Marie Singer (415) 372-8805

January 24-February 6
21st Annual Cairo Interna Book Fair
Interna Fair Grounds, NASR City, Egypt
Samir Sand Khalil, General Egyptian Book Org, Corniche El Nil, Bolac, Cairo, Egypt (00202) 775371

January 28
California Lawyers for the Arts Annual One-Day Writers' Conference
Fort Mason Center
San Francisco, CA 94123
(415) 775-7200

FEBRUARY

February 18-22
San Francisco Annual Gift and Stationery Show
Gift Center, 2181 Greenwich
San Francisco, CA 94123
(415) 346-6666

February 24-26
Asilomar Conference
Northern Calif. Chapter of the Society of Children's Book Writers, Asilomar, CA
Weekend for Writers, Noted Speakers, critiques. Gay Finkleman, Box 505, Saint Helena, CA 94574 (707) 963-0704 or Bobbie Kinkead, Box 5252, Berkeley, CA 94705.

MARCH

March 2-3
Mid-America Publishers Association Annual Spring Conference, Chicago, IL
Peggy Glenn, John Kremer, McHugh, Harold Moe, Jeff Sweet, noted experts in marketing and promoting books, publish-ers, plus editors and other speakers.
Deadline for registration: February 20th.
(800) 624-5893

March 4
3rd Annual National Writers Union Conference, San Francisco Chapter
San Francisco State University
Workshops & other activities for writers & publishers, 236 West Portal Ave, #232
San Francisco, CA 94127 (415) 654-6369

March 4-12
Annual International Book Fair of Mexico, Palacio de Mineria, Mexico
Sergio Tirado Ledesma, IBFM, Tacuba 5, Box 20-515, Mexico 06000 D F
Phone (905) 591-0155

March 11-19

21st Annual Brussels International Book Fair, Centre International Rogier, Brussels, Belgium, D Hauwearts, BIBF, 111 Avenue du Parc, 1060 Brussels, Belgium 02-538 92 93

March 11-12

"Writing to Sell", Pacific NW Writers' Conference, 17345 Sylvester Road, SW Seattle, WA 98166 (206) 242-9757

March 12-18

14th Biennial Jerusalem International Book Fair, Jerusalem Convention Center, Jerusalem, Israel, Zev Berger, JIBF, 212 Jaffa Road, Box 1241, Jerusalem, Israel 02-380896

March 18

American River College "Sell What You Write" Workshop, Annual seminar, 350 participants, various topics of interest to writers and publishers, including "How I Made a Million in Self-Publishing". Noted writers, publishers, editors. Bud Gardner, 4700 College Oak Drive, Sacramento, CA 94841 (916) 484-8643

March 13-16

Asian World Publishing Congress #05-07 Beach Centre, 15 Beach Road Singapore 0719 Phone 339-4377

March 20-22

Small Press & Journal Publishing Expo '89, "Conference and Exposition for Book, Scholarly Journal & Literary Magazine Publishers", New York Penta Hotel, New York City, l Meckler Publishing, 11 Ferry Lane West, Westport, CT 06880 (203) 226-6967. Full days of workshops with noted experts: book & magazine production, marketing, planning, management, distribution, specialty publishing (audio, video), foreign rights, fulfillment, plus vendor exhibits. Sponsored by Small Press magazine.

March 28

"The Editorial Process," seminar. Writers Connection, Cupertino, CA (408) 973-0227

March 31-April 1

University of North Texas Creative Writing Seminar, Book Publishers of Texas, Statewide Association Annual Meeting. One-day seminar conducted by PMA. Desktop Publishing, design, management, publishing, vendors, exhibits, presentations. Lee Anne Hammons, 3208 Amberway Drive, Arlington Texas 96014 (817) 467-2495

March-June, Sept-Dec

editcetera Workshops for Writers/ Publishers, International House, UC Berkeley. Series of beginning and advanced courses, simple copyediting, substantive editing, proofreading, indexing, art & photography. Hazel White, (415) 849-1110

APRIL

April 3-5

The Annual London International Book Fair, US Pavilion, shared booth available, representation for sales/rights, $50 per title. United States Department of Commerce, TD/AACG/OCG Room 4327 14th St Constitutional Ave, NW, Washington DC 20230

April 5-9

Oregon Library Association Conference Salem, OR (503) 378-2112

April 6-9

26th Annual Bologna Children's Book Fair, Bologna Fairgrounds, Bologna, Italy Francesca Ferrari, BCBF, Piazza Costituzione 6, 40128 Bolonga, Italy

April 18-23

Annual Quebec International Book Fair Quebec Municipal Convention Center, Quebec, Canada. Lorenzo Michaud, QIBF, 2590 Boulevard Laurier, Suite 760, Ste–Foy, Quebec, Canada GIV 4M6 (418) 658-1974

April 25

"How to Writer Better News Releases,"
seminar, Writers Connection
(408) 973-0227

April 26-30

Booklovers Convention, (romance
books), Phoenix, Arizona
Romantic Times, 162 Joralemon Street,
Brooklyn Heights, NY 11201

April 26-29

Washington Library Association Conference, Lynwood, WA
Valerie Stevens, Exhibits Manager
(206) 778-2148

MAY

May 5-7

3rd Latin American Book Fair
Women Writers from Latin America,
Spain and elsewhere. Division of
Humanities, City College of New York
(212) 690-8172

May 12-18

Annual Torino National Book Fair
Torino, Italy. Erica Giacosa, Salone Del
Libro Torino, Largo Regio Parco 9,
10152 Torino, Italy

May 13

**Marin Self-Publishers Assoc. Annual
Day of Seminars and Workshops**
Keynoter, Dan Poynter, author of The
Self-Publishing Manual. Workshop
subjects include: production, foreign
rights/sales, desktop publishing, how to
find and choose a printer, traditional and
non-traditional marketing. Karen
Misuraca (415) 381-4601, Jayne Murdock
(415) 454-1771.

May 17

**Bookbuilders West Annual Crash
Course in Production**
Box 883666, San Francisco, CA 94188
(415) 995-4208 Paul Butzler. Several
other annual events; free newsletter.

May 19

American Society of Indexers
Annual meeting, San Francisco,
nancy Mulvany, (415) 524-4195

May 17-22

**34th Annual Warsaw International
Book Fair**, Palace of Culture and Science,
Warsaw, Poland. Wladyslaw Bienkowski,
WIBF, Krakowskie Przedmiescie 7,
Box 1001, Warsaw, Poland
Phone #178641

May 20

"A Look Ahead: Publishing Opportunities in the 1990's" Sunnyvale Hilton,
9 a.m. to 5 p.m. Publishing trends, Role
of Small Presses, Writing to Sell, Literary
Agents, What Editors Want, more.
Writers Connection, 1601 Saratoga-
Sunnyvale Rd, #180, Cupertino, CA
95014, Meera Lester (408) 973-0227

May 20-21

Para Publishing Seminars
Weekend intensives, also offered in
March, August and November, for small
groups of independent publishers and
entrepreneurial publishers, by two
industry experts: Dan Poynter and Mindy
Bingham, authors of The Self-Publishing
Manual and Is There a Book Inside You?
Free information kit and free newsletter.
Para Publishing, Box 4232, Santa Barbara, CA 93140-4232 (805) 968-7277,
FAX (805) 968-1379

JUNE

June (1990)

Biennial Interna Feminist Book Fair
Barcelona, Spain
Info: Feminist Bookstore News, Box
882554, San Francisco, CA 94188
(415) 626-1556

June 3-6

89th Annual American Booksellers
Association Convention, Washington
Convention Center, Washington DC
Eileen Dengler, ABA, 137 West 25th
Street, New York, NY 10111
Phone (212) 463-8450
PMA co-op exhibit: (213) 372-2732.
COSMEP co-op exhibit: (415) 922-9490

June 10-15

Special Libraries Association Convention New York, 1700 18th St, NW
Washington, D.C. 20009 (202) 234-4700

June 13

"Publishing Power w/Ventura", seminar
Writers Connection (408) 973-0227

June 15-18

Textbook Authors Annual Convention
Menger Hotel, San Antonio, TX
Contact TAA HQ (904) 546-1000

June 22

**Canadian Library Association Annual
Show**, 151 Sparks Street, Ottowa
(613) 232-9625

June 24

**"Creating Books to Match California's
New History/Social Science Framework"**. Diane Brooks, Cal. Dept. of
Education, San Francisco, CA.
Society of Children's Book Writers, Box
505, Saint Helena, CA 94574

June 24-28

**American Library Association Annual
Convention**, Dallas, TX
ALA, 50 E Huron St, Chicago, IL 60611

June 25-August 5

**Clarion Workshop in Science Fiction &
Fantasy Writing**, Lynman Briggs School,
MSU, E-29 Holmes Hall, East Lansing, MI
48825-1107. "Best known and most
highly regarded of sci-fi workshops in the
country". Albert Drake, Director
(517) 353-6486

JULY

July 13-23

**Centrum Foundation Summer Writers'
Conference**, Box 1158, Port Townsend,
WA 988369 (206) 385-3102

July 14-16

California Writers' Club Conference
Pacific Grove, CA. Biennial weekend,
featuring noted editors, agents, publishers, writers. Panels, seminars, private
appointments, exhibits. 450 participants.
Dorothy Benson, 2214 Derby Street,
Berkeley, CA 94705

July 16 -29

Stanford Publishing Course
Intensive in-residence seminars, workshops, presentations with editors, publishers, noted experts in publishing field.
Participants must qualify with experience
and/or background. Justin O'Brien, (415)
723-2300, Bowman Alumni House
Stanford, CA 94305

July 17

**Sonoma State University Writers'
Conference**, Annual week of workshops:
morning fiction & poetry, afternoon
panels on all phases of writing, evening
readings. Accommodations avail. SSU,
Rohnert Park, CA 94928, (707) 664-2507,
Jonah Raskin

July 23-26

6th Annual Writers' Institute Conference, Biola University. Largest Christian
writers' conference in the nation. Biola
University, 13800 Biola Avenue,
La Mirada, CA 90639, (231) 944-0351,
Ext 3441

July 24-28

Napa Valley Poetry Conference
July 31-August 4, Napa Valley Craft of
Fiction Conference, Annual writers' conferences featuring noted writers, editors,
poets. Napa Valley College, Napa, CA
94558 (707) 253-3070

July 29

Video Festival, San Francisco
Speakers from national conferences
Society of Children's Book Writers,
Box 505, Saint Helena, CA 94574

AUGUST

August 5-9

San Francisco Annual Gift and Stationery Show, Gift Center, 2181 Greenwich, San Francisco, CA 94123 (415) 346-6666

August 12-18

4th Annual Edinburgh Book Festival
For the public. Theme for 1989 is North American authors, special exhibition from and about North America. Arrangements available to send books for exhibition and sale. 25A S West Thistle ST Lane, Edinburgh EH2 1EW, Phone 031-225-1915, FAX 031-220-0377 Jerry Brown, Director

August 11-13

Writers' Connection Screenwriting Conference, "Selling to Hollywood"
Sunnyvale Hilton, Sunnyvale, CA
Motion picture & TV producers, Hollywood agents, story editors, screenwriters.
Meera Lester (408) 973-0227

August

Society of Children's Book Writers National Conferencem Los Angeles
SCBW No. Cal Chapter, Gay Finkleman, Box 505, Saint Helena, CA 94574
(707) 963-0704

SEPTEMBER

September 2-10

Annual Singapore International Book Fair, World Trade Center, Singapore
N T S Chopra, 865 Mountbatten Rd, #05-28 Singapore 1543   #344-1495

September 9

Southwest Booksellers Association Trade Show, Dallas Convention Center
Booksellers from a 9-state region. Steve Davis, Box 190831, Dallas, TX 75219
(214) 954-4469

September 9-11

Pacific Northwest Booksellers Trade Show, Tacoma, WA, PNB, RT 1, Box 219B, Banks, OR 97106
Debby Garman (503) 324-8180

September 17-18

Northern California Booksellers Association Trade Show 89, Oakland Convention Center. Info: Cody's Books, 2454 Telegraph, Berkeley, CA 94704
(415) 845-7852

September 28-30

COSMEP Annual Publishers' Conference
Bismarck Hotel, Chicago. COSMEP, The International Association of Independent Publishers, Box 703, San Francisco, CA 94101, (415) 922-9490, Henry Berry

September 30

"The How-to's for Picture Book Writing and Illustrating", San Francisco, CA
Society of Children's Book Writers, Box 505, Saint Helena, CA 94574
(707) 963-0704

September 30

Comedy/Humour Writers' Conference
Annual. Features noted professional comedy writers. Sponsored by: Comedy/ Humour Writers' Association, Box 211, San Francisco, CA 94101 (415) 751-6725

September

Biennial Moscow International Book Fair, Fairgrounds of USSR, Exhibition of Economic Achievment, Moscow, USSR
Takred G Golenpolsky, MIBF, 16 Chekov Street, Moscow 103006 USSR

September

Annual Liber Salon Internacional
Evelyn De L'Epine, Liber '89, Paseo de la Castellana 82, 28036 Madrid, Spain
Phone (91) 457 44 04

OCTOBER

October 11-16

41st Annual Frankfurt Book Fair
Frankfurt Fairgrounds, Frankfurt/Main, Fedederal Republic of Germany, Peter Weidhaas, FBF, Reineckstrasse 3, D-6000 Frankfurt am Main 1, Federal Republic of Germany 069-2102-217 Co-op exhibitors: USA Book Expo, 86 Millwood Rd, Millwood, NY 10546 (914) 762-2422. Co-op exhibits through PMA (213) 372-2732. Accommodations: Caravan Travel (212)889-4880, reserves blocks of rooms

October 14-16

2nd Annual San Antonio Inter-Amer Bookfair, Hemisfair Park, San Antonio, TX. Includes readers/panelists: Carlos Fuentes, Larry McMurtry, etc. Exhibits, panels, more. Rosemary Catacalos (512) 271-3151.

October 19

Society of School Librarians International, San Antonio, TX Registration deadline for PMA exhibit : September 16. (213) 372-2732

October 24-30

The 34th Annual Belgrade International Book Fair, Belgrade Fairgrounds, Belgrade, Yugoslavia. Vojislav Vujovic, Association of Yugoslavian Publishers and Booksellers, Kneza Milosa 25, Belgrade 11000,Yugoslavia 011-642-248/642-533

October

Association of American Publishers
"Booktech - A Publisher's Forum", high-tech applications specific to publishing industry, vendor fair, demos, speakers. San Francisco, CA (415) 689-8920

NOVEMBER

November 13-19

National Children's Book Week
Children's Book Council, 67 Irving Pl., New York, NY 10003
(212) 254-2666

November 12

California Library Association Convention, Fresno, CA. PMA exhibit registration deadline : October 14. (213) 372-2732

November 15
National Young Reader's Day
(800) 4-BOOK-IT

November 23-December 4
6th Annual Cairo International Children's Book Fair, International Fair Grounds, NASR Egypt. Samir Sand Khalil, General Egyptian Book Organization, Corniche El Nil, Bolac, Cairo, Egypt (00202) 775371

November
Computer Press Assoc annual meeting, Las Vegas, Saul Feldman, (415) 681-5364

November
Guadalajara International Book Fair
500 booth exhibit. Extensive conference schedule, FIL 89, Apartado 39-130/Ave Hidalgo 1417, Guadalajara 4417 JAL, Mexico

DECEMBER

December 2,3
Small Press Book Fair, The Small Press Center, (non-profit exhibitor of independently pub books), 20 West 44th St., New York, NY 10036 (212) 764-7021

December
Bookbuilders West Annual Book Show
Many awards in several categories of books, book covers. (see May 17 info)

MISCELLANEOUS

Computer Alliance
Ongoing classes for every popular Macintosh software program, MAC lab. Newsletter, schedule of classes. Fort Mason, Bldg D, San Francisco, CA 94123 (415) 771-1671 Director, Lee Haskell

Media Alliance
Bldg D, Ft Mason, San Francisco, CA 94123. Wide array of classes re writing, publishing, promotion, desktop pub, rights, taxes, editorial—everything related to the media. Monthly newsletter, news, schedule of events, classes.
(415) 441-2557

Communication Unlimited
120 seminars annually in California Variety of topics in interest to writers & publishers: "Self-publishing the TCE Way," "How to Sell 75% of Your Freelance Writing," "Before You Write That Book,", etc. Through Calif colleges & universities. Gordon Burgett, Box 6405, Santa Maria, CA 93456 (805) 937-8711

Folio Book Publishing Seminars
6 River Bend, Box 4949
Stamford, CN 06907-0949.
All aspects of publishing, production, promotion, management, editing, design and more. Conferences held in a number of U.S. cities, including Los Angeles. Faculty: Tony Bove, Cheryl Rhodes, Publish magazine, John Huenefeld, publishing consultant, Peter Jacobi, Don Ranley, journalism professors.
Folio, Box 4949 Stamford, CT 06907-0949 (203) 358-9900

Seybold Seminars
Nationwide conferences for publishing professionals: Technology, products, vendors, trends, systems. Typical attendee involved in high-volume, high-quality, full-time prepress production of periodicals and books. 6922 Wildlife Rd, Box 578, Malibu, CA 90265 (213) 457-5850.

The information listed here on events, classes and conferences was obtained from the sponsoring organizations. The editor and publisher takes no responsibility for inaccuracies or changes.

12 Books for Publishers

The Building of a Book:
Always One More Mountain to Climb

By Jayne May Murdock

Jayne and her husband, Dick, helped found the Marin Self-Publishers Association. Their company, May-Murdock Publications, has produced fourteen books, including "Smoke in the Canyon," "Shannon: What's It All Mean?" and "Love Lines." May-Murdock also publishes the Northwestern Pacific Railroad Historical Society magazine. May-Murdock Publications, Box 1346, Ross, CA 94957.

When you're self-publishing your 'steenth offering and the text has already appeared as columns in the local newspaper, it's a comparatively simple task, right? Wrong!

For over a year, my husband Dick's Sunday column, "Outdoors in Marin," had been keeping an enthusiastic following of Bay Area readers advised as to where to go, how to get there and what to do when you've arrived.

We saw a fine opportunity in Dick's material, and received permission from the paper to convert sixty-one columns into book form. As this would be our fourteenth self-published book, we thought it would be easy. Straightforward. Run'em off, design a book. No problem.

Wrong, again.

For one thing, our expectations were higher this time. A bigger book, more pages, a photograph on every page, full color cover and so on; class all the way.

We drew up a schedule with lots of built-in leeway, with lists of things to be started and completed each month.

We chose a January publication date so it would be new for the longest possible time, but we wanted the book to be in the stores by late October or early November at the latest, to hit the Christmas trade.

For this, camera-ready copy was needed by the printer in September, manuscript had to be ready for the typesetter early in August, editing and design done by July, and all copy in place by June. And here it was nearly April already!

Nothing insurmountable, yet who would guess there would be mountains to climb? Valleys to be plunged into?

Task number one was to run off each column, in chronological order, on the dot matrix printer, in draft form.

Then, arrange the hard copy in a binder, geographically, tossing out inappropriate columns. The editing began, and I found there is a world of difference between a "line-the-birdcage" life expectancy of a newspaper story and the long shelf-life of a reference book.

Much had to be changed. This could never have been accomplished, at least not by me, in the days before computers made rewriting a comparative breeze.

We chose a title and sub-title for the book — From Point Bonita to Point Reyes: Outdoors in Marin — then, for good measure, added 61 Places to Visit , so there would be no doubt about the subject matter.

Next, we named each chapter, assigned the ISBN, designed the format, figured the page count and set the retail price. We filled out the ABI (Advance Book Information) form, made copies for future use and sent the original off to R.R. Bowker.

Dick and I try to travel one week a month in our VW Adventurewagen, and while traveling along, discuss our current project. During one trip, we chose the persons we wanted to write the preface and foreword, plus those holding positions in Marin's great outdoors, making them naturals to read excerpts from the manuscript and give us blurbs for the back cover and to use on publicity fliers.

We got rough chapters to the appropriate people, waiting more or less patiently for each reply. Once, toward the end, a slow mail delivery cost us six crucial days. (For anything of this nature, we advise allowing much more time than seems necessary, then add more time.)

Concurrent with this, once a week we took pictures of the destinations described in the book. Luckily, the first roll of black and white film, a medium I wasn't familiar with, provided eight great pictures. I was encouraged by this success to go on.

Later, photo safaris were not so productive and we had to return again and again to achieve what was needed. We were still taking pictures, almost desperately, while the book was being typeset.

About midway in the production, working with a small dummy copy of the front and back matter, I discovered pages had not been allotted for the table of contents. No amount of juggling could fit them in. A call to the printer, whose bid we had already accepted, informed us that expanding the book from 144 pages to 160 was more economical than going to 152 pages. So, now I had another problem: filling those extra pages.

This meant changing page numbers throughout — text, contents, index and other lists — on the scanner-ready finished copy as well as in the computer. And, we needed to submit a corrected ABI form to Bowker. And, we raised the price by a dollar. Just a little valley in our journey!

At the beginning of a late June trip, a burned-out clutch on our RV stranded us in Auburn for three 107-degree days. We spent this enforced downtime sitting in the shade at a picnic table by a lovely lake, writing the sixty-one chapter subtitles.

Never, at home, could we have stolen that much uninterrupted time; a fortuitous accident, indeed. Whenever we read a subtitle, we remember how it came into being.

Built around a color photo of one of Marin's loveliest lakes, the cover turned out to be a Mt. Everst type mountain to overcome. It involved four-color separation, a process with which I'd been badly burned in a previous book and was now approaching with apprehension.

An accomplished photographer-friend had taken the cover photo, but it was not a slide, and a transparency was needed.

I took another photo, but the change in seasons made it less beautiful, without a reflection of the mountain and sky in the lake. We then took slides of the photo but the color was off. Finally, we sent the original negative back to the lab and they made a slide from it. Expensive, but perfect!

By this time we were rushed, and after one bad experience with the U.S. mails (a week to receive a first class letter from our typesetter in San Francisco), I ran a delivery service to and fro and also spent hours sitting beside the charming lady typesetter, adjusting, formatting and correcting glitches.

Proofreading at every step of the way turned up more errors than imaginable, and still there were more! Big ones, like the wrong chapter number in large type!

The worst was saved till last, however, when a tiny, but potentially horrendous error wasn't spotted until almost too late.

Camera-ready copy at the printer, art work at the color separator, gloating over a black and white copy of the cover, my eyes fell on the words "foreword by." I realized with a sinking feeling that it read "foreward." On the cover! And on the title page!

Between hysteria about the error and thankfulness I'd spotted it, I phoned the printer, the typesetter and the cover person to alert them.

This little blip cost over $100 to correct.

How did we fare on our pre-planned calendar formulated ten months before?

A few days late getting the copy to the typesetter, ten days late getting it back from them, resulting in a later press run, brought the shipment of books to us late in November, barely ahead of the hoped-for Christmas season.

This gave us three days to mail and deliver over 200 books promised by Thanksgiving, to individuals and bookstores.

Buy the end of the following week, copies had been placed in all local bookstores, a distributor was handling the rest of the Bay Area, and mail orders were dispatched.

Wonderful things happened. One bookstore owner swept a pile of Sonnets From The Portuguese off the counter and placed a stack of Point Bonita to Point Reyes there instead.

Another made space in the window between Danielle Steele's latest and Jerry Graham's Backroads. Good company!

In six weeks, nearly half the books were gone and we were at the break-even point.

There are still mountains to climb, but the view from here is great!

Books for Publishers
(including order form)

The Decision to Publish, *By Mary Bold, 6 X 9, plastic comb binding, foldouts, 1989, 2nd edition, 160 pages, $14.95. (order form #1)*

Trying to decide whether or not to self-publish? Want to explore non-traditional as well as traditional publishing options? Need a user-friendly explanation of desktop publishing?

This book is for writers who need concrete information before making the decision to publish, whether the motive is profit or personal fulfillment.

Bold is an experienced, successful publisher, and her style is particularly up-beat and fun to read. ("Publisher: he who risks money.") She emphasizes realistic expectations and the need for planning.

There is a step-by-step procession through financial considerations, expense projections, royalties, agents, self-publishing, market analysis, start-up activities, planning, budgets, press runs, all aspects of production, book design, distribution, promotion, and more.

Descriptions are brief, clear and nothing is missed. Included are many real life examples and anecdotes. The book is nicely laid out, with plenty of room for personal notes, and there's a whole raft of full-size fold out sample news releases.

The Decision to Publish won a Special Book Award from the National Association of Independent Publishers, and for good reason. This book makes it possible for you to come to an informed decision about whether or not to publish.

Financial Feasibility in Book Publishing, *By Robert Follett, Alpine Guild, 8 1/2 X 11, 64 pages, perfectbound, film laminated two-color cover, 1988, $12.95. (order form #2)*

Written by a man with years of experience as an editor, copywriter, designer, marketing manager and CEO of a large publishing company, owner of a small publishing company and teacher of many workshops and seminars on financial analysis, this is a workbook for publishers looking to make a profit.

It's a nuts and bolts approach to estimating revenues, projecting expenditures and setting financial objectives.

Charts, formulas, examples, forms and worksheets are interspersed with true stories, explanations and advice.

Some subjects covered are sales, discounts, pricing, returns, expenditures, editing, design, typesetting, manufacture, marketing, royalties and distribution.

Of particular interest is an in-depth discussion of exploring and testing the potential market for a book, how to determine market size, print run quantity and pricing.

Other useful inclusions are guidelines for estimating book length, and real numbers to help determine what to pay typesetters, designers, printers, editors and other outside contractors.

The series of worksheets is invaluable for figuring out, planning and implementing book projects.

Before you invest in your first or your tenth attempt to make money as a publisher, get a copy of Follett's book.

THE SELF-PUBLISHING MANUAL, How To Write, Print & Sell Your Own Book, *by Dan Poynter, Para Publishing, 352 pages, 5.5 X 8.5, perfectbound, film laminated four-color cover, $14.95. (order form #3)*

If you can buy just one book, this is it, the classic reference on writing, publishing, marketing, promoting & distributing books, by one of the industry's most renowned experts and an eminently successful self-publisher.

New publishers should approach the book with a highlighter pen, as every page is a gold mine of essential information. Experienced publishers will keep it handy for constant reference.

Poynter goes step-by-step from idea through manuscript, printing, promotion and sales, offering numerous innovative book marketing formulas and tons of resources. There are illustrations of many essential forms, and something that's missing in many books for publishers — a calendar checklist with which to plan production and promotion months in advance.

Book design and promotional materials are covered, how to choose a printer, how to deal with bookstores and distributors, rights, reviews, media coverage, direct mail and more.

Poynter conducts workshops for self-publishers and small presses, and produces several books a year. *The Self-Publishing Manual* is a distillation of his knowledge, sources and secrets of the trade.

The Illustrated Handbook of Desktop Publishing and Typesetting,

By Michael L. Kleper, TAB Books, 8 1/2 X 11, 770 pages, film laminated four-color cover, 3rd printing, 1987, $29.95. (order form #4)

This is a sourcebook, a comprehensive analysis of desktop publishing by an internationally recognized expert in computerized typesetting and production.

In-depth is what you have here, definitive explanations and illustrations of Macintosh and IBM desktop publishing systems, including all basic software. The objective of the book is to show the products available for producing typographic output using a personal computer, what they do, and how they can be beneficial.

There is a complete history and description of typestyles, typefitting, printers, modems, keyboards and other hardware, principles
of layout, design, graphics, business applications and costs, data manipulation, and more, much more.

If computerized word processing and typesetting is going to be a significant part of your life, this tome will acquaint you with basic concepts and help you make hardware and software buying decisions. If you read it straight through, you'll be able to award yourself a degree and start teaching desktop publishing yourself.

Illustrations are profuse and extremely helpful, and the book is written for the common man, not the technical expert.

Especially valuable are the chapters on making typesetting decisions, determining costs, accessory products and devices, and the appendix of sources - vendors, publications, organizations, etc.

By the pound, this book is already worth more than the purchase price. But, the real value lies in the tools you get with which to evaluate a desktop publishing or typesetting program, and how to use one effectively.
And, if you're already set up with hardware and software, you'll learn to make the most of what you've got.

"If you can afford only one book on desktop, this would have to be the one to buy."

Directory of Book, Catalog and Magazine Printers, *edited by John Kremer, 92 pages, perfectbound, 8 X 11, film-lam cover,* **$15.** *(order form #5)*

Whether you're seeking a printer for the first time or for reprints and new books, publishing expert John Kremer's directory of printers is of inestimable value. A thousand printers are listed, described in detail and indexed in several ways, enabling you to come up with an informed selection from which to solicit price quotes.

Complete, easy instructions, forms and recommendations set up the request-for-quote process for you, and the listings provide every bit of information about printers specializing in your size and type of book. He also lists foreign printers and printers specializing in brochures, direct mail pieces, labels, tabloids, posters, booklets, manuals and so on.

Save yourself a lot of time, money and finding-out-the-hard-way by making use of Kremer's book.

Small Time Operator, How to start your own small business, keep your books, pay your taxes and stay out of trouble, *33rd printing, Bernard Kamoroff, Bell Springs Publishing, 1988, 8 1/2 by 11, film-lam cover, perfectbound, 192 pages,* **$10.95.** *Free updates available. (order form #6)*

"The most popular small business guidebook ever published," it's of special value to entrepreneurial publishers because profitability in the publishing business can be illusive, to say the least. 250,000 copies are said to be in print.

It's updated frequently and crammed with advice, instructions, facts, resources and recommendations on startup, marketing, financing, licenses, insurance, bookkeeping, partnerships, expansion and more. Also included is a year's worth of ledgers and worksheets.

The author is an experienced tax accountant and financial advisor to start-up businesses. He writes in an approachable style, for the layperson, while providing all the detailed, technical information you could possibly need — cash flow, inventory control, accounting systems, employees, corporations, taxes in depth, acquiring capital and much more.

You won't be able to read it all in one sitting. It's a reference book and workbook, an education in itself. Frequent free updates are included with this book.

How to Self Publish and Make Money, *by Crook and Wise, Sandhill Publishing/ Crook Publishing, 136 pages, 6 X 9, film lam cover, perfectbound, 136 pages,* **$12.95.** *(order form #7)*

Written for the Canadian market but almost completely applicable to the U.S., this is a startup book: reasons why to publish, whether or not to go ahead, attitude and mind-set, goal setting, what to expect, planning, marketing, promotion, production, working with printers, design and layout. Especially useful are the discussions of the experienced authors' mistakes and their recommendations.

The book includes organizations and sources in Canada, plus an invaluable perspective of the Canadian book market. A must for any press thinking about plunging in North of the border.

Free Help From Uncle Sam to Start Your Own Business (Or Expand the One You Have), *by William Allarid, 3rd edition, 1988, Puma Publishing, film lam cover, perfectbound, 160 pages, 6 X 9,* **$9.95.** *(order form #8)*

As a starting point and reference book for soliciting public assistance in the form of loans, grants and direct payments, this book is essential. Included are 100 ways the government will help aspiring or established entrepreneurs, with many examples and descriptions of the programs.

Zillions of financial opportunities are available through Federal programs. You just need to find the one which applies to you. This book will enable you to do that in record time, by helping to identify the program and the appropriate agency or office.

Endorsed by the Service Corps of Retired Executives, the book gives actual examples and straightens out the bureaucratic maze between you and Federal loan programs, loan guarantees, direct payment programs, grant programs, information services and counseling services.

Looking Good in Print, A Guide to Basic Design for Desktop Publishing,
Ventana Press, 1988, 210 pages, 7 3/8 by 9 1/4, film-lam cover, perfectbound, $23.95. (order form #9)

This book will help you, painlessly, to become a better designer of books, flyers, ads and all kinds of promotional materials. A graphic design primer for desktop publishers, it introduces you to white space, bullets, typefaces, effective use of photos and illustrations and much more.

There are many good books about desktop publishing design; this is one of the best, because it incorporates good, simple ideas and lots of examples into an easy to read, attractive format.

You'll learn how to produce appealing, persuasive printed materials, and down-to-earth solutions for nearly every design project. There are dozens of tips and tricks for improving your newsletters, brochures, flyers, ads, charts, graphs, etc.

Over 200 illustrations, several design makeover examples and 10 common design pitfalls are all especially useful. It's a main selection for the Graphic Artists Book Club and an alternate selection of the Writers Digest Book Club.

Publishing on Command, *By Carole C. Marsh, Gallopade Publishing Group, 1989, $14.95 paperback or $24.95, 3-ring binder. (order form #10)*

The author of this exciting, unusual book was named Communicator of the Year, operates several companies and has produced many books and articles on the subject of entrepreneurial publishing.

Of the many types of short press run options available to small publishers, in-house, on-demand printing has many advantages—beating your competition, speeding up your receivables, avoiding inventory, instant updating, etc.

Marsh describes the essential details of how and why to publish "on-command" books, a system used by Gallopade to produce hundreds of titles over the last few years.

"You can be perpetually profitable, keep your space needs limited to your home or small office, put investment money in the form that is your best asset (new copyrights) in case you decide to sell out, and take advantage of unanticipated opportunities."

Business Guide to Print Promotion, *by Marlene Miller, Iris Communication Group, 1988, 6 X 9, film lam cover, perfectbound, 224 pages, $19.95. (order form #11)*

This is a classic reference book and guide to producing promotional materials, the technical aspects (type, paper, printing), creative elements (copywriting, photography, design) and production, including 100 examples and illustrations, glossary, resource materials and case studies (logo, letterhead, brochures, direct mail, ads, etc.).

It covers all the basics for beginners plus specifics and new ideas for the experienced — print advertising, direct mail, brochures from start to finish, use and production of photography, and probably more about type and paper than you thought you needed to know.

The author is a long-time consultant to businesses, a specialist in promotional materials and communications. She'll teach you how to write powerful, market-oriented copy that sells, how to use photography and illustration more effectively, how to plan and execute successful direct mail campaigns, how to save money when ordering printing, and a whole lot more.

A Graphic Artist's Book Club selection, and featured in the Adweek/Book series.

The Ultimate Black Book, The Only 400 Telephone Numbers You'll Ever Need To Find Most of the Information You'll Ever Want, *1st edition, by Godfrey Harris, The Americas Group, 1988, 80 indexed pages, saddle stitched, $5.95. (order form #12)*

Destined to be the most dogeared book (really, a booklet) in your library, this one will enable you to hunt up factual, public information on just about any subject. There is an index of hundreds of topics, keywords and categories, from the specific - sunbathing, pipelines, gambling, to the general - publishing, religion and public relations. There are helpful instructions on dealing with monster organizations and corporations - how to get the right person, how to find out what you need to know.

It's the only directory of its kind, and worth a lot more than $5.95.

New Age Yellow Pages, *Marcia Gervase Ingenito, Editor, Highgate House, 8 1/2 X 11, 2nd edition, 1988, 256 pages, perfectbound, film laminated four-color cover, **$12.95**. (order form #13)*

The first and most complete of its kind, this is a directory and a guide to services, products, businesses, organizations and resources of a consciousness raising nature.

Publishers of New Age books and tapes will find hundreds of targets for news releases and direct mail materials—associations, book distributors, wholesalers, bookstores, other New Age publishers for co-op opportunities, mailing lists, gift shops, catalogues, magazines, seminars, businesses by geographical location and dozens more categories.

Also included are 50 money-saving coupons for consumer discounts and free offers. There is a glossary from Absent Healing to Zen, an advertisers index and a raft of articles by New Age leaders

If you're selling books to New Age readers, *The New Age Yellow Pages* is worth hundreds, maybe thousands of dollars in sales to you. (Your competition already has one— 6500 copies of this new edition sold in ten weeks.)

The International Directory of Little Magazines and Small Presses, *Len Fulton, Editor, 24th edition, 1989, Dustbooks, 892 pages, 6 X 9, perfectbound, film laminated cover, **$22.95**. (order form #14)*

The standard reference used by writers, publishers, libraries and the trade for more than twenty years, it describes in great detail over 4600 magazines and small book publishers.

There are cross references by geographical location and subject, making it a snap to locate those periodicals or publishers with whom you might explore co-op activities, or to whom you might send news releases and flyers.

There are a hundred reasons why your publishing company will want to have access to many of the publications listed here.

This directory comes from the dependable publisher of several small press related books and resources, including the monthly news and reviews magazine, *Small Press Review*.

California Publishing Marketplace, *Writer's Connection, 240 pages, 6 X 9, 1989, **$14.95**. (order form #15)*

This is a guide to free-lance markets for writers, compiled by one of the most important writers' organizations in Northern California, Writers Connection. There are hundreds of detailed listings of book, magazine and newspaper publishers in the state of California, plus literary agents, professional organizations and other resources.

Every writer and publisher in the West needs *California Publishing Marketplace* in their reference library; it's the only directory of its kind.

Eveready Editorial, A New Book A Day Keeps Bankruptcy Away, *By Carole C. Marsh, Gallopade Publishing Group, 1989, $14.95 paperback or $24.95, 3-ring binder. (order form #16)*

Another book from the author of dozens of titles on the subject of entrepreneurial publishing, this one details her system for producing a perpetual stream of new books (she puts out about 60 books a year).

Marsh details how to organize raw research, notes and ideas into instant books and instant profit—what to keep, what to discard, what format to use. The Marsh method is adaptable to any type publishing operation and any number of authors, in-house and outside.

"This book gives you a competitive edge, it gets a money-making series out of an author, instead of just a single title, it challenges all your systems and it's fun."

Small publishers find themselves at the leading edge of a new age of opportunity. *Everyready Editorial* outlines one way to take full advantage of the flexibility and quick response characteristic of entrepreneurial publishers.

1001 Ways to Market Your Books, *by John Kremer, Ad-Lib Publications, 1989, 448 pages, film-lam cover, $14.95 perfectbound, $19.95 hardbound. (order form #17)*

An experienced publisher and noted expert in the field of book marketing and promotion, the author knows of what he writes. There isn't a publisher of any size or type who won't benefit from this one, a treasure chest of original and tested bookselling ideas and suggestions, a stimulating compendium of marketing tips and real-life examples.

Included in the updated 1989 edition are ideas for advertising, promotion, distribution, book design, spinoffs and more. It's targeted to booksellers, but there is lots in here for producers of all kinds of other services and products.

You'll learn how to work effectively with the bookstores, providing them with copy for their newsletters, point-of-purchase materials to aid sales, audio and video excerpts, author appearances, flyers, co-op advertising and inserts in their mailers.

There are dozens of ideas for selling subsidiary rights, conducting special sales, attending trade fairs, mail order catalogs, offbeat advertising, special offers, getting reviews, sales aids, TV and radio, alternative retail outlets, selling to schools and libraries.

Over a thousand tips and suggestions for marketing your books are illustrated with good examples, and you won't find them anywhere else but here in Kremer's bottomless cache.

Book Fairs, *by Dan Poynter, Para Publishing, 96 pages, 5.5 X 8.5, perfectbound, film lam cover, $7.95. (order form #18)*

By the bestselling author of *The Self-Publishing Manual,* this book is an exhibiting guide for publishers, everything you need to select, arrange and operate a booth at a bookfair or trade show.

Required reading for first time exhibitors, the book includes pre-show preparation, equipment and calendar checklists, resources for display materials and exhibition services, contact information for book show organizers, good ideas for shipping, setting up, taking orders, giving freebies, what to wear, training staff, how to approach book buyers, and more.

Of immeasurable value to veterans and beginners alike are the inside tips on how to work a fair to maximum advantage, in the booth and on the floor.

Don't leave home for a trade show or book fair without it.

New Age Marketing Opportunities, *By Sophia Tarila, First Editions, 1988, 240 pages, 8 1/2 X 11, perfectbound, film laminated cover,* **$59.95.** *(order form #19)*

The subtitle of this book is "A Comprehensive Directory," an understatement if there ever was one.

While putting together a bookselling plan for her own publishing company, the author found this directory just didn't exist, so she jumped in and filled the niche herself, on an impressive scale.

There are 6000 detailed listings from the New Age marketplace: publishers, periodicals, book reviewers, wholesalers, catalogs, bookstores, events, directories, mailing lists, services, associations, consultants and electronic media.

If your book, service or product is New Age related in any way, *New Age Marketing Opportunities* is absolutely essential for your marketing campaign.

Writer's Northwest Handbook, The Only Complete Guide to Northwest Writing and Publishing. *3rd edition, 1988, Media Weavers. 8 1/2 by 11, 224 pages, film-lam cover,* **$14.95.** *(order form #20)*

Everything has been expanded in this new edition of a bestseller. There are now 2600 book and periodical publishers, 500 resource listings, including calendar of events, organizations, classes, awards and contests, 45 essays and profiles on writing, publishing, teaching, art and craft. A fat volume of information, ideas and most of all, resources, it's useful and interesting to writers and publishers nationwide.

There are also sample news releases, book proposals, manuscript formats, query letters, photo releases, a freelance rate chart, and expense reports.

Some of the most productive and celebrated writers and publishers in the Northwest have contributed articles about every aspect of the business: getting published, book design, literary agents, self-publishing, copyrights, writing for children, poetry, play writing, editing, publicists and many more.

And last, but not at all least, the comprehensive directory of periodicals can be used to target a marketing campaign in the Northwest, making the book an incredible bargain.

Book Marketing Made Easier, *by John Kremer, Ad-Lib Publications, 160 pages, 8 X 11, perfectbound, film-lam cover,* **$14.95.** *(order form #21)*

By a prolific and respected producer of guides and directories for small press and self-publisher, this is a workbook with everything you need for planning and executing a book marketing campaign.

There are over 70 forms and records, for directory listings, copyrights, financial projections of various kinds, expense records, cost estimates, checklists, sales analyses, marketing timetable, spinoffs checklist, fact sheets, news release formats, response cards and much more.

Kremer is one of the recognized experts in his field, and he leads you carefully through the entire process of planning, setting up, monitoring and following through on book-selling operations. He gives you the raw materials for preparing your marketing strategy, working on your budget, forecasting your sales, copyrighting and registering your book, researching the media, sending releases, obtaining reviews, organizing author tours and distribution, submitting your books to catalogs and directories, dealing with bookstores, reviewers and authors and obtaining testimonials, among other things.

This is a basic reference tool to go along with Kremer's other invaluable publications for small publishers.

Copyright Not Copycat, *By Sally Stuart and Woody Young, Joy Publishing, 100 pages, 8 1/2 by 11, 1987, perfectbound, film lam cover,* **$9.95.** *(order form #22)*

"Copyright law is most confusing, frustrating and frightening to the average writer," says author Stuart.

Stuart and Youngs' publication is a workbook/sourcebook for writers, but 99% of the information is appropriate for self-publishers. With an easy to understand, non-intimidating question-answer format (and droll cat cartoons), the book explains the basics of the copyright act of 1978.

You start by looking up your own most pressing questions at the beginning of the book; simple answers are provided, followed by quotes and explanations from the official government text.

Some interesting tidbits: what the copyright office can and cannot do, fair use, quoting without permission, copyright protection in other countries, what info to provide the copyright office when making certain types of requests.

There are descriptions of zillions of government circulars specific to copyright issues, an extensive bibliography of references, a raft of forms and detailed instructions for completing them.

Copyright not Copycat is a good basic for any writer/publisher's library, answering all your most worrisome questions in non-technical, down to earth language.

The Guide to Writers Conferences, *Shaw Associates, 2nd Edition, 1989, 343 pages, 6 X 9, perfectbound, $14.95. (order form #23)*

This guide lists and describes in detail hundreds of writers' conferences, workshops, colonies, retreats and organizations, with chronological, geographical and subject indexes.

More than 850 events are included, with complete information. You'll find conferences and workshops in more locations and on more writing-related subjects than you ever dreamed existed.

There a comprehensive section on 120 organizations and associations, and several dozen listings of scholarship awards and writing contests.

This is a good reference book to keep, as most of the events are annual. You can plan your next vacation around a writers' conference in some scenic part of the U.S.

And, if you sell books, audios, videos or other products of interest to producers of writers' conferences, you definitely need the 1989 Guide to Writers' Conferences.

Commercial Translations, A Business-like Approach to Obtaining Accurate Translations, *by Godfrey Harris and Charles Sonabend, The Americas Group, 1985, 136 pages, 6 X 9, film lam cover, perfectbound, $9.95. (order form #24)*

For books and audio tapes distributed to foreign markets, or business communications to non-English readers, successful translations can be as important as the original text itself.

This book will help you understand the complexities of translations and assist you in finding the right translator, especially in regard to time and cost involved. "Verified" translations are discussed, and the characteristics of computer-generated translations compared to "from scratch" translations.

The two author/experts go into how much a translation should cost, how long it should take, soliciting bids, questions to ask (excellent), a checklist for choosing a service and instructions to give your translator.

Harris is a former diplomat and president of an international consulting firm, and Sonabend is managing director of one of the largest and most technologically advanced full-service translation firms in the world.

Self-Publishing by the Seat of the Pants, *By Carole C. Marsh, Gallopade Publishing Group, $14.95 paperback or $24.95, 3-ring binder. (order form #25)*

Carole Marsh does it again. She's a veteran entrepreneurial publisher, and in this book shares her secrets and new ideas for success in the business.

Marsh has published almost 600 books in the last several years, after having started a small company as a complete novice, experimenting, getting involved in every aspect of the publishing process, and figuring out first-hand how to make money at it.

She lets you in on how to avoid the traps which prevent small publishers from making a profit, how to deal with production, how to take advantage of the subjects you know and care about, how to market successfully, and how to do it all in record time with the least amount of paperwork.

How to Make Big Profits Publishing City & Regional Books, *By Marilyn and Tom Ross, Communication Creativity, 141 pages, 8 1/4 X 5 1/4, perfectbound, $14.95. (order form #26)*

Marilyn and Tom Ross are two famous entrepreneurs in the publishing business. They've helped hundreds of clients produce and market books, and their own books on the subject of self-publishing are bestsellers.

This is a particularly timely and practical book, especially for publishers casting about for new profit-making ideas. Frequently updated, short run regional publications that fill a specific need can make lots of money.

The Ross book starts with how to zero in on a great marketable idea, market research and positioning, with lots of real examples and ideas–tourist guides, regional cookbooks, consumer books, activity guides, etc.

Directories and resource guides are also explored in depth.

Next, they get into capitalization, advertising, selling subsidiary rights, cash flow, direct mail and various funding methods. Other subjects covered are research, format, production, doing business, marketing, franchise rights, repackaging and spinoffs.

There is a comprehensive appendix of sources—organizations, suppliers, marketing contacts, exhibit services, catalogs and more.

The aathors write in a straightforward, approachable style, and this book makes fascinating reading. It's packed with new ideas and tried-and-true methods.

Publishing a regionally-oriented book is one of the best ways to take advantage of what you already know. The Rosses tell you exactly how to do it.

How To Earn $50,000 Profit From Your First Book, Then Double It, *by Gordon Burgett, 80 page workbook and five 60-page cassettes, $75. (order form #27)*

The nitty-gritty, boiled down heart of Burgett's nationwide seminars given over a period of years. If you can't get to this professional speaker and publisher, he comes to you with this workbook and set of tapes.

Which markets you should write for, promotion, how to give your book an angle, market testing, facts, hints, cost analyses, guides, advice re speeches, seminars and consulting, promotional tools—all of this and more.

Make yourself and your book(s) famous and profitable by following Burgett's tested advice and down-to-earth recommendations.

Publish Your Own Handbound Books, *By Betty Doty, The Bookery, plastic wrapped bookbinding kit, 127 pages, 5 3/4 X 4 1/2, $8.95. (order form #28)*

Handbound itself, this book illustrates and instructs you in the process of producing small quantities of special books - your own cookbook, for example, poetry or short stories, your grandchildren's drawings, the family history.

Using a plain paper copier, you can become a publisher of hardbound books over-night—the ultimate self-publishing experience.

The author not only gets into the hands-on how-to of making books, she also discusses copyrights, editing, layout, style, distribution, selling to bookstores, advertising, reviews and interviews.

This is a charmingly put together great idea, filling a need for particularly short runs and low-cost printings.

Books for Publishers

Please send the following books.

To: _____ Phone _____

Address _____ City _____ State _____ ZIP _____

Title	Quanity	Price	Total
1. The Decision to Publish		$14.95	
2. Financial Feasibility in Book Publishing		$12.95	
3. The Self-Publishing Manual		$14.95	
4. Illustrated Handbook of Desktop Publishing & Typesetting		$29.95	
5. Directory of Book, Catalog & Magazine Printers		$15.00	
6. Small Time Operator		$10.95	
7. How to Self Publish and Make Money		$12.95	
8. Free Help From Uncle Sam to Start Your Own Business		$ 9.95	
9. Looking Good in Print		$23.95	
10. Publishing on Command (paperback)		$14.95	
Publishing on Command (binder)		$24.95	
11. Business Guide to Print Promotion		$19.95	
12. The Ultimate Black Book		$ 5.95	
13. New Age Yellow Pages		$12.95	
14. Interna Directory of Little Magazines & Small Presses		$22.95	
15. California Publishing Marketplace		$14.95	
16. Eveready Editorial (paperback)		$14.95	
Everready Editorial (binder)		$24.95	
17. 1001 Ways to Market Your Books (paperback)		$14.95	
1001 Ways to Market Your Books (hardcover)		$19.95	
18. Book Fairs		$ 7.95	
19. New Age Marketing Opportunities		$59.95	
20. Writer's Northwest Handbook		$14.95	
21. Book Marketing Made Easier		$14.95	
22. Copyright Not Copycat		$ 9.95	
23. The Guide to Writers Conferences		$14.95	
24. Commercial Translations		$ 9.95	
25. Self-Publishing by Seat of the Pants (paperback)		$14.95	
Self-Publishing by Seat of the pants (binder)		$24.95	
26. How to Make Big Profits Publishing City & Regional Books		$14.95	
27. How To Earn $50,000 Profit From Your First Book		$75.00	
28. Publish Your Own Handbound Books		$ 8.95	

Please send your check to:

Jacpoon PUBLICATIONS
9 Channel Landing
Tiburon, CA 94920

Subtotal _____

Shipping ($2 per book) _____

Tax (6% in Calif.) _____

TOTAL _____

WOULDN'T YOU LIKE YOUR OWN COPY OF *SELLING BOOKS IN THE BAY AREA?*

Please send your check for **$17.95**,
plus **$2.00** shipping and **$1.08** tax in California to:

Lagoon PUBLICATIONS
9 Channel Landing, #6
Tiburon, CA 94920

Your Name: _____

Address: _____

Phone: _____

Would you like a sample copy of SPEX, the Marin Small Press Association newsletter? _____

- -

WOULDN'T YOU LIKE YOUR OWN COPY OF *SELLING BOOKS IN THE BAY AREA?*

Please send your check for **$17.95**,
plus **$2.00** shipping and **$1.08** tax in California to:

Lagoon PUBLICATIONS
9 Channel Landing, #6
Tiburon, CA 94920

Your Name: _____

Address: _____

Phone: _____

Would you like a sample copy of SPEX, the Marin Small Press Association newsletter? _____

- -

WOULDN'T YOU LIKE YOUR OWN COPY OF *SELLING BOOKS IN THE BAY AREA?*

Please send your check for **$17.95**,
plus **$2.00** shipping and **$1.08** tax in California to:

Lagoon PUBLICATIONS
9 Channel Landing, #6
Tiburon, CA 94920

Your Name: _____

Address: _____

Phone: _____

Would you like a sample copy of SPEX, the Marin Small Press Association newsletter? _____